STONEHENGE

THE STORY SO FAR

STONEHENGE

THE STORY SO FAR

Julian Richards

ENGLISH HERITAGE

For Richard Bradley – who introduced me to the Age of Stonehenge

First published in 2007 by English Heritage, Kemble Drive, Swindon SN2 2GZ

10 9 8 7 6 5 4 3 2 1

English Heritage is the Government's statutory adviser on the historic environment.

ISBN 978 1 905624 00 3

Product code 50965

A CIP catalogue for this book is available from the British Library.

Edited by Val Horsler
Designed by Michael McMann
Indexed by Julian Richards
Brought to press by Adele Campbell
Printed by Cambridge Printing

Front cover: © Paul Trendell
Back cover: Hot-air balloon flight commemmorating the first aerial photograph taken over Stonehenge in 1906. © English Heritage

Contents

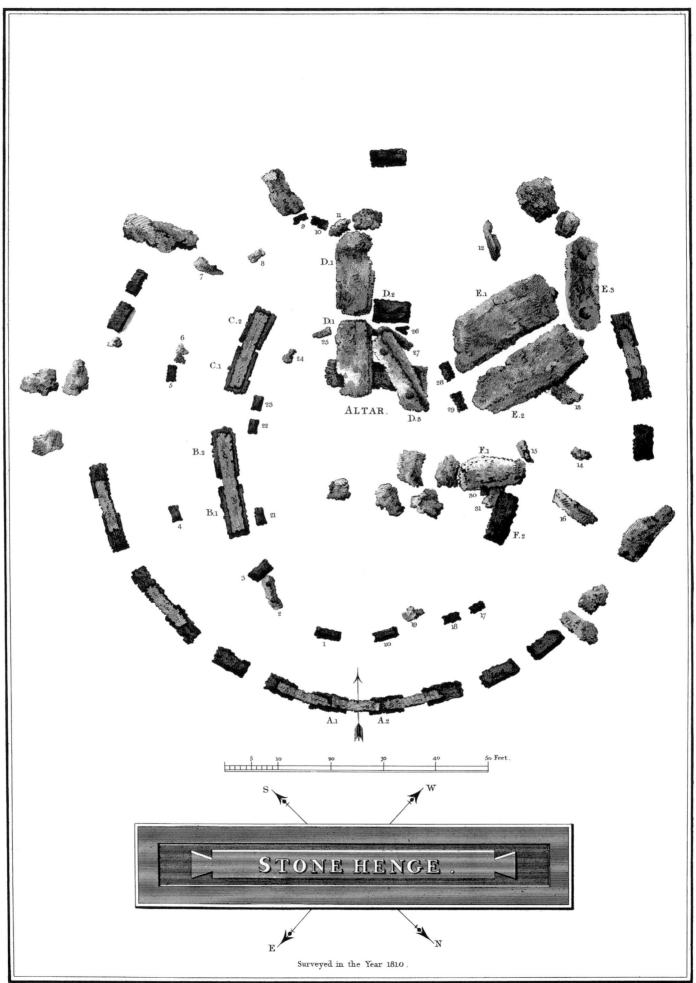

STONE HENGE.

Surveyed in the Year 1810.

P. Crocker del.

J.S Basire Sc.

OPPOSITE
Philip Crocker's 1810 plan of Stonehenge from Sir
Richard Colt Hoare's *Ancient History of Wiltshire*.

Introduction

Stonehenge is undeniably the most famous prehistoric site in the world. It has survived, even if now in a semi-ruined state, for nearly 5,000 years since building started, and in the early 21st century has almost a million visitors a year. Stonehenge has never really been forgotten. Romans and Saxons visited it, medieval monks drew it and over the last four or five centuries it has been the subject of endless investigation and speculation by antiquarians and pioneering archaeologists and scientists, as well as mystics, stargazers and all those who seek its spirituality and meaning. There are countless theories about when and how it was built, who built it and why so much effort was expended. In the 20th century there were many archaeological investigations at varying scales and of varying quality. Many books have been written, some scholarly and reflecting the understanding of the age in which they were written, others imaginative and eccentric.

This book attempts to answer in detail some of the fundamental questions about Stonehenge, based on the understanding that has been gained through centuries of study. In writing this book, 15 years after my earliest written offering on the subject of Stonehenge, I have had the enormous benefit of the results of all the 20th-century excavations carried out at the stones, fully analysed and finally published by English Heritage in 1995. But even with all these new data I am all too aware that this book is not the final answer. It reflects our current understanding of Stonehenge, but future investigations both at Stonehenge itself and within its surrounding landscape will undoubtedly change our understanding, perhaps in quite radical ways. The title, *Stonehenge – the story so far*, is therefore a very carefully considered choice.

This book is written from the perspective of 25 years of close involvement with Stonehenge and its surroundings. This involvement started with excavations and fieldwork in the 1980s, a decade in which it was a privilege and a pleasure to camp within sight of the stones, and slightly less of a pleasure to spend freezing winter months surveying bare and windswept fields. We made many exciting finds and the fieldwork was followed by several years of analysis and finally the publication of the results: not a course that has always been completed by previous investigators. During these years I have experienced the contrast between a peaceful midwinter sunset and a throbbing midsummer dawn in the company of 20,000 celebrants. I have been able (courtesy of the BBC) to investigate on a grand scale how Stonehenge might have been built and have amassed, under the collective term 'Stonehengeiana', a vast and varied collection of hideous souvenirs and strange ephemera. Fifteen years ago, as the author of the first *Stonehenge* for English Heritage, I rather pompously described myself as a 'pragmatic prehistorian'. I think I would like to change that. This book has been written by an archaeologist, and one with his feet firmly on the ground. But I am also an enthusiast, with a genuine passion for Stonehenge itself and for our ancient past and a huge respect for our prehistoric ancestors. After all these years and countless visits I still find Stonehenge a profoundly moving place and I hope that I always will.

PAGES 8–9
Mist and mystery – Stonehenge in winter.

At the summer solstice Stonehenge becomes a place of wild celebration.

An explanation of the book's structure

In starting to write about Stonehenge I have the advantage of believing that (almost) everyone who picks up the book will have heard of the place and, as its unique arrangements of stones are instantly recognisable, will probably know what at least parts of it look like. They may well have visited it or be intending to pay a visit; they may already have formed their own ideas about what it means to them. In 1967 the archaeologist Jacquetta Hawkes, reflecting on the way that the interpretation of Stonehenge changes with time, said that 'every age has the Stonehenge it deserves'. Indeed, so varied are the personal views that perhaps every individual has the Stonehenge that he or she desires. For some it is nothing more than another brief stop on a tourist itinerary, for others a reminder of the achievements of the ancient past, while yet others regard it as a living temple, as spiritual today as when it was first built.

When writing the story of Stonehenge it may seem logical to start at the beginning, with its origins, and end up in the present, the early 21st century. But there are problems with this simple scheme, rooted in the fact that, although since at least the 12th century Stonehenge has been described, drawn and painted and been the subject of endless speculation and investigation, it is only since the development of the comparatively new science of archaeology, mainly during the 20th century, that we have been able to achieve any real understanding of it. So the *history* of

Stonehenge today – hemmed in by busy roads and cut off from its surrounding landscape.

Stonehenge is the study, speculation and description, over the last nine centuries, of the ancient monument, the enigmatic ruin from the dim and distant past. But its *pre*history, the study of how and when, and even why, it was built – before written records in the ages of stone and bronze between 5,000 and about 3,500 years ago – and of the people who built it, all has to come from archaeology, the investigation of the physical remains of the past.

A further component of the study of Stonehenge is its place in the rich landscape that surrounds it, a palimpsest of prehistoric remains that are an inseparable part of Stonehenge, its history and its meaning. This landscape too has a parallel history of discovery and investigation, and is integral to the overall picture.

There is therefore a logic in firstly looking at the structure of Stonehenge, to help the reader to become familiar with its components and layout, before then placing it firmly in its surrounding landscape. What follows is the history of Stonehenge, from earliest times to the most recent investigations and scientific analysis. From these centuries of study a huge body of information has accrued that allows some of the major questions to be addressed. Finally, the threads are woven into an imaginative narrative: the story of Stonehenge.

The book is divided into twelve chapters.

Chapters 1 and 2 examine in detail the Stonehenge that we see today, together with an introduction to the surrounding landscape and the ceremonial monuments and burial mounds that were built before or during the Age of Stonehenge. Here Stonehenge and its landscape are not only placed in their local context but are also shown as part of a wider prehistoric world. This section also introduces the idea of prehistory and the ways in which it is subdivided, and offers a guide on how to date events in prehistoric times.

Chapters 3 and 4 look at the history of Stonehenge, from its first mention in the 12th century through to the end of the 19th. Medieval mysticism, which saw Stonehenge built by Merlin, is overtaken by the studies of 17th- and 18th-century antiquarians such as John Aubrey and William Stukeley. They in turn make way for Sir Richard Colt Hoare and William Cunnington, pioneering archaeologists who laid the intellectual foundations for the future study of Stonehenge. The 19th century also saw the popularity of Stonehenge increase and the first attempts to protect it.

The 20th century is the subject of chapters 5–8, a time of investigation that was ushered in by the fall of yet another stone on 30th December 1900. Linked to the excavations of first William Gowland, then William Hawley and, from the 1950s, Richard Atkinson and Stuart Piggott were major restorations that would change the face of Stonehenge. From the 1920s onwards aerial photography revealed a lost prehistoric landscape around Stonehenge, and in the 1990s a great study was carried out of the results of all the 20th-century excavations that would bring us as close as we can now be to an understanding of Stonehenge in all its complexity.

Chapter 7 also includes a more detailed look at the Stonehenge landscape and the ways in which our understanding of it has increased during the 20th and early 21st centuries.

Chapters 9–11 ask, and attempt to answer, the big questions. Who built Stonehenge? How was it built? And perhaps the most difficult of all, why?

Chapter 12, subtitled 'the story so far', draws together all the evidence, from antiquarian observations to the latest radiocarbon dates and investigations in the surrounding landscape, in a single narrative. Firmly based on archaeological facts, this story is an attempt to bring to life the Age of Stonehenge.

Acknowledgements

Writing the text of a book is only one part of the team effort that culminates in its publication. In writing this one I have attempted to get the facts right but suspect that I may not have succeeded in every case. All I can say is that I tried and, if informed of my errors, won't make the same mistakes again.

On the production side I owe an enormous debt to my editor, Val Horsler, who has not only been extraordinarily patient with me but edited what I eventually produced with a rarely found combination of firmness and friendliness. I would also like to thank Annette Lyons and Sue Lobb who both read and commented on the text as it developed.

Stonehenge is rich in imagery, both past and present, and I would like to thank Elaine Willis for obtaining so many of the earlier images and also all those who have been so helpful and generous in response to my requests, including Javis Gurr and Jonathan Butler in the English Heritage photo library and Katy Whitaker and colleagues in the NMR. Many thanks are also due to the designer, Michael McMann. Working so closely with Michael to integrate text and images was a great pleasure and I feel that he has made the book a visual treat. I would also like to acknowledge the help and once again patience of Adele Campbell, who brought the book to press, and Rob Richardson, both from English Heritage's publications team.

Other English Heritage staff to whom I would like to offer thanks include David Batchelor (Stonehenge team), Alex Bayliss (scientific dating), Isabel Bedu (World Heritage Site team), Bob Bewley, Simon Crutchley and Lindsay Jones (aerial photography), Gill Campbell (environmental studies), Peter Carson (Stonehenge manager) and Andrew David and Neil Linford (geophysics). Jane Evans of the British Geological Survey commented on the Isotopes science box.

I am also very grateful to Mike Parker Pearson, Joshua Pollard, Colin Richards and Julian Thomas of the Stonehenge Riverside Project for sharing their ideas and in particular the results of the 2006 excavations with me. There are many more of my archaeological friends and colleagues who have talked about Stonehenge with me over the years. To each and every one of you I say thanks – every conversation and shared idea has helped me with this book.

Finally I would like to acknowledge the debt that all those who are fascinated with Stonehenge owe to the generations of 'Stonehengers' who have gone before: Aubrey, Stukelely, Cunnington and Colt Hoare, Gowland, Hawley and Atkinson. Thank you all for your efforts and ideas, your triumphs and frustrations. Such is archaeology.

CHAPTER I   **Welcome to Stonehenge**

What is it about Stonehenge that draws nearly one million visitors a year? Why does it continue to intrigue and frustrate archaeologists and inspire passions, beliefs and theories both plausible and wild? There is a simple answer: it is because Stonehenge is the supreme achievement of prehistoric design and engineering, the Stone Age equivalent of Canterbury Cathedral, the physical manifestation of what can be built by ingenious people with strongly held beliefs, simple tools and the ability to organise great labour forces.

Stonehenge is unique. To archaeologists it is a 'henge', a prehistoric ceremonial site, of which there are many examples of varying size and complexity throughout the British Isles. A henge is a circular or oval enclosed space defined by a ditch and bank but with the bank on the outside, the reverse of what would be found in a site constructed for defence. These enclosures can have a single entrance, or two, usually on opposite sides, and in some cases as many as four. Inside there are often regular circular arrangements of upright stones, while many that have been excavated have revealed evidence of similar structures made of wood, now surviving only as buried traces of upright posts. The majority of these sites were built and used during the later part of the Neolithic or New Stone Age, some time between 3000 and 2300BC. Some henges are considerably larger in overall scale than Stonehenge, and some have even more massive stones, but there are several ways in which Stonehenge is unique and in many ways superior.

Firstly there is its longevity. The first construction work took place around 3000BC, but while other henges lapsed into disuse and decay, Stonehenge continued to be modified into the Bronze Age, until at least around 1600BC. No other henge was built and used over such a long span of time. Then there are the stones. Most other henges incorporate locally available building materials, moved over a distance of perhaps a few miles at most. But some of the smaller stones at Stonehenge come from as far away as Wales, 240km (150 miles) away. No other henge has stones that were brought from such great distances. Finally, at no other prehistoric site in Britain and Ireland were stones shaped and jointed together to create structures of such sophistication and elegance. This is why Stonehenge is so special.

Now, in the early 21st century, visitors arrive at Stonehenge by car or coach, by bike and occasionally even on foot, travelling along the roads and tracks that eventually converge and maroon Stonehenge in a triangle of grassland. To the south is the A303, the main route to the south-west, with traffic that is often almost at a standstill and along which Stonehenge is a prominent way-marker. To the north lies the A344, the old turnpike road from Amesbury to Devizes (which until at least the 1920s was a more important route than the A303). This runs right past Stonehenge, almost within touching distance of one of the outlying stones, and cuts it off from its landscape setting to the north. The third side of the triangle is formed by an old byway, now a roughly surfaced track. Within the surrounding landscape of gently undulating chalk hills and shallow dry valleys lies an extraordinary collection of sites – mostly ignored by visitors to the area – many constructed during the time that Stonehenge was built and used. These include ceremonial and burial sites that are even older than Stonehenge, and at least three more henges. Most prominently, whether in tight clusters, strung out along the low ridge tops or occasionally in lonely isolation, are round barrows – burial mounds that create a landscape of the dead. And at the heart of this landscape, just beyond the intrusions of the 21st century, lies one of the world's most spectacular prehistoric structures.

What is Stonehenge?

At first glance Stonehenge may seem to be just a jumble of stones, some upright, some fallen and lying broken on the grass. There are gaps where stones are obviously missing and some concrete evidence of recent repairs. But sufficient survives to recognise an order: arrangements of circles and horseshoe shapes in the centre, outlying isolated stones and the low rise and fall of ancient and eroded banks and ditches. Stonehenge is not simply a monument of hard and enduring stone; it is partly a place of softer elements, of chalk and soil and long-decayed timber.

So what are the components that make up the ancient monument known as Stonehenge? Starting from the outside, the first structure to be encountered is the ditch and bank of a circular earthwork enclosure about 110m (360ft) in diameter. It consists of a ditch dug into the underlying chalk rock, with an inner bank made of material dug out of the ditch and, in places, a low exterior or 'counterscarp' bank. So Stonehenge is unlike other henges in having its ditch outside its bank. The only tools available for the builders of the time to loosen the chalk were picks made from red deer antlers, many of which, broken and discarded, have been found buried in the ditch. How the chalk was moved is less certain, as the skins or baskets that must have been used have not survived.

When first dug the ditch would have been steep and flat-bottomed, about 1.2m to 1.3m (just over 4ft) deep on average, and varying considerably in width up to a maximum of 4.2m (14ft). The bank is a simple structure, a dump of chalk rubble without any obvious signs of having been faced in any way. It is difficult to calculate its original height but, although now much eroded, it still stands in places to a height of nearly 1m (over 3ft).

There are two entrances into the enclosure. One, on its north-easterly side, is very obvious, a wide gap from which parallel ditches and banks run out and down across the sloping grassland. These are the earthworks of the first straight section of the Avenue, a ceremonial approach way to Stonehenge that then follows a curving course, crosses the line of the A303 beyond the nearest ridge and finally reaches the banks of the River Avon about 2.3km (1¼ miles) away. The second entrance is a simple narrow gap in the ditch and bank on the southern side of the enclosure.

In stark contrast to their appearance today, the ditch would have been deeper and narrower when first dug and the banks would have been higher, and these earthworks and those of the monuments in the surrounding landscape would have gleamed brilliant chalk white. Today the profiles of much of the Stonehenge enclosure and the first section of the Avenue are softened by millennia of erosion:

Stonehenge viewed up the line of the Avenue. This link with the wider landscape is unfortunately cut by the A344.

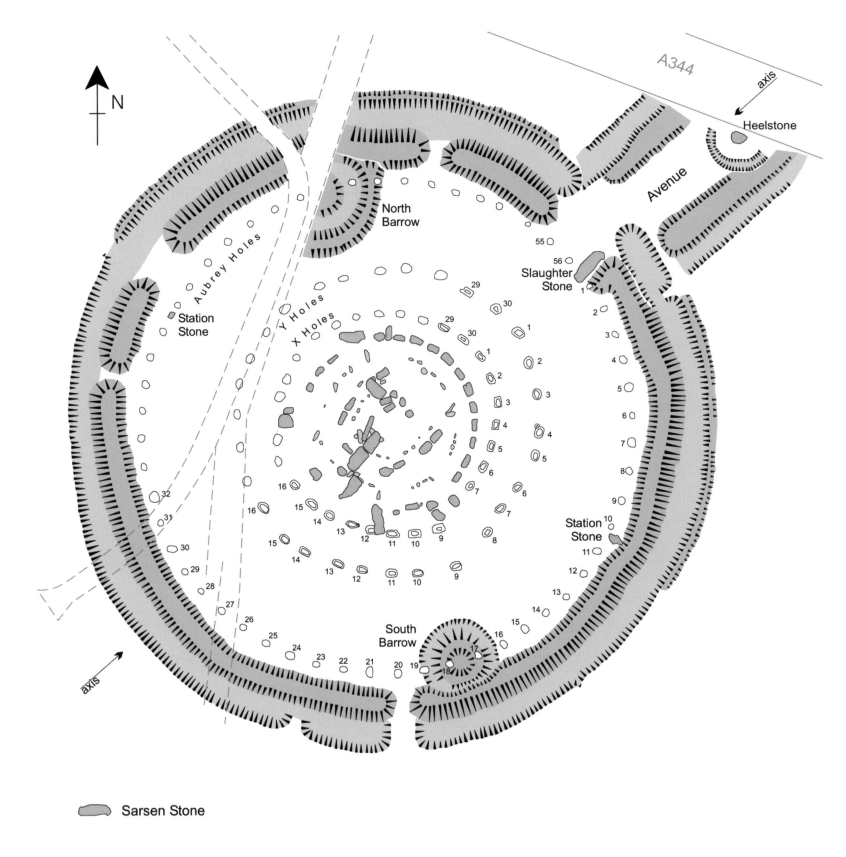

N

A344

axis

Heelstone

Avenue

North
Barrow

Aubrey Holes

55

56

Slaughter
Stone

Station
Stone

Y Holes

X Holes

29

30

29

30

32

31

30

29

28

27

26

25

24

23

22

21

20

19

16

16

15

14

13

15

14

13

12

12

11

11

10

10

9

9

8

7

6

5

4

3

2

1

Station
Stone

South
Barrow

17

18

16

15

14

13

12

11

10

9

8

7

6

5

4

3

2

1

axis

Sarsen Stone

Stonehenge from the south-west under a light dusting of snow that helps pick out the earthworks of the enclosure and the Avenue.

OPPOSITE
The major components of Stonehenge.

the banks have slumped and spread, the ditches have silted up and their sides have weathered to gentler slopes. Soils have formed and grass has grown. There is, however, a noticeable difference in the present appearance of the ditch on the southern side of the enclosure and round the eastern side as far as the line of the Avenue. This part of the ditch was incompletely filled in after being excavated by the archaeologist William Hawley in the 1920s, and consequently has a sharper profile.

These then are some of the 'soft' elements of Stonehenge; but now for the stones. The first stone seen by visitors approaching along the A344, which stands just outside the entrance to the enclosure within the line of the Avenue and close by the fence along the road, is a massive unshaped boulder, nearly 5m (16ft) high. It leans

The Heel Stone, a great block of unshaped Sarsen that stands just outside the main entrance to the earthwork enclosure.

in towards the centre of the monument but presumably originally stood more upright. This is the Heel Stone, a great lump of 'sarsen', a hard red-brown stone. Sarsen is found within the Stonehenge area in small boulders weighing no more than a few tons, but it is likely – although still the subject of debate – that the source of the sarsen used to build Stonehenge is on the Marlborough Downs, some 30km (19 miles) to the north, centred on Wiltshire's other great complex of prehistoric monuments at Avebury.

There have been suggestions that the Heel Stone's name derives from the Greek 'helios', meaning sun, perhaps a reference to the midsummer sun with which Stonehenge is so strongly associated. But in fact its name refers to an ancient folk tale which had the Devil, in the process of building Stonehenge, interrupted in his work by a friar. In a rage the Devil hurled a stone at the friar which struck the unfortunate man on the heel, leaving an imprint in the stone. This tale originally referred to one of the central stones (where the heel-shaped imprint can still be seen) but was later transferred to this outlying stone that then became known as the Friar's Heel, or more simply the Heel Stone.

The Heel Stone, which is surrounded by a shallow circular ditch, was originally one of a pair, the empty hole for which was discovered in the roadside verge during the digging of a cable trench in 1979.

Also of sarsen, and with an equally imaginative name, is the stone that lies beyond the Heel Stone, half submerged in the grass within the entrance to the enclosure. This is the Slaughter Stone, its name the product of Victorian over-imagination that saw sacrificial blood in the rusty-red puddles that collect on its dimpled surface. Unfortunately for a good story this particular stone, the sole survivor of three that were positioned in the entrance to the enclosure, originally

Sarsens in their natural habitat – half buried in the ground on the Marlborough Downs.

The Slaughter Stone, its name the product of Victorian imagination, lies half submerged in the entrance to the earthwork enclosure.

The small Station Stone on the eastern side of the enclosure, one of four that originally stood just inside the encircling bank.

stood upright; it could therefore never have functioned as a sacrificial altar, and the red colour of the 'blood' is simply caused by the reaction of rainwater to iron within the stone.

Inside the enclosure, on opposite sides and close to the inner edge of the bank, lie two small sarsens, both of which show some slight traces of having been shaped. These are the two survivors of a regular arrangement of four, known as the Station Stones. The two stones that are now missing were, like the Heel Stone, each surrounded by a shallow circular ditch, creating the appearance of low mounds that became known, rather misleadingly, as the North and South Barrows. 'Barrows' in the archaeological sense of the word, are burial mounds, but these low mounds appear to have had nothing to do with burial.

Between the bank and the central stone structure lie three circular arrangements of pits, discovered during 20th-century excavations but not visible on the ground except where their position has been marked. Just inside the inner edge of the bank, on much the same line as the Station Stones, is a circle of 56 small pits. These are the Aubrey Holes, originally called the X Holes but now named after the antiquarian John Aubrey. As far back as the 17th century he noted shallow, regularly spaced depressions in the grass close to the bank and suggested that these might be the holes of missing stones. Strangely, these depressions were not noted by the early 18th-century antiquarian William Stukeley, normally the most keen-eyed of observers, but excavations in the 1920s showed that Aubrey had been right and that the depressions did mark substantial holes, spaced 4–5m (13–16ft) apart. But they had originally held upright timber posts, not stones as Aubrey suggested. Strangely, at a slightly later date, when the posts had either rotted or been removed, the hollows that were left became places of burial for cremated human bones. The 34 Aubrey Holes that have been excavated, mainly on the southern and eastern sides of the circle, are now marked on the ground with small circular spots of concrete.

Further in towards the centre, immediately outside the central stone structure, lie two more circles of comparatively shallow pits known as the Y and Z Holes which were again discovered in the excavations carried out in the 1920s. These pits are a puzzle. They appear to have been dug around 1600BC, very late in the period of Stonehenge's construction, and show no evidence that they ever held uprights of stone or timber.

This brings us to the central stone settings, the components of an amazing structure that may, from its current jumbled and ruinous appearance, seem difficult to understand. In reality things are not as complex as they appear. Quite simply, there are two concentric circles, one of the hard red-brown sarsen and the other, just inside it, of bluestone – an enigmatic Welsh rock that is discussed in detail below. Within these two circles are two more concentric arrangements, open-ended 'horseshoes' again with the outer of sarsen and the inner of bluestone.

The stone structure as it may have looked when completed around 2000BC – viewed from the south.

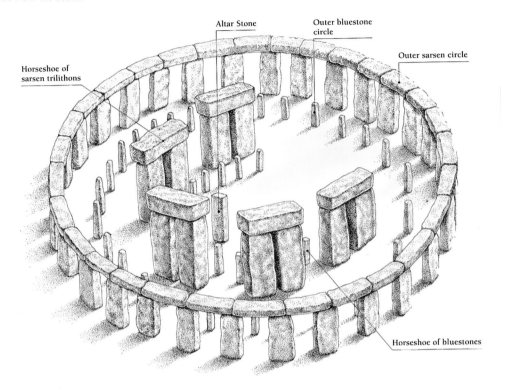

The structure as it is today – viewed from the south.

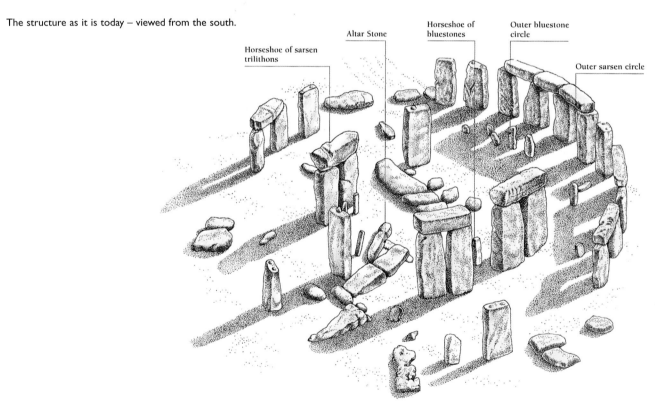

The central stone structure – viewed from the north.

Detailed plan of the central stones employing the numbering system devised by Petrie in 1880.

Fortunately for those who wish to refer to specific stones, in 1880 Professor Flinders Petrie published a plan allocating numbers to all those that survived, even those that were fragmentary. In his scheme the uprights of the outer sarsen circle are stones 1–30 and their corresponding lintels are numbered 101–130. The bluestones of the outer circle are numbers 31–49 with alphabetical suffixes (32a–e for example) where additional stones have been found or where a single stone has been broken into pieces. The uprights of the sarsen trilithons are numbered 51–60 (Stone 56 is the surviving upright of the tallest trilithon) and their lintels are stones 152, 154, 156, 158 and 160. Finally, the bluestones of the inner horseshoe are numbered 61–72 and the Altar Stone is numbered 80 although it is usually referred to by its name.

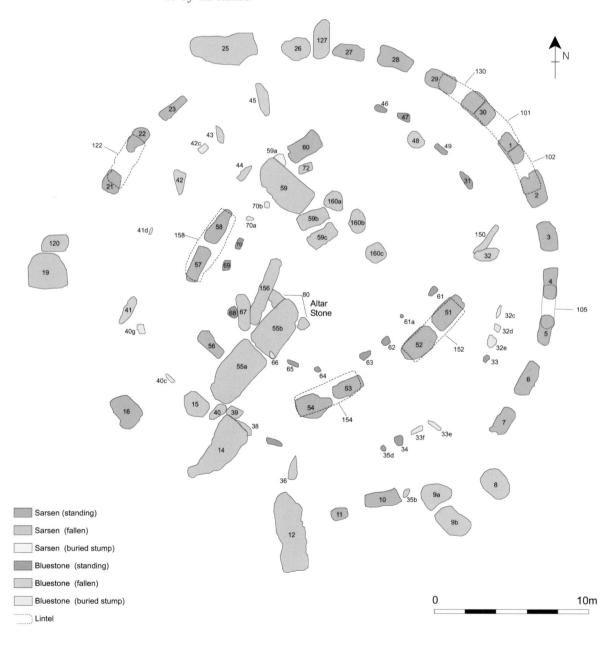

Sarsen (standing)
Sarsen (fallen)
Sarsen (buried stump)
Bluestone (standing)
Bluestone (fallen)
Bluestone (buried stump)
Lintel

0   10m

Stone 56, the elegant pillar with its pronounced tenon, framed in the gap between stones 1 and 30 of the sarsen circle.

The outermost setting is the sarsen circle which, if the symmetry of the surviving elements continued for the full circuit, would have consisted of 30 carefully shaped and closely spaced uprights capped by an equal number of horizontal lintels. The uprights are of differing sizes and shape, but show a consistency in having their smoothest face turned inwards. The distance from their central points is precisely equal around the circumference of the circle, the only exception to this symmetry being between the two stones (numbers 1 and 30) that face directly out towards the entrance to the enclosure and which are spaced slightly wider apart, as if to create an entrance. These uprights appear to have straight parallel sides, whereas in fact their sides are each worked into a slight outward curve. This is 'entasis', a design technique that counteracts the optical effect that causes genuine parallel-sided pillars to appear as if their sides have a slight inward curve. As represented by the uprights still standing, this circle is very fragmentary, particularly on its south and south-west sides where many stones are missing completely. In all, only 17 of the original 30 stones survive, and of these there is one (Stone 11) that is far shorter than the others.

The elaborate joints found in the sarsen circle.

These remarkable uprights were capped with lintels that would, if all in place, have created the effect of a continuous ring of stone, 30m (98ft) in inside diameter, suspended about 4m (13ft) above the ground. Today only five lintels are still *in situ*, two in isolation and a well preserved run of three on the north-east side facing the entrance to the enclosure. The lintels, just one of Stonehenge's unique features, may look as if nothing more than gravity holds them in place but they are in fact locked onto their uprights by means of joints more commonly found in woodwork. On the top of each upright are two protruding knobs or tenons that fit into corresponding sockets or mortice holes worked into the underside of the lintels. Even more remarkably, the ends of the lintels are locked together by means of tongue and groove joints, also derived from carpentry, where a vertical tongue fits into a corresponding vertical groove.

As further evidence of the care that has gone into the construction of this circle, the individual lintels are not simply straight blocks but have had their inner and outer faces worked into a gentle curve: all the better to complete the illusion of a continuous ring of stone. The surveying of the circle is also quite remarkable as care has been taken to level the tops of the stones, overcoming the effects of the gentle north-facing slope on which Stonehenge lies. As a result there is no more than a few centimetres' difference in height across the diameter of the circle. In its surveyed and engineered precision and its jointing techniques the sarsen circle is perhaps the single most elegant element of the stone settings that lie at the heart of Stonehenge.

If the outer sarsen circle is remarkable for its elegance, then the circle of stones that lies just inside and concentric with it is remarkable in other ways. It too is very fragmentary: although it may originally have included as many as 60 stones, only six still stand. At first glance they seem insignificant. They vary in size and shape and most appear to be in their natural state with no signs of having been shaped. They are dwarfed by their towering neighbours and, encrusted with lichen, are virtually indistinguishable from sarsen. But they are not sarsen: they are the celebrated 'bluestones' known to have come from the Preseli Mountains in Wales, over 240km (150 miles) to the west of Stonehenge. Since their average height is less than 2m (just over 6ft) it can be seen why 19th-century archaeologists, who knew nothing of the journey they had made, referred to them as 'inferior stones' or 'pigmy pillars'. They are a strangely mixed bag, a motley collection of volcanic

The surviving run of three linked lintels in the sarsen circle clearly shows the gentle curve of their long sides.

The 'pigmy pillars' – the north-east side of the fragmented bluestone circle flanked on either side by the much larger sarsens.

rocks, spotted and unspotted dolerite, rhyolite and a variety of ash stones. Some are attractive, others dull, and some so soft that they have dissolved above ground and have been seen only as buried stumps. But when fresh and clean they would have looked quite different: slaty greys and blues, interspersed with white-flecked blue-green tones, something strange and 'foreign'.

Although most of the stones within the bluestone circle appear to be unshaped, there are two exceptions, both finely worked stones with deep mortice holes. These were clearly shaped to be used as horizontal lintels before being set upright as pillars.

Where the bluestones come from is not disputed, but the means by which they arrived on Salisbury Plain is still the subject of heated debate. Some geologists argue that they were transported glacially, carried from Wales on ice sheets and then dumped as the climate warmed and the ice retreated. In contrast, most archaeologists are happy to accept that they were moved by human energy and motivation.

The mortice hole in this fallen bluestone pillar provides the evidence that it was originally a lintel, part of a miniature bluestone trilithon.

The boulder-strewn summit of Carn Menin in the Preseli Mountains of Wales.

25

Raking sunlight picks out the tooling marks on a surviving upright of the sarsen circle.

OPPOSITE
A trilithon on the southern side of the horseshoe showing the contrast between the two uprights: one rough, the other smooth.

Further towards the centre, the next setting is the most impressive: a horseshoe of five huge sarsen structures known as trilithons (from the Greek for 'three stones'). Each trilithon resembles a giant doorway, with two great closely spaced uprights supporting a massive lintel. Three trilithons stand complete, but the other two each have only one stone still standing. Once again there is great sophistication in the choice of stones and in the way in which they were shaped and arranged. Among these uprights are Stonehenge's largest individual stones, some over 8m (25ft) in overall height, and averaging about 2m (6ft) wide and 1m (3ft) deep. They now weigh as much as 40 tons, and would have weighed considerably more in their original unshaped state. There are no stones of anything approaching this size surviving in their original location on the Marlborough Downs today. Even in prehistoric times, before so many were cleared away to create fields for cultivation or as building material, finding matched stones of this size must have been very difficult.

Where they survive to be compared, there is a contrast between the two uprights of each individual trilithon. Facing outwards from the centre the left-hand stone is often smoother and more carefully shaped, in contrast to the slightly rougher state of its pair. There are suggestions, based on the observation of similar 'pairing' within the Avebury henge and its stone avenue, that this may represent a male/female association. Once again though, echoing the outer circle, the smoother faces of the stones are turned inwards. The individual trilithons are also not all of the same height; they are gently graded with the shortest pair marking the open end of the horseshoe and the tallest, known as the Great Trilithon, standing at its closed end. Only one stone of the magnificent Great Trilithon still stands (Stone 56), the tallest standing stone in Britain, over 7.3m (24ft) high above ground. Ironically, it is the ruined state of this part of the structure that provides so many clues to the whole trilithon horseshoe. The tenon that so obviously projects from the top of the tall surviving upright and the large mortice holes visible on the fallen lintel show that these stones were locked together using the same joints employed in the outer circle. A huge lump protruding from the base of the fallen upright of the Great Trilithon (Stone 55a) shows very clearly how much stone must have been removed to create the regular, parallel sides that showed above ground.

RIGHT
The graded heights of the sarsen trilithons can be appreciated more easily when they are viewed from above.

In the same way that the outer circle of sarsens is mirrored by an inner circle of bluestones, inside the horseshoe of sarsen trilithons lies a horseshoe of bluestones. There were originally 19 upright pillars, all of spotted dolerite, of which six still stand and a further six survive below ground as eroded stumps. These bluestones are generally taller than those in the outer circle and reflect the graded heights of the surrounding trilithons: the tallest stones set at the closed side of the horseshoe, in the shadow of the Great Trilithon. They include a number that have been elegantly shaped: slender columns with smooth rounded sides. The tallest (Stone 68) now leans a little, the legacy of centuries spent propping up a 40-ton sarsen, and has a deep vertical groove running from top to bottom. Another, one of the stumps, has traces of a corresponding tongue, leading to the suggestion that together they may originally have formed a composite stone. On the tops of some of these taller bluestones are traces of battered-down tenons suggesting they once supported lintels, though not in the position where they stand today.

Finally, at the closed end of the innermost horseshoe, in the shadow of the Great Trilithon and now partly buried beneath its fallen upright and lintel, lies the Altar Stone (Stone 80). This is the largest of the non-sarsen stones, a great slab of greenish-grey Cosheton Bed sandstone from the Welsh coast near Preseli. The Altar Stone has never been seen in its entirety, only glimpsed during excavations. In reconstructions it is most frequently shown standing as an upright pillar, but it is possibile that it may have lain flat on the ground and genuinely looked like an altar.

Stone 68, vertically grooved and the most elegant of the slender pillars that make up the bluestone horseshoe.

Excavations in 1958 provided the clearest view to date of the Altar Stone, buried under the collapsed remains of the Great Trilithon.

The shaping and jointing of the stones is obvious, but until comparatively recently it was not realised that some of the stones were also decorated. The names that are deeply carved on the smooth faces of many of the upright sarsens date from the last few centuries and were clearly made with metal tools, but it was as late as 1953 that carvings of a much earlier date were discovered by Richard Atkinson. These included the outlines of daggers and axes, a few at first on Stone 53 and then, as more systematic searches were carried out, more carvings on more stones. All the known examples are at or below eye level, suggesting that they were carved after the stones had been set upright. There are at least 44 axe blades, of a type of axe that dates to around 1500BC, all shown with the cutting edge uppermost. There is also a highly unconvincing 'mother goddess', a 'small knife' and a single dagger that was originally thought to be a representation of a Mycenaean dagger of around 1500BC. This dagger, which may in reality be two separate axe carvings, was seen at the time of its discovery as proof of contacts between Britain and the eastern Mediterranean until radiocarbon dating demonstrated that Stonehenge was older than the culture that was supposed to have influenced its construction. The fact that Stonehenge was decorated in this way should not be surprising; what is remarkable is that the carvings were not spotted earlier, as they are clearly visible on photographs taken some 70 years before Atkinson saw them.

So far over 40 carvings, mainly of axes, have been found. Most are on Stone 53 (left) and Stone 4.

These then are the visible components of Stonehenge: the circular earthwork enclosure with its main north-easterly entrance emphasised by the ditches and banks of the Avenue. There are the peripheral stones – the Heel Stone, the Slaughter Stone and the Station Stones – and the now invisible circles of pits – the Aubrey Holes and the Y and Z Holes. There are circles and horseshoes of sarsen and bluestone that make up the great central structure. But this is not the complete picture. The excavations carried out during the 20th century revealed hundreds of small holes dug into the underlying chalk, each of which originally held an upright timber post. They occur in neat rows across the entrance causeway, in meandering parallel lines inwards from the southern entrance and in incomprehensible profusion among the central stones. These, and even older postholes found in the area of the present car park, are evidence of a Stonehenge before stone, an enigma that will be investigated in more detail in later chapters.

How old is Stonehenge?

In historical times dates can be assigned to events or structures with some precision; 1066 is the date of the Norman Conquest of England, the Houses of Parliament were built between 1840 and 1888. But this is not possible with prehistory, the time before written records, so other means must be found to divide up the long span of time before history begins in Britain, traditionally with the Roman invasion of AD43.

For centuries, those who studied the past had no way of understanding the span of ancient time, often trying to divide it up by reference to biblical events such as the Great Flood. Great emphasis was placed on the identification of flood deposits and the consequent ability to define events as 'antediluvian' (before the flood). There were also problems in ordering the vast collections of ancient artefacts accumulated in European museums from centuries of collecting and digging. Then in the early 19th century the Danish archaeologist, Christian Jurgensen Thomson, devised a logical dating system of three separate ages, characterised by the surviving materials that were most commonly used. The most ancient was the one where tools were made of stone, followed by an age of bronze and finally one where the majority of metal tools were of iron. This simple 'Three Age System' has remained in use ever since, although Thomson's main divisions have now been subdivided and refined. In these terms the Age of Stonehenge, the time during which Stonehenge was built and used, starts in around 3000BC, during the Neolithic or New Stone Age period, and carries on until around 1600BC, the middle of the Bronze Age.

The Three Age System is what is known as a *relative* chronology. It enables events to be placed in order but does not give any idea of when, in real time, these events happened. So in different parts of the world the three ages can occur in the same sequence but at very different times. What is needed to fix these events in time is an *absolute* chronology, a way of dating events. This became possible in the 1950s with the development of radiocarbon dating.

The sequence and dates of events in the construction of Stonehenge have been worked out by combining evidence from excavation and radiocarbon dates. Careful observation during excavation may show that the hole dug to receive a stone, for example an upright sarsen, cuts through a hole originally dug for a timber post. This provides a sequence: the timber post must have been raised before the sarsen stone. But what was the gap between these two events: days, months, years or centuries? There is the possibility that the gap could be measured by using clues from dateable objects found in the holes, but in the case of Stonehenge radiocarbon dating offers the best clues.

RADIOCARBON DATING

Radiocarbon dating is a scientific dating technique that can be applied to the surviving remains of anything that was once alive. All living things, whether animals, plants, trees or people, take up carbon from the environment during life, including an isotope that is naturally radioactive. When a living thing dies, that radioactivity gradually fades away. For radiocarbon (carbon 14), half of its radioactivity will have faded away over a period of 5,558 years and half of what is left in another 5,558 years. So, if the amount of radioactivity remaining can be accurately measured then it is possible to calculate how many years have passed since the organism died.

Samples for radiocarbon dating can come from any surviving organic material. On dry sites such as Stonehenge, where wood does not survive, these are usually of charred wood (charcoal) or the solid remains of living creatures – bone or antler. Unlike dates obtained from tree-rings, which can pinpoint a specific year and even a season within that year, radiocarbon measurements do not give a single precise date but suggest a date range.

Because the amount of radiocarbon in the environment is not always the same, the radiocarbon dates have to be calibrated using a reference curve made of measurements on tree-rings of known date.

Take, for example, one of the recent radiocarbon dates obtained for Stonehenge. OxA-4878 is the identification number of a sample of animal bone from a stone hole of the bluestone circle and indicates that the measurement is number 4878 in the database of the Oxford Radiocarbon Accelerator Unit. The amount of radiocarbon in this sample is 3740+/-40BP (with BP standing for 'before present'). When calibrated, this date comes out as 2290–2030 cal BC, there being a 95% chance that the true date actually lies between these limits. When a series of dates are obtained these can be combined with the relative order obtained from the sequence of archaeological layers to provide more exact dating.

At Stonehenge, while the stones themselves cannot be directly dated, the holes in which they stand can, by using organic finds from the soils that fill them. These are mostly animal bones or the fragments of the antler picks that were presumably used to dig the holes. The most reliable sample for radiocarbon dating was the tip of an antler pick that had broken off and was still embedded in the chalk in the side of a stone hole. There was no doubt in this case that the date obtained from the pick was the date that the hole was dug.

Radiocarbon dating is a process that involves the total destruction of the sample, so a careful balance has to be struck between the need for dating and the preservation of fragile and irreplaceable archaeological finds.

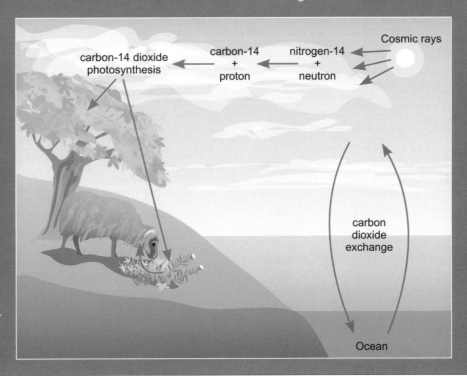

Radiocarbon is found in the upper atmosphere and enters the food chain, and so all living things, through photosynthesis

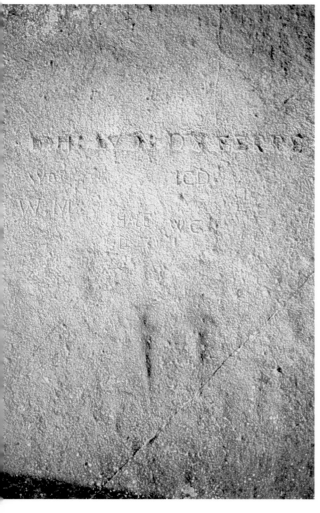

Framed by more recent graffiti, the axe and the dagger first spotted by Richard Atkinson in 1953.

LICHENS

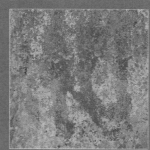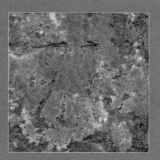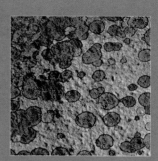

Even from a distance, visitors to Stonehenge can see that the surfaces of the stones do not have a uniform appearance. They are mottled with a wide variety of colours, created by different species of lichen covering virtually every exposed surface.

Every lichen consists of a fungus and a green alga (or a *cynobacterium*), living together in a mutually beneficial – or symbiotic – association. The algal partner contains chlorophyll and, like plants, has the ability to convert the sun's energy into sugar. The fungal partner constitutes the body of the lichen, protecting the alga from the harsh environments in which lichens live. Most lichens grow very slowly, increasing by between 0.5 and 5mm (0.02 and 0.2in) a year, depending on the species. They can be found In every climatic zone throughout the world, from arctic tundra to tropical rainforests, and each species is adapted to its specific type of environment.

A lichen survey at Stonehenge in 2003 found that there were 77 different species growing on the stones, several of which are nationally rare or scarce. Although it is hard to date lichens, as new growth is constantly replacing old, it will have taken hundreds of years for this range of species to become established on the stones. The lichen types at Stonehenge are broadly similar to those at the nearby stone circle at Avebury, but with some interesting exceptions.

Buellia saxorum, a type of lichen that specialises in colonising sarsen stones and which is widespread at Avebury, is totally absent from Stonehenge for no apparent reason. Equally surprising, many of the lichen species found at Stonehenge usually grow only on exposed coastlines. It is possible that the prevailing winds at Stonehenge, blowing in from the Atlantic, may have encouraged these species to grow, but again, specialists have not been able to find a convincing explanation. So not all the mysteries of Stonehenge are archaeological.

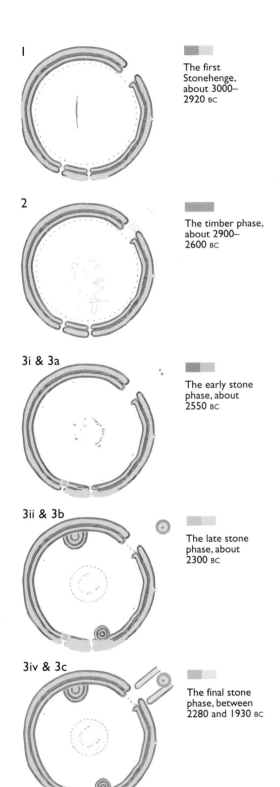

1

The first Stonehenge, about 3000–2920 BC

2

The timber phase, about 2900–2600 BC

3i & 3a

The early stone phase, about 2550 BC

3ii & 3b

The late stone phase, about 2300 BC

3iv & 3c

The final stone phase, between 2280 and 1930 BC

The construction of Stonehenge starts with the excavation of the ditch and the building of the bank, some time between 3000 and 2920BC. By radiocarbon dating standards this date range is very precise and was defined by using a large number of dating samples from antler picks and by carefully combining the results.

The next stage in Stonehenge's development includes the Aubrey Holes and presumably many of the postholes, the settings for upright timbers that lie within the enclosure. Unfortunately, despite the excavation of many of these timber settings, there are no radiocarbon dates for this phase. Logically its date must lie between the end of building the enclosure and the beginning of the next stage of construction, the arrival of the first stones. So on this basis it must date to between 2900 and 2600BC.

According to the most recent information, the first stones, a collection of bluestones and a small number of sarsens, including the Station Stones, the Heel Stone and its now missing pair, started to arrive around 2550BC. The bluestones were first set up in two concentric arcs, a peculiar and undated arrangement that appears never to have been completed and which was dismantled before the next stone phase, the arrival of the 75 massive sarsens that would make up the central building. Again, there is no precise dating for the sarsen circle and the horseshoe of trilithons, but until recently they were thought to have been raised around 2300BC. However, a recent revised scheme of dating (discussed in detail in chapter 8) suggests that these structures could have been built as early as 2600–2500BC which, if true, would mean that previous phases of construction would have had to have taken place at an earlier date. In effect the earlier chronology would be squashed into a much shorter time span. The final arrangement that saw the reintroduction of the bluestones, the repositioning of stones around the entrance to the enclosure and the construction of the Avenue took place between 2280 and 1930BC.

This effectively marked the end of construction at Stonehenge, with the exception of the Y and Z Holes which appear to have been dug as late as 1600BC.

From this time onwards Stonehenge appears to have slipped slowly and gently into retirement. Obsolete and decaying, it awaited the medieval scholars who would usher in the beginnings of its new life, as an object of wonder and curiosity.

CHAPTER 2   Landscape

The majority of visitors to Stonehenge are drawn by the stones themselves and may not even notice the subtle traces of the earthworks that surround them. Very few venture beyond the confines of the car park to explore the surrounding landscape – a landscape so rich in prehistoric remains that much of it, in recognition of its international importance, was classified in 1986 as a World Heritage Site.

The richness of this backdrop to Stonehenge was recognised by antiquarians and pioneering archaeologists as far back as the 18th century. They discovered, and in some cases dug into, the more obvious remains of ditches, banks and mounds that to their eyes all appeared to be concerned with burial and ritual. In fact, until the early years of the 20th century Stonehenge appeared to be surrounded by a landscape inhabited solely by the prehistoric dead, in which the living – the people who raised the stones and worshipped there – had no place. Then, in the early years of the 20th century, the invention of aircraft and the proximity of several early airfields led to photographs being taken from the air, with startling results. Suddenly, alongside all the ceremonial and burial sites (including some new discoveries) were the more mundane traces of prehistoric life: boundary ditches, trackways, fields and farmsteads.

In recent years more evidence, of a different kind, has come from 'fieldwalking' the ploughed fields that surround Stonehenge. This is a method of investigation more correctly known as 'surface collection', in which artefacts are systematically collected from the surface of bare winter fields. Large areas have been covered, producing hundreds of thousands of artefacts, mainly more durable types such as fragments of worked flint and stone, but also fragile pottery and rare metal finds. Shattered flint flakes reveal where the raw material was mined and where tools were made, while the tools themselves show where different domestic tasks were carried out. Burnt stones provide evidence of hearths and fragments of pottery show where food was stored and cooked. This is another layer of evidence to help in the understanding of how the landscape developed and was used during the Age of Stonehenge.

This chapter is intended as an introduction to the main prehistoric monuments that lie close to Stonehenge, explaining how they can be recognised, what we understand of their function and how they relate to the long timescale during which Stonehenge was built and used. Particular attention will be paid to those monuments that are not only still visible but are also accessible to visitors. Their discovery and early investigation will be explained in more detail in chapters 3, 4 and 7 and they will also reappear, in their original form, alongside the evidence from aerial photography, fieldwalking and environmental studies, as part of the story of the developing Stonehenge landscape in chapter 12.

In terms of timescale the monuments can be divided into three broad groups. The first, either predating or contemporary with the earliest phase of Stonehenge – the simple enclosure and its timber structures – includes earthwork enclosures of various forms and elongated burial mounds called long barrows. The second group, which were built and used at the same time as the timber and early stone phases at

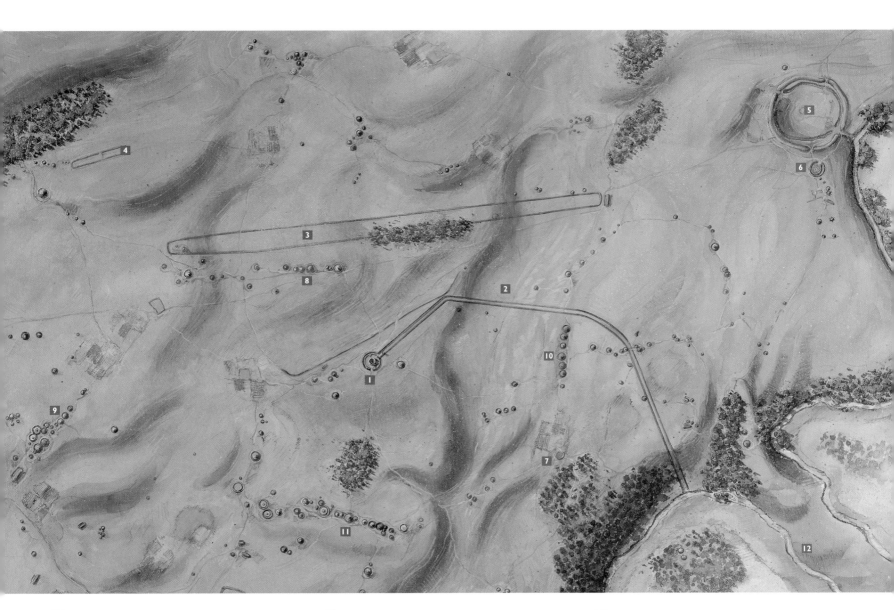

1 Stonehenge

2 The Avenue

3 The Cursus

4 The Lesser Cursus

5 Durrington Walls

6 Woodhenge

7 Coneybury Henge

8 The Cursus Barrows

9 Winterbourne Stoke Crossroads Barrows

10 New King Barrows

11 Normanton Down Barrows

12 River Avon

OPPOSITE
The Cursus viewed from its western end. The gap in the wood in the foreground shows its width and the eastern end is marked by a straight belt of trees.

Stonehenge, consists mainly of other henges – ceremonial sites of various sizes and forms that date to the later part of the Neolithic period. The third group of monuments, which date from the time when Stonehenge was being rebuilt in stone right through to the final minor alterations, should strictly include some of the late henges but consists mainly of the hundreds of Bronze Age round barrows that pepper the landscape or cluster together in complex cemeteries.

Enclosures and long barrows

Robin Hood's Ball

Robin Hood's Ball is an earthwork enclosure that lies within the Salisbury Plain military training area (SPTA) on the summit of a low ridge about 4km (2.5 miles) north-west of Stonehenge. It is a type of site known as a 'causewayed enclosure', consisting of roughly circular or irregular earthworks that can have one, two or three circuits of ditch and bank. Their most distinctive feature, however, is the way in which the ditches were dug, reflected in the 'causewayed' element of their name. Rather than being dug as a continuous circuit, they appear as a series of short segments separated by causeways, while the banks are also often discontinuous and

Robin Hood's Ball, a Neolithic causewayed enclosure to the north-west of Stonehenge.

have a rather lumpy profile. Most were constructed in the earlier part of the Neolithic, between about 4000 and 3500BC, but some continued in use until around 3000BC. Small excavations were carried out at Robin Hood's Ball in the 1960s, producing fragments of the characteristic round-bottomed pots known as 'Windmill Hill Ware' after the causewayed enclosure in north Wiltshire where pottery of this type was first recognised.

Exactly how sites like this were used is difficult to understand. Some, sited on steep hilltops, appear to have had a defensive function and examples at Crickley Hill in Gloucestershire and Hambledon Hill in Dorset show evidence of large-scale attack. Hundreds of the finely-worked, leaf-shaped flint arrowheads that also characterise this period were found close to major entrances and, in the case of Hambledon, part of the defensive circuit appears to have been deliberately destroyed. A human skeleton, found in the ditch under collapsed chalk rubble, had a flint arrowhead lodged in its ribs. Other sites of this type contain evidence that they were lived in. But the majority, like Robin Hood's Ball and the first Stonehenge, a very late example of this type of site, appear to have had some form of ceremonial function. Parts of Hambledon, for example, may have been used as places where human corpses were exposed and reduced to skeletons before burial in long barrows (*see* below). In some cases their ditches contain deposits of pottery and animal bones, perhaps the remains of feasts that were not simply thrown away as rubbish but were regarded as important and disposed of in an organised manner. More evidence of the special nature of causewayed enclosures comes from some of the exotic artefacts found in excavation. These include axes found in southern England made of stone that has to have come from as far away as Wales or the Lake District, and fragile pottery made from clay that is only found in Cornwall. Finds like these show the importance of causewayed enclosures in long-distance trade networks.

The Cursus and the Lesser Cursus

In around 3000BC Robin Hood's Ball and the first Stonehenge were joined by two even stranger enclosures. The first, called the Cursus, is a hugely elongated earthwork about 100m (330ft) wide and 2.7km (1.7 miles) long that runs roughly east–west across the downland to the north of Stonehenge. The long sides of the enclosure are each marked by a low bank and, outside it, a shallow ditch. Along much of its length these slight earthworks have been flattened by cultivation, although their position has been marked in places by carefully placed fence lines. Towards its western end its width is marked by a gap in Fargo Wood beyond which the ditch and bank of the western terminal have been partly reconstructed. Both here and at the opposite end the ditch is more substantial and the bank appears to have been correspondingly larger, which means that, despite the central section of the Cursus dipping into a shallow dry valley, each end can be seen from the other. The eastern end is generally thought to stop just short of a Neolithic long barrow that lies north–south, parallel to the Cursus terminal. But this mound, now much eroded and traversed by the track that runs along the King Barrow Ridge, may simply be the eastern bank of the Cursus rather than a separate long barrow. Only excavation can tell.

The Lesser Cursus has been ploughed almost flat but a detailed plan of its ditches has been revealed by geophysical survey.

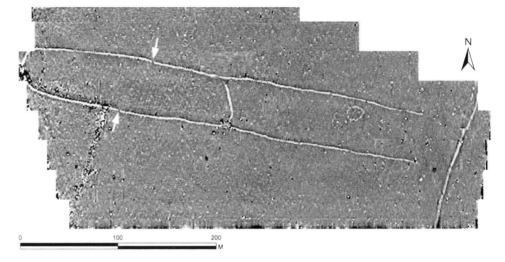

This strange monument was first spotted by the early 18th-century antiquarian William Stukeley, who decided that it was Roman in date and gave it the name Cursus or Hippodrome (both Latin names for racetrack). He was entirely wrong about the date, as radiocarbon dating has shown that it was built around 3000BC. Its function, however, still remains uncertain, even after six separate small-scale excavations (three by the author). It appears to be aligned on the sunrise at the equinox, the times in spring and autumn when day and night are of equal length, but may just as well have been laid out for processions, echoing Stukeley's original idea of its function. It has also been suggested that it may have functioned as a symbolic barrier, separating the two enclosures of Stonehenge and Robin Hood's Ball, each with its attendant clusters of long barrows.

The Cursus lies wholly within the National Trust's Stonehenge Estate and it is possible to follow in the footsteps of its Neolithic builders and walk from one end to the other.

Considering that they are rare monuments, it is remarkable that there is a second cursus within the Stonehenge landscape, just to the north-west of the western end of the one described above. This one, which is much smaller – only about 400m (1300ft) long and 60m (200ft) wide – is known as the Lesser Cursus. Although its earthworks have been levelled by ploughing and the site can no longer be seen on the ground, excavations by the author in 1983 revealed that, when first built, it was even shorter. Initially a mere 200m (650ft) in length, its sides were defined by a tiny ditch that was then considerably enlarged at the same time as its overall length was doubled. Strangely, at its eastern end the ditches simply stop, leaving an open end as if it was never completed. The newly-dug ditches then appear to have been rapidly filled in with the recently excavated chalk, which in one area covered a collection of antler picks neatly and deliberately laid out in a line on the ditch floor. Radiocarbon dates from these picks suggest that the Lesser Cursus was also built in around 3000BC.

Abandoned Neolithic digging tools: antler picks found on the floor of the Lesser Cursus ditch.

The Lesser Cursus lies on private land.

West Kennet long barrow in the Avebury area, close to the source of the sarsens. Around Stonehenge the burial chambers inside long barrows are likely to be made of timber.

Long barrows

Apart from these assorted enclosures which, in the apparent absence of any practical use must be regarded as having some sort of ceremonial function, there are also a number of burial sites from this period in the vicinity of Stonehenge. Long barrows are elongated mounds of varying size, often flanked by deep and sometimes irregular ditches that acted as quarries for the material used to build the mound. In areas where suitable stone is available, for example around Avebury in north Wiltshire, the mounds often cover stone chambers, some quite complex in their structure, that could be repeatedly opened up to allow more burials to be introduced. In areas where no suitable building stone is readily available, such as around Stonehenge, the mounds tend to cover similar structures made of wood, which were less easy to open and reseal. These structures, best interpreted as houses of the dead, often contain collections of human remains arranged in ways that suggest that bones rather than complete bodies were placed inside them. There is evidence that the transformation from corpse to bare bones, by the simple process of exposing the body to the forces of nature, may have taken place in some causewayed enclosures. The most obvious function of long barrows seems to have been as ancestral tombs, but they may also have been a means of establishing a claim to the territory on which they stood, the Neolithic equivalent of a title deed.

Within the Stonehenge landscape there are at least ten long barrows, ranging in size from one only 16m (50ft) long, hidden within the group of round barrows on Normanton Down, to the largest and best preserved example at Winterbourne Stoke Crossroads. This huge mound, over 85m (280ft) long, was perhaps as much as 1,000 years old when it provided both the focus and the alignment for an impressive cemetery of Bronze Age round barrows.

The barrow diggers of the early 19th century tended to avoid long barrows as they grew to realise that their excavation usually meant much effort for little reward. Finding the place of burial (usually at the broader end) was not easy, and if they did locate it all they could expect was bones and the occasional pot or stone tool. But a little later in the 19th century it was precisely these contents that would attract the attentions of John Thurnam, a Wiltshire doctor fascinated by the skull shapes of the ancient Britons. None of the long barrows in the Stonehenge area has been examined scientifically.

Plan of Woodhenge revealed by excavations in 1926 and 2006.

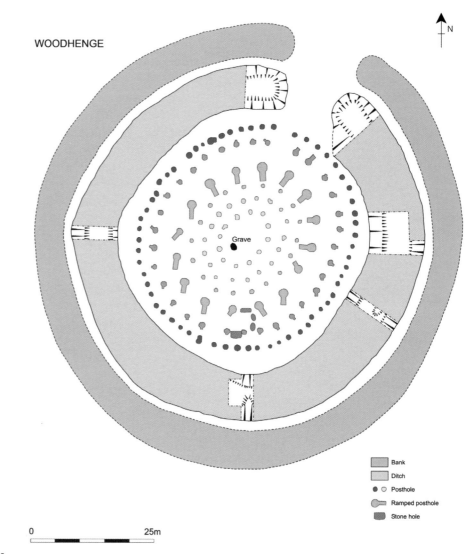

WOODHENGE

N

Grave

Bank
Ditch
Posthole
Ramped posthole
Stone hole

0   25m

Henge monuments

Woodhenge

Woodhenge – aerial camera view of the 2006 excavations

Perched on a bluff above the River Avon nearly 3km (2 miles) to the north-west of Stonehenge lies Woodhenge. In the early 19th century it was realised that there was a site of some sort here, but even by this time it had been ploughed for many years and it was decided that it was simply the remains of a large, flattened 'druid' barrow. Then in 1925 aerial photographs, followed shortly afterwards by excavation, showed that it was a roughly circular ditched enclosure about 50m (160ft) in diameter with a single north-east facing entrance. Within the enclosure, which had traces of an external bank, were 168 postholes arranged in six concentric rings. The oak posts that they had originally contained varied considerably in size from ring to ring. The smallest were only 23cm (9in), the largest as much as 85cm (nearly 3ft) in diameter. Within the enclosure, on the south-east side, there were also two pits that were interpreted as the sockets for upright stones and further stone holes were found during excavations carried out in 2006.

Human remains were found at Woodhenge – a crouched skeleton in a grave dug into the floor of the ditch and cremated bones in one of the postholes. But perhaps the most disturbing find was a grave that lay at the centre of the enclosure under a small flint cairn. It contained the skeleton of a young child – perhaps a natural death, perhaps a sacrifice.

The site gained the name 'Woodhenge' quite soon after its discovery, due to the similarity of its plan to that of Stonehenge. The highly decorated 'Grooved Ware' pottery that was found in its postholes indicated a construction date towards the end of the Neolithic period, during the Age of Stonehenge. This has subsequently been confirmed by radiocarbon dating which suggests that it was built around 2300BC.

Today Woodhenge is in the guardianship of English Heritage. There is free access and it is displayed as it was shortly after the excavation, with the positions of the posts marked by low, colour-coded concrete pillars of appropriate diameter.

The timber posts at Woodhenge, which may have supported wooden lintels, need not have been plain but may have been elaborately decorated.

Durrington Walls

Close to Woodhenge, straddling a hollow on the sloping valley side above a loop in the River Avon, lies a massive enclosure over 500m (roughly 1,440ft) across at its widest point. The bank, which lies outside the ditch, is over 30m (100ft) wide in places and there are four entrances. The widest and most obvious faces south-east, downslope towards the river, and another faces in the opposite direction to the north-east. To the north is a blocked entrance and the fourth looks south towards Woodhenge. This is the super-henge of Durrington Walls, the largest in the British Isles and a site that, despite its scale, is very difficult to appreciate at ground level.

Trenches dug through the bank in 1917 and 1951 produced pottery that suggested a similar date to the stone phase at Stonehenge, but Durrington would have remained an enigma if it had not been for the huge excavations carried out in the mid-1960s when the road that ran through the centre of the enclosure was straightened. An area over 760m (2,184ft) long and up to 40m (115ft) wide was excavated. A 34m (98ft) length of ditch was emptied and at this point in the circuit was shown to be up to 6m (20ft) deep and varying in width from around 7m (23ft) at its base to nearly 18m (60ft) wide at the top.

Inside the enclosure excavation revealed the remains of two circles of timber posts. The Southern Circle, lying just inside the south-eastern entrance of the enclosure, initially consisted of five rings of comparatively small but deeply set posts; this was replaced by a circle with six rings, the outermost nearly 40m (133ft) in diameter. Some of these later posts were nearly 1m (over 3ft) in diameter and set in postholes 2.5m (8ft) deep. A second, smaller circle lay about 120m (400ft) north and consisted of a square central setting of four large posts surrounded by a ring of smaller posts about 14.5m (48ft) in diameter. There are many conflicting ideas about the original appearance of these circles, but it was always considered unlikely that they would be all that lay within the earthwork enclosure. It was hardly surprising, then, that in 1996 and again in 2005 geophysical surveys revealed a range of enclosures, postholes and pits lying within the unexplored parts of the site.

Large-scale excavations from 2004 onwards, carried out by a team led by Mike Parker Pearson, have re-examined the southern timber circle and, within the enclosure, have identified a range of ditched enclosures that contain not only the pits for huge wooden posts but also traces of small rectangular houses with central hearths. Similar houses, with floors made of hard-packed chalk and walls of closely spaced wooden stakes, lie just outside the south-eastern entrance, flanking a wide metalled 'avenue' that leads down towards the river. These new excavations are the most exciting recent developments in our understanding of the Stonehenge landscape during the later Neolithic period.

Whether Durrington Walls, which was built around 2500BC, was a place where people lived or where they gathered to conduct elaborate ceremonies is uncertain; it may have been a combination of both.

Durrington Walls can be viewed from the car park adjacent to Woodhenge.

Magnetometer plot of Coneybury Henge shown deliberately upside down so that the higher and lower readings of the ditch and outer bank appear like physical contours.

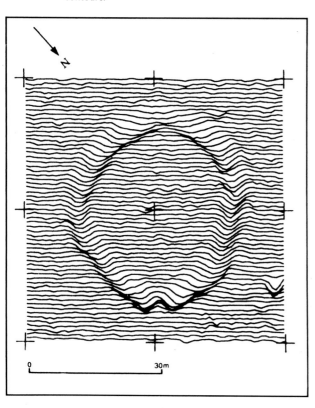

0   30m

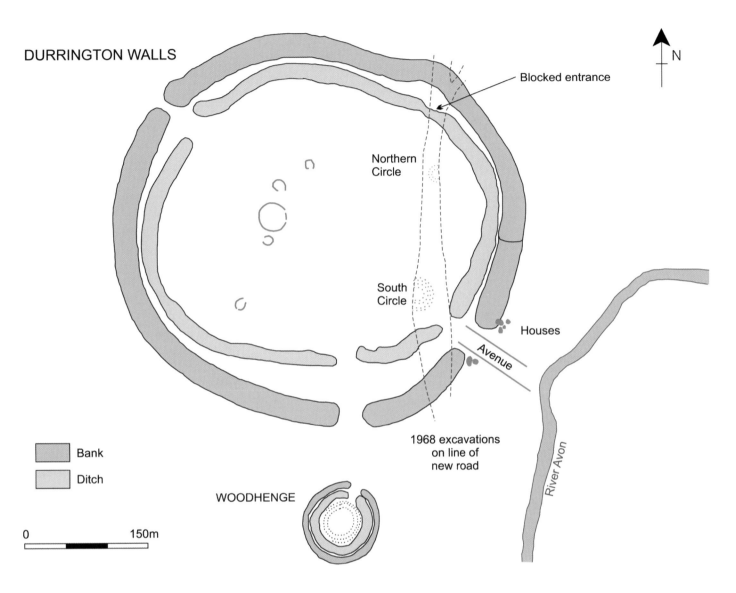

DURRINGTON WALLS

Blocked entrance

Northern Circle

South Circle

Houses

Avenue

1968 excavations on line of new road

River Avon

Bank

Ditch

WOODHENGE

0   150m

Durrington Walls and the complex of Neolithic monuments on the west bank of the River Avon.

Coneybury Henge

A third henge lies on the summit of Coneybury Hill, about 1.4km (0.8 miles) to the south-east of Stonehenge. Like Woodhenge, this site was for many years thought to be the remains of a ploughed Bronze Age round barrow, until aerial photographs taken in the 1970s showed that its ditch was not circular but oval and that there was a single north-east facing entrance. The shape and the alignment, shared with both Woodhenge and Stonehenge, suggested that Coneybury was yet another henge monument and this was confirmed when the site was partially excavated by the author in 1980. The ditch was deep and steep-sided, and inside it were postholes and pits containing Grooved Ware pottery. A single radiocarbon date suggests that Coneybury was built around 2700BC, an early date for a henge monument.

Coneybury Henge lies on farmland and is not visible on the ground.

Round barrows

There are hundreds of Bronze Age round barrows around Stonehenge, contemporary with its later phases and peppering the landscape or clustering together in complex cemeteries. Unlike the earlier Neolithic long barrows that contain groups of burials, most Bronze Age round barrows were initially the tombs of individuals. The remains were either buried or cremated, and they were accompanied to the next world by a wide variety of personal possessions, including pottery vessels, tools of stone, bone or bronze, and ornaments made of exotic materials such as jet, amber and gold. Finds like these excited antiquarians and early archaeologists, with the result that almost all the barrows in the Stonehenge area were at least partially excavated during the 18th and 19th centuries. Some survivors, much damaged by ploughing, were completely excavated in the 1950s and 1960s.

When first built the barrows, like earlier monuments, would have stood out gleaming white in a predominantly green landscape, especially when they were carefully positioned on prominent ridges and hills. Their earthworks, although all circular in plan, exhibit an amazing variety of combinations of ditch, bank, mound and hollow.

The most common type is the bowl barrow, a simple circular mound that can vary considerably in size and is usually surrounded by a ditch, the quarry for the mound material.

Bell barrows have a flat or slightly sloping area, known as a 'berm', separating the mound from the surrounding ditch and creating a bell-shaped profile. Bowl and bell barrows are the most visible types of round barrow and the ones that survive in the greatest numbers, largely due to the size of their mounds which can be over 5m (16ft) high and present a real obstacle to ploughing.

In contrast, disc and saucer barrows are shallow in profile and consequently very vulnerable, and survive comparatively rarely. Disc barrows, which can be over 50m (160ft) in diameter, have a ditch with an external bank that defines a flat circular area in the centre of which lies a small mound or 'tump'. Saucer barrows are generally smaller in diameter and also have an external bank, but have a low gentle mound rising up from the inner edge of the ditch.

Perhaps the strangest form is the extremely rare pond barrow, where instead of a mound there is a shallow circular hollow surrounded by a low bank. The rarity of this type of barrow may be because, especially when eroded, it is impossible to distinguish from a genuine pond.

In their original form, even if gently eroded, the different types of barrows can be easily distinguished. It is far less easy, and sometimes impossible, when they have been heavily eroded or flattened by ploughing. What often survives, even when all the above-ground structure has been removed, is the filled-in ditch; as a result, during the 20th century aerial photography has added many barrows, showing up as 'ring ditches' in bare fields or growing crops, to the already impressive total.

BARROW TYPES

Within the Stonehenge landscape the most numerous and spectacular prehistoric monuments are undoubtedly the Bronze Age round barrows of a variety of shapes and sizes.

When first built, their gleaming white chalk mounds would have been highly visible in the landscape, especially when carefully and prominently positioned.

Many of the fine barrow groups that surround Stonehenge lie on National Trust open access land.

Bowl barrows can vary considerably in size, They have a mound usually surrounded by a ditch

Bell barrows have a flat or slightly sloping area separating the mound and the surrounding ditch

Disc barrows have a small mound lying within a flat circular area surrounded by a ditch and an external bank

Saucer barrows have a low mound surrounded by a ditch and external bank

Pond barrows, an extremely rare form, have a shallow circular hollow surrounded by a low bank

Barrow groups

The area around Stonehenge can be regarded as one huge cemetery, consisting of several hundred individual round barrows of every type known in southern Britain. But within this general spread several well defined clusters can be identified, usually referred to as groups or cemeteries and going by the names they were given by the early archaeologists who first explored them.

The Cursus Barrows, as their name suggests, lie close to the Cursus, on the crest of a low ridge that runs parallel to its southern side. There were originally at least ten barrows in a meandering east–west line but ploughing has levelled some of the smaller ones and today the most prominent feature of this group is the line of large and closely spaced bell barrows that mark its eastern extent. These, including an unusual twin bell barrow with a single ditch encircling two mounds, are the closest accessible barrows to Stonehenge. A similarly impressive bell barrow, known by early explorers of the landscape as 'the Monarch of the Plain', lies on the edge of Fargo Wood and marks the western end of the Cursus Barrows.

Moving clockwise around the landscape, the massive mounds of the New King Barrows can be seen to the east of Stonehenge among the trees that lie on the crest of the closest ridge. These are part of a group (including the Old King Barrows to the north) that meanders along the ridge for a distance of over a kilometre. Within this overall group there were originally at least 22 barrows including, at the southern end, some of the largest bowl and bell barrows within the Stonehenge landscape. These are the only barrows that escaped excavation in the 19th century, because even at that time they were protected by a covering of trees and a landowner unwilling to fell them to satisfy antiquarian curiosity. The only clues to their date and structure have come from holes torn in the mounds when trees were toppled by storms in 1990. Investigation then suggested that some of the mounds were of an unusual construction, built largely of turf stripped from the surrounding area and capped with ditch-dug chalk. There is no firm evidence for when they were built, but their size suggests that it would have been early in the Bronze Age, perhaps between 2300 and 2000BC.

The Cursus Barrows, lying parallel to the southern bank of the Cursus.

In the surviving fragments of an ancient beech wood lie the massive mounds of the New King Barrows.

The King Barrows can be viewed from the track that runs along the ridge from the eastern end of the Cursus to the north, and southwards as far as the A303.

To the south of Stonehenge, on the crest of a low ridge, lie the Normanton Down Barrows, described by the early 19th-century antiquarian Sir Richard Colt Hoare as 'a noble group – diversified in their forms, perfect in their symmetry, and rich in their contents.'

Within this group, as well as the smallest long barrow in the Stonehenge area, are some spectacularly large disc barrows – Colt Hoare's 'druid barrows'. The finds discovered in their tiny mounds, including beads and other personal ornaments, convinced him that they were the burial places of females. The most westerly of the disc barrows in this group is regarded by present-day Druids as the 'Mother Barrow'.

The Normanton Down Barrows. Beyond the two magnificent disc barrows and crowned with a single bush lies Bush Barrow, where spectacular finds were made in 1808. The 'Mother Barrow' is in the foreground.

Colt Hoare's comment on the 'rich contents' of these barrows is largely due to the finds that came from a large mound known as Bush Barrow in 1808. These included bronze daggers with surviving wooden handles decorated with complex patterns made up of minute gold pins. There was a bronze axe and what may have been a stone-headed 'sceptre' with bone decorations on its wooden handle. But the most spectacular finds were three objects of pure gold: a 'breastplate', a smaller lozenge-shaped sheet and a 'belt hook'. Bush Barrow, which today alone of all the barrows in the Normanton Group still has a bush growing on it, produced the richest single burial in the immediate vicinity of Stonehenge.

The Normanton Down Barrows are privately owned, but Bush Barrow and the adjacent disc barrows (including the Mother Barrow) can be viewed from nearby bridleways and footpaths.

The position of the cemeteries on Normanton Down and the King Barrow Ridge, together with the Cursus Barrows, is quite deliberate. To an observer standing at Stonehenge and looking around the surrounding landscape, the barrows of all of these groups are silhouetted on the skyline.

Further south, beyond Normanton Down and its intimate relationship with Stonehenge, lie the cemeteries of Wilsford and Lake. Lake lies in privately owned woodland, at the western edge of which can be seen the prominent mound of the Prophet Barrow, while the spectacular disc barrows of the Wilsford group have suffered badly from ploughing in the recent past.

Barrows of the Lake Down group to the south of Stonehenge.

The final great cemetery, the Winterbourne Stoke Crossroads group, lies to the south-west of Stonehenge, close to the roundabout at the junction of the A303 with the Salisbury to Devizes road. The location and subsequent structure of the entire cemetery is defined by the long barrow that lies closest to the crossroads. The alignment of its mound was followed, perhaps more than 1,000 years later, by a line of large bowl and bell barrows that stretches off to the north-east. Then, over several hundred more years as burial fashions changed in the earlier part of the Bronze Age (between 2000 and 1600BC), other more elaborate barrow types were added. As well as smaller bowl barrows there are discs and saucers, their beautiful but shallow forms best appreciated by standing on the summits of some of the larger mounds. There are even two pond barrows, including one that is dug through the ditch of a bell barrow, a rare example of a visible sequence of construction. This spectacular and well preserved barrow group, which contains every type of round barrow found in southern England, has a burial history that could span as much as 2,000 years. Part of the cemetery is owned by the National Trust and is accessible to visitors.

From long barrow to pond barrow, the Winterbourne Stoke Crossroads group is the most complex in the Stonehenge landscape and represents at least 1,500 years of burial history.

This then is the immediate context of Stonehenge. But, just as Stonehenge itself must not be viewed in isolation but as part of a surrounding landscape, so must both Stonehenge and its landscape be viewed as part of a much wider phenomenon.

The background to the whole tradition of building monuments, whether in stone or timber but all essentially involving communal labour and a sense of organisation, lies in the origins of agriculture. By and large people who practised a Mesolithic (Middle Stone Age) hunter-gatherer economy had no tradition of building substantial structures though some communities, particularly those with access to rich resources such as those living in coastal areas, clearly lived in complex and quite settled groups and developed a rich tradition of burial. It can be argued that the mounds raised over some Mesolithic graves represent the first monuments, but their scale is small compared to what was to follow.

Generally, farming is the key, the change in economy being just one part of the Neolithic 'package' that included the production of pottery and changes in the ways of making and finishing stone tools. Farming, both of domesticated animals – sheep or goats, cattle and pigs – and cereals such as wheat and barley, together with the associated ideas of territory and land ownership, originated in the Near East and reached Crete, Greece and Iberia (Spain) by around 6000BC, before spreading across Europe. The first plough agriculture in Brittany dates to around 4500BC and shortly afterwards this Neolithic (New Stone Age) economy reached Ireland and then Britain. There were several ways in which these ideas could have spread. Indigenous hunter-gatherer populations could take them up; alternatively they could have been spread by the movement of people who took their new ways with them to new lands. So there is no simple answer, and likewise much uncertainty about the routes that were taken. Across the European mainland agriculture may have spread across areas of fertile soils, but the ideas, together with seed corn and breeding animals, had to travel by sea to reach Britain and Ireland.

One result of the interaction between well established and successful groups of hunter-gatherers (with their established burial traditions) and the new ideas and new people that represented the Neolithic (with its concept of territory and a potentially more productive economy) was the development, some time shortly after 5000BC, of a new cultural phenomenon: megalithic architecture. The first megalithic ('big stone') structures were the long mounds of the Carnac region of Morbihan in Brittany and the passage graves first found in the west of the region. Long mounds were, as their name suggests, long low rectangular mounds of earth, their sides supported by drystone walls or upright slabs. The mounds covered a variety of structures including slab-built boxes (cists) containing human remains.

At the same time as these mounds were being built, between 4700 and 4400BC, a series of huge upright stones, or menhirs, were being erected, further components of what were becoming ritual landscapes. The most spectacular of these was Le Grand Menhir Brisé, originally over 20m (66 ft) high and weighing 348 tons. It was pulled down and broken in around 3800BC and its pieces used as the capstones for three separate passage graves. These are the second distinctive type of burial monument that emerged at this time, complex structures in which stone mounds covered one or more chambers for the dead, each of which was accessed from outside by means of a long passage. Passage graves, which individually could have a complex history and become highly elaborate, were destined to become a far more widespread and lasting tradition than the earlier long mounds and their accompanying menhirs. But perhaps the most celebrated examples of megalithic architecture in Brittany are the extraordinary alignments at Carnac where, in around 3800BC, over 3,000 stones were erected in long lines that snake in parallel rows across the landscape. Alongside these stone rows are enclosures of upright stones, perhaps the very first stone circles.

These structures, which required huge labour input (perhaps as many as 2,000 people to move the Grand Menhir) and were mainly for the glorification of the ancestral dead, soon spread throughout what is often called the Atlantic zone. In Ireland the megalithic tradition is represented by dolmens, stone-built burial chambers, some simple and others more elaborate, and by passage graves. Both show a distinctly coastal bias in their distribution and, reflecting the time taken for ideas to travel, appear some time after 4000BC. Ireland has over 200 passage graves, including the spectacularly large and elaborate examples of Knowth, Dowth and Newgrange. Newgrange incorporates 450 stone slabs each weighing up to 5 tons and its complex and highly decorated burial chambers are capped with a mound that is estimated to contain 200,000 tons of earth and boulders.

Evidence of the spread of ideas during the fourth millennium BC can clearly be seen in the similarity between the distinctly Irish 'court cairn' and the Clyde cairns of the

The elaborately decorated interior of the passage grave at Gavrinis in Brittany.

west coast of Scotland. From Brittany through Ireland and into Scotland, the tradition of megalithic building spread further north to the islands of the Hebrides and Orkney.

Orkney, its fertile soils already being farmed early in the fourth millennium BC, also has many stone-built tombs, houses for the dead that in some ways reflect the living architecture seen in Neolithic villages like Scara Brae. But around 3000BC there is a change of emphasis, from tomb building to the creation of ritual landscapes. The tomb of Maes Howe, considered by many to be the finest piece of megalithic architecture in prehistoric Europe, is now recognised as simply one component of a complex ritual landscape that represents an increase in cooperation and effort. There are even more tombs, as well as standing stones and three great henges – the Ring of Bookan, the Stones of Stenness and the massive Ring of Brodgar, over 100m in diameter and surrounded by a deep, rock-cut ditch.

This pattern is repeated on Lewis in the Hebrides where, on the hill of Callanish, lies the 'Stonehenge of the north', a circle from which four stone rows radiate out and close to which lie other stone alignments. This is yet another example where the focal monuments are just one part of a landscape of great complexity and subtlety, in which built structures relate in a very deliberate way to the natural landforms.

So traditions that develop in Orkney take root and blossom in Wessex. Henges reach gigantic proportions; the whole idea of communal effort on an increasingly vast scale can be seen in monuments like Silbury Hill, the largest artificial mound in Europe. And then there is Stonehenge itself which, it can be argued, is a monument that embodies many of the ideas that were first realised in Brittany so many centuries before. If those who had raised the Grand Menhir could have seen Stonehenge in its final form they would have recognised their skills and ideas taken to new heights. Just as the surroundings of Stonehenge took the concept of a ritual landscape to a new level, so Stonehenge itself can be regarded as the ultimate expression of the Atlantic tradition of megalithic architecture.

The Ring of Brodgar in Orkney

WORLD HERITAGE SITES

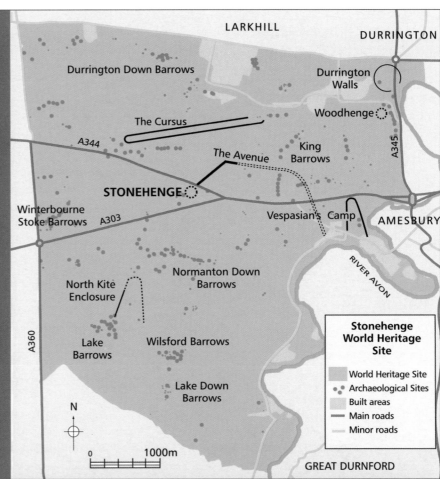

Stonehenge World Heritage Site

- World Heritage Site
- Archaeological Sites
- Built areas
- Main roads
- Minor roads

The World Heritage Convention was established in 1972 by UNESCO (United Nations Educational, Scientific and Cultural Organisation). It defines World Heritage Sites as places of international importance for the conservation of mankind's cultural and natural heritage. They are places that need to be preserved for future generations, as part of a common universal heritage.

There are over 800 such sites worldwide, with 27 in the UK including The Giant's Causeway in Ireland, Hadrian's Wall, the Jurassic Coast of Dorset and Devon and the City of Liverpool.

To become a World Heritage Site, a place has to be nominated by its government to the World Heritage Committee who take advice from specialist international bodies.

The Stonehenge and Avebury landscapes were inscribed on the World Heritage List in 1986 for their outstanding prehistoric monuments, in particular for Stonehenge itself which, with its shaped stones, lintels, unique jointing and perfect geometry, is the most sophisticated stone circle in the world. The ceremonial landscape that surrounds it, with its dense concentrations of archaeological remains, was also recognised as being of outstanding importance.

To protect such an incomparable testimony to prehistoric achievement, the Stonehenge World Heritage Site covers 2600 hectares (6500 acres) of chalk downland, woodland and arable fields. The ownership is shared between English Heritage, the National Trust, the Ministry of Defence, farmers and householders.

World Heritage status brings international recognition and prestige, and encourages national governments to improve the protection of their sites. The management plan that has been prepared for Stonehenge and its surrounding landscape is designed to help conserve and manage the site for present and future generations. The plan has already been responsible for the return of previously cultivated areas to grassland, improving the management of ancient monuments and helping to improve biodiversity.

CHAPTER 3   **The discovery of Stonehenge**

The last changes at Stonehenge, the digging of the two circles of pits known as the Y and Z Holes, took place some time around 1600BC. But these additions, which seem more like an afterthought than part of any great reorganisation, may not have marked the end of Stonehenge's use, merely its modification. Medieval cathedrals and churches were not built, altered and then immediately abandoned; they carried on in use long after the fabric of their buildings ceased to change. But was this the case at Stonehenge? If what appear to be the last alterations in 1600BC really were its final form, then what went on after it was completed? Were there rituals and ceremonies that have left no trace in the archaeological record? And when did the stones finally start to lose their importance? Within the surrounding landscape there are clues that point to a change of emphasis towards the end of the Bronze Age, around 1000BC. By this time land was being parcelled up and small farmsteads were appearing, established on what may until then have been sacred ground, their fields spreading over ancient ceremonial sites. This may mark a decline in the spiritual importance of the entire area and it may be at this time that Stonehenge finally became obsolete.

On a low ridge adjacent to the River Avon near Amesbury lies Vespasian's Camp, a hillfort with earthen ramparts that, despite bearing the name of a Roman emperor, was built and occupied during the later part of the Iron Age, the centuries immediately before the Roman invasions. To the people who lived in the fort Stonehenge must have been just a local curiosity. But it is possible that its fame had spread abroad, into the classical world. In the 5th century BC the Greek historian Hecateus of Abdera wrote of a 'magnificent sacred precinct of Apollo and a notable temple which is adorned with many votive offerings and is spherical in shape'. The spherical temple could be Stonehenge, and Apollo is the god of the Sun which fits well with what we think may have been its function (*see* chapter 11). But beyond this there are problems. Hecateus's temple is described as lying in the land of the 'Hyperboreans', a legendary people believed to have lived 'beyond the north wind in a land of unbroken sunshine'. This does not sound like Britain, and overall there is no convincing evidence to suggest that Hecateus really did know of Stonehenge.

By the time of the Roman invasion in AD43 Stonehenge must have long ceased to be a relevant spiritual centre and would have been, at best, something strange and rare. Over the years excavations at Stonehenge have produced finds of coins, brooches and surprisingly large quantities of pottery dating to the time of the Roman occupation. But there are no signs of structures and no evidence for the deliberate removal of stones, and so these finds must be seen as little more than casual losses by curious visitors. By this time, after perhaps more than 1,000 years of neglect, stones may have started to fall and Stonehenge may have started to take on a ruinous appearance. Even so, it would still have been recognised by those familiar with the classical world as an ancient and unique structure of extraordinary sophistication.

From being a curiosity in Roman times, Stonehenge may have become the focus of more macabre activities. In November 1923 a burial was found in a shallow grave just outside the sarsen circle and adjacent to Y Hole 9. Two postholes were also found

Merlin building Stonehenge in a 14th-century manuscript illustration. Or is he dismantling a stone circle in Ireland?

close to the grave. The skeleton was at first thought to be Roman or later in date and therefore of little interest, and the bones were then mislaid. However, they have recently been tracked down, re-examined and radiocarbon dated, and the skeleton turned out to be that of a man aged about 30 who had been decapitated very efficiently by a single blow from a sharp blade, struck from behind and to his right. The radiocarbon date indicates that he was killed some time during the 7th century AD, the Saxon period, around the time the influence of Christianity was spreading across southern England. But was Stonehenge the place of his execution, or was he killed elsewhere and brought to this ancient place for burial? It has been suggested that the postholes found close to the grave may be the remains of a gallows, and although this seems to be stretching the evidence, there is perhaps some significance in the Old English derivation of the name Stonehenge. There are two components: 'stan' is consistent and means stone, while the other part of the name is either 'hencg' meaning hinge, which could apply to the right-angled joint between upright and lintel, or 'hen(c)gen' meaning gallows. Did Stonehenge, during the time that is often referred to as the 'Dark Age', become a place of execution where hangings and beheadings took place, and did it, in the process, gain a suitably dark name?

Stonehenge, which appears in early manuscripts spelt in a variety of ways (Stanenges, Stanheng or Stanhenge), emerges from this dark and ill-defined period of its history in about AD1130, when Henry of Huntingdon described the four wonders of Britain in his *Historia Anglorum (History of the English)*:

> the second is at Stonehenge, where stones of an amazing size are set up in a manner of doorways, so that one door seems to be set upon another. Nor can anyone guess by what means so many stones were raised so high, or why they were built here.

This rather puzzling reference to doors set on top of each other is presumably Henry's literary license, as there is no evidence that Stonehenge ever had a second storey.

Stonehenge was clearly well known to Norman scholars. Its unique structure ensured that, unlike any other stone circle in the British Isles, it had a name by which it could easily be recognised, and soon there were bold attempts to explain its construction and purpose. In 1136, in his *History of the Kings of Britain*, Geoffrey of Monmouth explained that Stonehenge was a memorial to a complicated feud that involved Saxons, led by King Hengist, Britons under the command of their king, Vortigern, and the rightful British king, Aurelius Ambrosius. Having explained the circumstances, Geoffrey was then able to calculate the construction date of Stonehenge by using detailed accounts of the rulers that succeeded Ambrosius (including King Arthur) and the lengths of their reigns. The date that he finally arrived at was AD485, and he also stated that the stones came from an Irish stone circle called the Giant's Round from where they were transported to Salisbury Plain by the wizard Merlin. Like many of Geoffrey's other stories, this account of Stonehenge's origins proved extremely popular and, despite the elements of magic which seem out of place in what was supposed to be an historical account, was widely circulated and accepted without criticism.

A schematic view of Stonehenge in a scala mundi of c.1340.

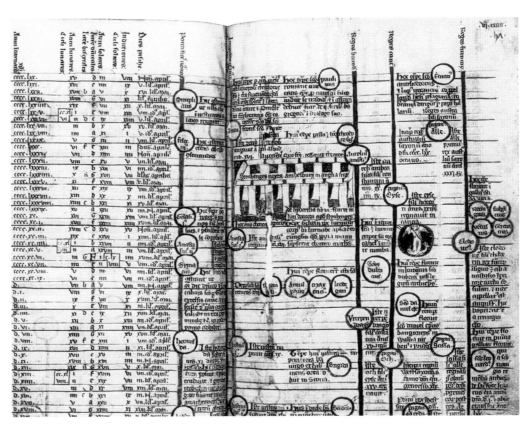

The first real representation of Stonehenge – the new discovery dating to c.1441.

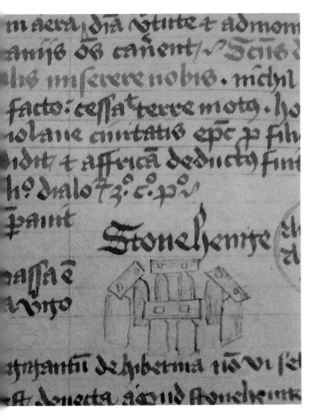

Until very recently only two medieval illustrations of Stonehenge were known, both schematic representations and firmly rooted in the story that the stones were raised by Merlin. In one, from the British Library's 1338–40 copy of *Roman de Brut*, the wizard is shown apparently placing a lintel at Stonehenge. In a scala mundi (chronicle of the world) of the same date, now in the library of Corpus Christi, Cambridge, Stonehenge is rectangular, again clearly not the product of first-hand observation. This is why a recent discovery by art historian Professor Christian Heck in a library in Douai, France, is so important. The drawing, which was only made public in 2007, is far from schematic, showing four trilithons with clearly visible tenons. There are some peculiarities – the tenons appear on the tops of the lintels for example – but it is sufficiently accurate to suggest that the artist had actually visited Stonehenge at a time when four compete trilithons still stood. So this drawing, executed perhaps a century after the other two, is a product of Renaissance observation rather than medieval mythology. This is also the first time that Stonehenge is referred to using its modern spelling.

In discussing all three early drawings Professor Heck suggests that the best known image (of Merlin lifting a lintel) may not show Stonehenge at all. In the *Roman de Brut* Merlin – 'not by force but by art, brought and erected the giants' round from Ireland, at Stonehenge near Amesbury'. So perhaps this shows not the building of Stonehenge but the dismantling of the stone circle on Mount Killaraus prior to its magical transportation.

Lucas de Heere's watercolour, apparently 'drawn on the spot' in the late 16th century.

Geoffrey of Monmouth's fantasies enjoyed lasting popularity and it was not until the 16th century that scholars started to demolish them. But even then there were still those who were prepared to accept some of his unfounded assertions. The Italian Polydore Vergil, for example, despite being one of Geoffrey's greatest critics, still believed that Stonehenge was the burial place of Aurelius Ambrosius. John Leland, King's Antiquary to Henry VIII, who gave an account of the ancient remains of England in his *De Antiquitate Britannica*, tried to explain the transportation of the stones to Stonehenge by non-magical means. But even he, despite sensibly suggesting the use of 'remarkable ingenuity and ... clever inventions', still involved Merlin, though as engineer rather than wizard.

It is also from this century that we have the first detailed written description of Stonehenge and, from the same source, a remarkable watercolour painting. Lucas de Heere was a Flemish refugee who, between 1573 and 1575, wrote the *Corte Beschryvinge van England, Scotland, ende Ireland*. *Corte Beschryvinge* roughly translates as 'short decription' and in this work, which survives only in manuscript form, de Heere describes the stones of Stonehenge and links his description to the watercolour of the stones 'as I have myself drawn them on the spot'. He describes them as being 'hard coarse material, of grey colour. They are generally about 18 or 20ft high and about 8ft wide over all sides (for they are square)'. This is puzzling, as the larger sarsen stones that he is describing are not square in plan, but are flat slabs more than twice as wide as they are deep. He writes of the arrangement and jointing of the stones that 'stand two by two, each couple having one stone across, like a gallows, which stone has two mortises catching two stone tenons of the two upright stones'. This is very accurate, but comparisons between his written description and the painting show some fundamental flaws. He identifies 'three ranks of stones, the largest of which comprises about three hundred feet in compass'. This must be the sarsen circle, the outer part of the central stone settings, which is just over 91m (100 yards) in circumference. De Heere describes this outer rank of stones as being 'mostly decayed', and shows seven lintels still in place, with a linked run of four on the north-east side, still today the best preserved section but now with only three lintels. He seems to have taken no note of the bluestone circle and shows only four upright pillars of the bluestone horseshoe. There are mistakes too in his depiction of the trilithons. Three are shown standing, but the tallest is shown in the wrong place and as fallen outwards rather than towards the centre. Of the remaining trilithon, of which there should be at least one standing upright, there is no sign at all. But despite these mistakes, and the earthwork that is shown crowding up against the outer stones – all of which cast some doubt on his assertion that the painting was 'drawn on the spot' – this is a valuable record of the state of Stonehenge after perhaps 3,000 years of neglect.

In 1625 the cartographer John Speed published a map of south Wiltshire that included 'Stonehinge' lying just to the west of the town of 'Ambersbury'. Speed had been warned that the stones were 'so dangerous that they may not safely be passed under', and that 'many of them are fallen downe, and the rest suspected of no sure foundation', but found that these fears were exaggerated. It was around this time that Stonehenge received the first of many royal visitors. In 1620 King James I, the guest of the Duke of Buckingham at Wilton House on the outskirts of Salisbury, became fascinated with Stonehenge. After attempting to persuade the owner, Robert Newdyk, to sell him the site, the Duke of Buckingham contented himself with commissioning the first recorded excavation within the stones. The hole that was dug, 'the bignesse of two saw pits', produced a variety of finds, from 'stagges hornes and bulls hornes and charcoales' (the familiar finds of later excavations) to 'batterdashers and pieces of armour eaten out with rust'. These are intriguing finds, many of them clearly not of prehistoric date, but there is the possibility that some, if not all, may have come from surrounding barrows rather than from Stonehenge itself. They have all subsequently been lost.

John Speed's map of 1625 showing the location of 'Stonehinge'.

THIS PAGE AND OPPOSITE TOP
The wider symmetry of Inigo Jones's overall plan of
Stonehenge.

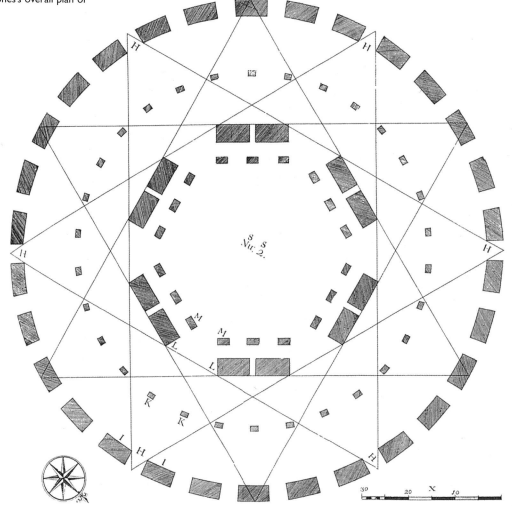

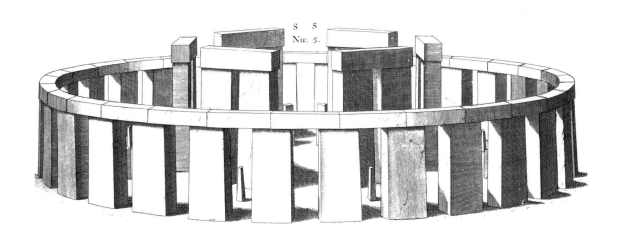

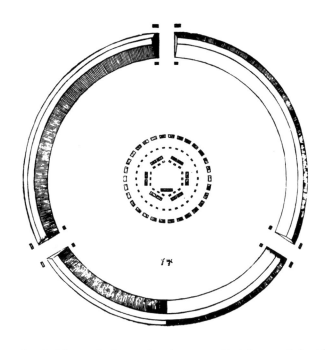

Inigo Jones, 1573–1652

One positive result of this early investigation was that James I decided that Stonehenge should be studied in detail, and engaged the architect Inigo Jones to carry out the work. Using an architect to carry out this work was quite logical as Stonehenge was seen at the time as a ruined building, an example of architecture. Jones worked on this commission until his death, after which his assistant, John Webb, completed *The Most Notable Antiquity of Great Britain, vulgarly called Stoneheng, on Salisbury Plain. Restored.* This is the first full-length book about Stonehenge, and it includes Jones's (and his disciple Webb's) explanation of who built it. The argument goes like this. From the descriptions of native Britons by classical authors, Stonehenge could not have been built by such a 'savage and barbarous people' who 'squatted in caves, tents and hovels, living on milk, roots and fruits'. Nor, according to Jones, could it have been built after the end of the Roman occupation as this was a time when 'all sciences were utterly perished' and there was nothing but 'universal confusion'. It thus stood to reason that Stonehenge had to fit within the period of comparative civilisation introduced to Britain by the Romans. Having come to this conclusion, Jones set about making the layout and structure of Stonehenge fit with the recognised rules of classical architecture. On a plan of the stones he superimposed an elaborate geometrical design, consisting of four equilateral triangles within a circle, based on proportions set out by the Roman architect Vitruvius. He needed a degree of imagination to do this: an extra trilithon, which did not exist and for which there was no evidence, had to be added to create the perfect symmetry required. But this was acceptable to Jones, as he was merely replacing stones that had gone missing owing to natural causes and 'the rage of men'. Inigo Jones was satisfied; here was all the necessary proof that Stonehenge must have been built by the Romans. However, although Jones might have been convinced by his own arguments the public were not. Surprisingly, considering the popularity of Geoffrey of Monmouth's earlier Stonehenge fantasies, when it was finally published the Jones/Webb theory was very badly received.

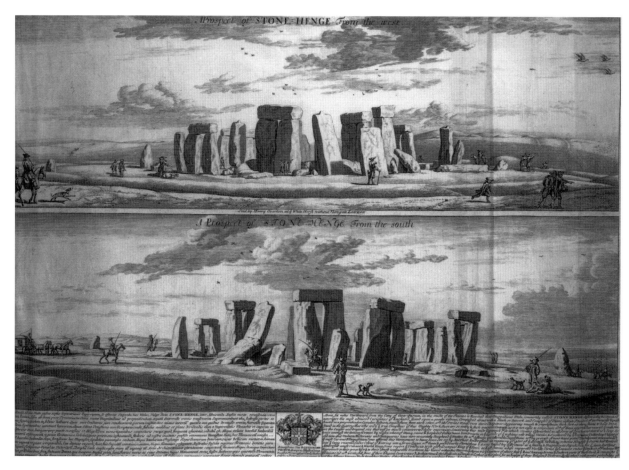

David Loggan's 17th-century engraving of Stonehenge,
complete with curious visitors.

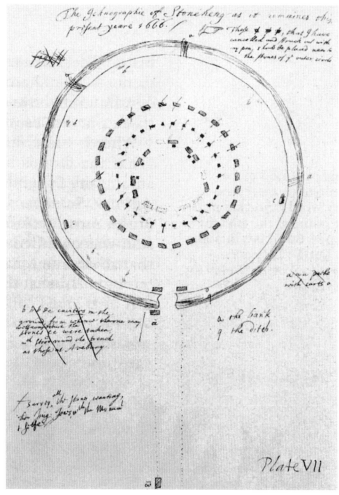

John Aubrey's sketched plan of 1666.

John Aubrey, 1626–97.

William Stukeley, 1687–1765, pioneering landscape archaeologist.

The 17th century progressed in a flurry of antiquarian speculation, and very soon Danes reappeared alongside the Saxons and Romans as potential builders of Stonehenge. There were others who argued that, as there was nothing else like Stonehenge known in the British Isles, its architects and builders had to have come from somewhere far away and exotic. So towards the end of the century the Phoenicians were introduced – the 17th-century equivalent of more recent extra-terrestrial explanations. But even at this time there were some who, in complete contrast, argued the case for the native British – for Stonehenge to be home-grown. Among them was John Aubrey, a Wiltshire-born antiquary who realised that searching in written historical records for the builders of Stonehenge was a fruitless exercise because such sites were 'so exceeding old that no Bookes do reach them'. Aubrey knew that the clues to understanding such ancient sites lay in observation and comparison, basic fieldwork that is still today one of the tools of prehistoric study. John Aubrey carried out his investigations at the command of his king, Charles II, and produced his first plan of Stonehenge in 1666. Although rather sketchy, it is one of the first accurate drawings ever made of the site. Like Inigo Jones, he wanted to find more symmetry in the arrangements of the stones than existed in reality. The positions of two extra (and imaginary) trilithons are outlined in order to turn the horseshoe into a neater circle. But he was also capable of acute observation, noting a series of 'cavities in the ground' close to the inner edge of the bank that he assumed were the holes for missing stones. Two hundred and fifty years later they were proved to be pits, but for upright timbers not stones, and were named 'Aubrey Holes' in recognition of his original discovery.

Aubrey's comparative studies of stone circles, from Stonehenge and Avebury in Wiltshire to others in England, Wales, Scotland and Ireland, led him to the conclusion that they were all temples. He also suggested, quite logically, that because stone circles were built in areas of the British Isles that had not seen occupation by Danes, Romans or Saxons, they must have been built by the native British. These people, despite being capable of building Stonehenge, were according to Aubrey 'almost as salvage [savage] as the beasts whose skins were their only rayment' and 'two or three degrees lesse salvage than the Americans'. But if he was basically correct about the builders of Stonehenge, where he went astray was in his assumption that the priests who attended these temples were most probably Druids. Aubrey never published his great work, the *Monumenta Britannica*, but his fieldwork had pointed the way towards a greater understanding of the ancient past and his pioneering methods were soon eagerly taken up by other scholars.

In the early years of the 18th century the Lincolnshire-born antiquary William Stukeley undertook his first topographical tours, travelling the countryside observing, measuring and recording the antiquities he came across. Stone circles, such as the Rollright Stones in Oxfordshire which he visited in 1710, made an instant impression. Its 'corroded' stones were probably 'an heathen temple of our Ancestors, perhaps in the Druid's time', an interpretation that remained and grew throughout his career in the field. In 1716, having never seen Stonehenge which seems surprising given his interests, he decided on a scheme to create firstly 'the groundplot of its present ruins', followed by 'a view of it in its pristine state' and finally, most ambitiously, to determine 'the original Architectonic scheme by which it was erected, together with design, use, Founders etc'. In other words, Stukeley intended to answer all the fundamental questions about Stonehenge: what did it look like, how was it built, who built it and what was it for?

On 18th May 1719 he finally visited Stonehenge where he was 'surprised ... beyond measure' (and possibly a little concerned about the magnitude of his self-imposed task). This visit, during which, with the help of Lord Pembroke, he drew his first plan, was the start of a long association with Stonehenge and its surrounding landscape. Between 1721 and 1724 Stukeley spent part of each summer surveying at Stonehenge and also at Avebury, the great stone circle about 40km (25 miles) north on the Marlborough Downs. His approach to Stonehenge was both analytical and romantic:

> When you enter the building, whether on foot or horseback and cast your eyes around, upon the yawning ruins, you are struck into a exstatic reverie, which none can describe, and they only can be sensible of it, that feel it. Other buildings fall by piece meal, but here a single stone is a ruin and lies like the haughty carcass of Goliath. Yet there is as much of it undemolished, as enables us sufficiently to recover its form, when it was in its most perfect state.

Lyricism apart, Stukelely had a great eye for detail. He noted that the uprights of the sarsen circle have their best (smoothest) faces turned inwards, and decided that the best way to refute ideas about exotic architectural influence was by carrying out a detailed measured survey of the stones. He argued, very logically, that 'if the proportions of Stonehenge fall into fractions and uncouth numbers, when measur'd by the English, French, Roman or Grecian foot, we may assuredly conclude the architects were neither English, French, Roman or Greeks'. So in 1723 he spent two and a half days at Stonehenge, taking 2,000 separate measurements with the help of his patron and friend, Lord Winchelsea. The plan that resulted, allowing for the changes that the stones had undergone over time (something that has not been allowed for by some more recent surveyors and interpreters) showed Stonehenge to be 'truly geometrical'. According to Stukeley, all of the dimensions that he recorded at Stonehenge could be divided into 'round and full numbers, not trifling fractions' using a unit of $20\frac{4}{5}$ inches. The Roman scale, by contrast, produced something 'ridiculous and without design'. He felt that he had proved his point: Stonehenge could not be Roman.

Stukeley also recorded the earthworks of the Avenue as far as they survived, from Stonehenge itself to the King Barrow Ridge. Shallow indentations in the grass close to Stonehenge were taken to be the impressions left by missing stones and a second branch of the Avenue, extending the first straight section further north east, was also identified. This was later proved to be a feature of the natural landscape and not part of the Avenue.

The 'detestable practice' of stone breaking as described by Stukeley in the early 18th century.

There were lighter moments in this serious study. With the aid of a ladder Stukeley and Lord Winchelsea climbed onto a trilithon where they went for a 'considerable walk on the top' (a slight exaggeration) before dining and leaving their tobacco pipes behind. On the instruction of Lord Pembroke, Stukeley also tried his hand at digging within the stones. Sensibly he refrained from excavating immediately next to any of the standing stones, realising that this was a sure way of making them unstable, and instead dug 'on the inside of the altar about the middle, 4 feet along the edge of the stone, 6 feet forward'. He saw the holes dug into the solid chalk that would keep stones upright 'as firm as if a wall were built around them' but found little in the way of artefacts.

Stukeley's consideration for the welfare of Stonehenge does not seem to have been shared by some other early 18th-century visitors. Not content with trying to count the stones (a favourite practice at many stone circles), some engaged in the 'detestable practice' of attacking the stones and 'breaking pieces off with great hammers'. Although this does not seem to have been carried out on the industrial scale that Stukeley had witnessed at Avebury, he realised that the stones had 'doubly suffered, from weather, and from the people every day diminishing all corners and edges, to carry pieces away with them'.

Stukeley did not confine his fieldwork to Stonehenge itself but roamed the landscape that surrounded it, the 'delightful plain' covered in the 'short grass continually crop't by the flocks of sheep ... the softest and most verdant turf, extremely easy to walk on, and which rises with a spring under one's feet'. He obviously had a great affection for this chalk downland; not only was it a pleasure to walk on but within it were preserved the remains of many ancient sites.

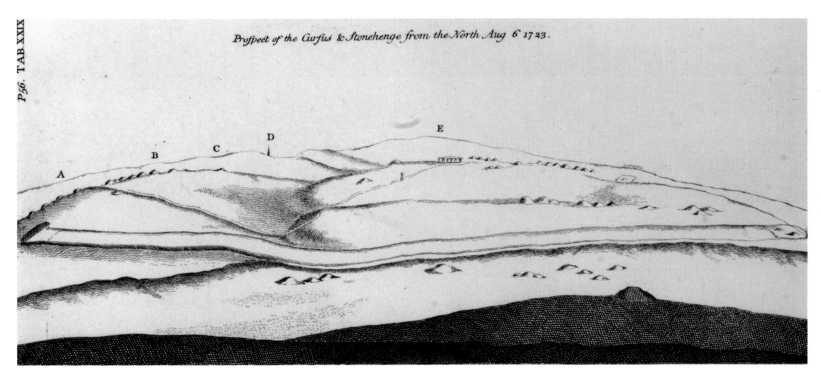

Proſpect of the Curſus & Stonehenge from the North Aug 6 1723.

Stukeley's 1723 'Prospect of the Cursus and Stonehenge from the North'. The Cursus was perhaps his greatest discovery in the Stonehenge landscape.

Slight traces of ditches, banks and mounds were clues to places of burial, ceremony or human habitation. They had survived for thousands of years, but with the changes in agriculture that came in later years many would become unrecognisable or invisible on the ground after only a few years of ploughing. So Stukeley's observations in the Stonehenge landscape and around Avebury were very timely. In August 1721 he was the first to notice the Avenue, charting its course from the entrance to Stonehenge downslope to a point at which he thought it branched, and beyond. He recorded a northern arm, no longer considered to be a part of the Avenue, and one that headed eastwards to the ridge on which the King Barrows lie. He never saw its whole length, because from this point onwards it had already been levelled by ploughing and would only be rediscovered when filled-in ditches showed up on 20th-century aerial photographs.

To the north of Stonehenge, on 6th August 1723, Stukeley made one of his most remarkable discoveries. Running in a broadly east–west direction across the undulating downs was a vastly elongated earthwork enclosure, over 2.7km (1.7miles) long and 100m (330ft) wide. This 'noble monument of antiquity', its long sides defined by a small bank and ditch with larger earthworks at either end, represented 'a fine design for the purpose of running'. It was obvious from the name Stukeley gave to this extraordinary structure that he had already made his mind up about its purpose. It was the 'cursus', or hippodrome, a race track for 'games, feasts, exercises and sports'. The larger mound that marked its eastern end was 'for the judges of the prizes, and chief of the spectators'. So the spectators had a grandstand seat and the British charioteers would not be hurt if they fell out owing to the 'exquisite softness of the turf'.

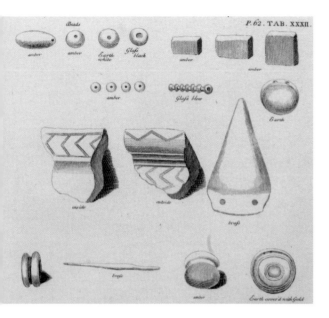

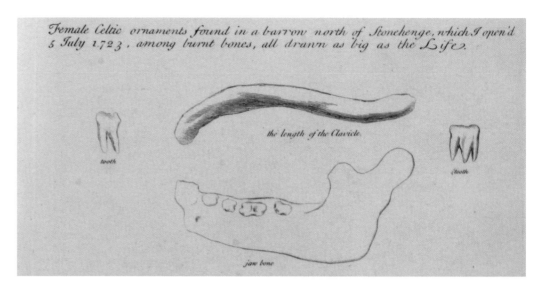

The bones and possessions of a young girl, excavated by Stukeley from a round barrow north of Stonehenge.

Stukeley in character as Chyndonax the Druid.

It was Lord Pembroke who had encouraged Stukeley to dig at Stonehenge and together, in 1722 and 1723, they examined some of the many round barrows that were 'set upon elevated ground and in sight of the temple'. Their investigations revealed details of construction: a consistent central mound of dark soil (thought to be turf stripped from a considerable area) covered with a thick coating of white chalk 'dug out of the environing ditch'. Below the mounds they found burials, skeletons and, from the double barrow north of Stonehenge, the burnt bones of a young girl, contained inside an urn that instantly crumbled to pieces. Her possessions, a selection of which were later illustrated by Stukelely in his 1740 publication *Stonehenge*, were buried with her: a bronze dagger and bodkin, beads of amber, glass and 'earth cover'd with gold'.

Stukeley's fieldwork was ahead of its time and he did attempt to order his findings, classifying barrows by their shape, recognising the unusual nature of the bluestones and using the orientation of monuments to suggest a date for their construction. He realised that the orientation of Stonehenge was significant: that its entrance pointed to 'the point where the sun rises, or nearly, at the summer solstice'. He also decided, on the basis of measuring changes over time in the direction of magnetic north, that a 700-year cycle could be identified and that, as Stonehenge was undoubtedly a monument of the ancient Britons, it had to have been built about 460BC.

It is very fortunate for future generations of archaeologists that Stukeley recorded his observations in notes and drawings that survive both as manuscripts and in published form. These are valuable records of a long-vanished landscape, the legacy of a remarkable man who was effectively Britain's first real field archaeologist. But by the time these observations came to print, Stukeley had developed obsessions that would heavily influence the rest of his life. In 1722, with a group of his antiquarian friends, he formed the 'Society of Roman Knights', an early example of role-playing, in which each member chose a suitably Celtic or Roman name. Stukeley decided to become Chyndonax, Prince of Druids, and by the time he took holy orders in 1729 had, rather peculiarly for a man of the church, started to believe in the reality of a Druid religion. His thinking pervaded his writing and by the time his great work on Stonehenge was published in 1740 it had gone from being *A History of the Ancient Celts* to *Stonehenge, a temple restored to the British Druids*. So, although it was Aubrey who had first suggested a connection between the Druids and Stonehenge, it was Stukeley who cemented this association and who is consequently responsible for nearly 300 years of confusion.

It is very easy now to dismiss Stukeley's Druidomania, but for the rest of the 18th century no-one wrote anything more sensible about Stonehenge. However, for the first time it had a custodian, of sorts. Gaffer Hunt, a carpenter from Amesbury, set up a small shelter within the stones where he provided drink, entertainment and tours of the site, and could even lend the curious visitor a set of measuring rods to conduct their own survey. A cellar to keep the drinks cool is said to have been dug out under one of the surviving uprights. Amazingly this did not destabilise it, and it was other stones that fell at the very end of the 18th century, ushering in a new chapter in the history of Stonehenge.

In Stukeley's later writings British Druids increasingly took over as the builders and users of temples like Stonehenge.

Surveying the damage – the aftermath of the trilithon collapse in 1797.

CHAPTER 4   Stonehenge in the 19th century

On 3rd January 1797 one of the three sarsen trilithons still standing after nearly 4,000 years collapsed, falling outwards and in the process hitting a bluestone and bringing down part of the outer sarsen circle. This particular trilithon had been leaning for some time and may have been further destabilised by gypsies camping within the stones who dug a hole to shelter in at its base. The final blow was probably a period of heavy frost followed by a rapid thaw. This is the first recorded collapse at Stonehenge: 70 or 80 tons of stone crashing to the ground with an impact that was said to have been felt by farm workers ploughing a field half a mile away.

The fall was the subject of much curiosity. Visiting local antiquarians were surprised at how shallowly the stones had been set in the ground, expecting more than the three feet or so (about 1m) that they observed. One of these visitors was William Cunnington, a successful wool merchant from the village of Heytesbury near Warminster in Wiltshire. He had a family and a comfortable house but he was not a well man, suffering from what is now thought to have been acromegaly, a disorder of the pituitary gland. His doctor advised him to 'ride out or die', in other words to get some fresh air, so he took to riding across Salisbury Plain where, like Stukeley years before, he observed ancient earthworks in the downland grass. His interest grew and he began to investigate some of the sites he had found, carrying out rudimentary excavations that produced collections of objects and interesting observations but no great enlightenment. So it was not surprising that he too was to be found at Stonehenge shortly after the collapse, 'digging with a stick under those two very large stones which fell down'. Cunnington was puzzled to find Roman pottery in the disturbed soil but unlike some of his contemporaries, who saw this as an excuse to resurrect the notion that Stonehenge was a Roman construction, he had a more practical interpretation. He suggested that his finds 'might have been fragments left on the ground as are glass bottles etc in the present day... and soon after the fall of the Trilithon the adjacent earth containing the pottery might fall into the excavation'. Cunnington understood the danger of what archaeologists now call 'intrusive finds', objects from a later period that somehow work their way into more ancient deposits, with confusing results.

Cunnington's skills as a self-taught excavator were recognised by H P Wyndham, the Member of Parliament for Wiltshire, who initially engaged him to uncover a mosaic at the Pitmead Roman Villa. They then went on to investigate ancient burial mounds. Like many antiquarian excavators both before and after, they found long barrows hard work and, as they only tended to produce bones and occasional scraps of 'rude' pottery, comparatively unproductive. Round barrows were a different matter. By 1801 Cunnington had opened at least 24 and, initially using Stukeley's classification, was becoming confident of knowing even before excavation what each different type would contain. Some, particularly the 'low barrows', often contained cremations and 'Druid barrows', the term used by Stukeley to describe disc barrows, were thought to be the 'burial places of ladies'. This was valuable work and in 1801, in recognition, Cunnington was elected a Fellow of the Society of Antiquaries of London.

At about this time, through his association with Wyndham, Cunnington was introduced to the Rev William Coxe, the Rector of Stourton. Coxe combined his

William Cunnington, 1754–1810, the merchant of Heytesbury and Colt Hoare's right-hand man.

Sir Richard Colt Hoare, 1758–1838, in his study at Stourhead. Every inch the antiquarian.

Philip Crocker's watercolour of Colt Hoare's barrow diggers at work.

clerical duties with a great interest in Wiltshire's antiquities. He raised a subscription to re-erect the newly fallen Stonehenge trilithon, though this scheme came to nothing when the owner refused permission. He also encouraged Cunnington in his barrow digging, realising that the discoveries that were being made would be vital to his long-term plan to write a history of Wiltshire's antiquities. But although this partnership started off well, tensions soon arose, Coxe lost interest and Cunnington found a new sponsor, collaborator and friend.

Cunnington had first met Sir Richard Colt Hoare, who was to have a huge impact on his life, in 1801. The two men could not have been more different: one a self-made merchant, very aware of his humble origins; the other a wealthy, travelled and aristocratic landowner, heir to a vast banking fortune and owner of (among other properties) the magnificent estate at Stourhead. Colt Hoare's wife and father had both died in 1785 and he had then spent many years travelling in Europe, particularly in Italy, before war and revolution meant that it was safer to come back to England and study English antiquities. Like Cunnington, Colt Hoare had a passion for the past and, like Coxe, was determined to write an ancient history of Wiltshire. He too was very aware of the difficulties of this task: there were no historical records to consult, just a bewildering variety of field monuments, camps and forts, villages and burial mounds and of course, more enigmatic than most, Stonehenge. He realised that what was needed was investigation – the systematic recovery, rather than the haphazard accumulation, of objects from the past. These he felt would provide evidence for the people who built and used these sites, and in Cunnington he found the partner who would retrieve this evidence.

Group of Barrows, South of Stone Henge.

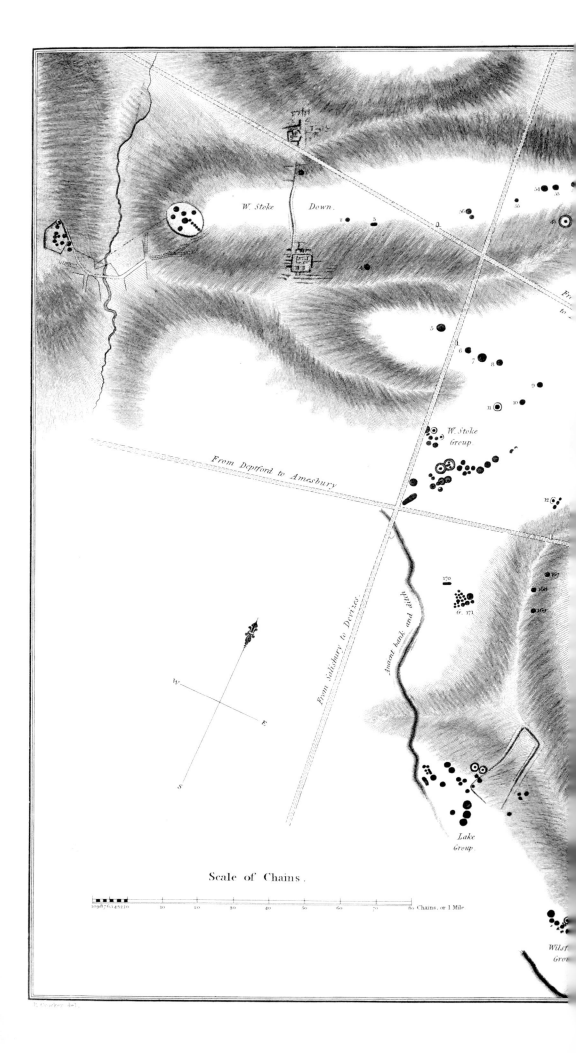

'Stonehenge and its Environs' from volume 1 of *The Ancient History of Wiltshire* published in 1812. A happy hunting ground for the 'barrow mad' team of Colt Hoare and Cunnington.

W. Stoke   Down.

W. Stoke
Group.

From Deptford to Amesbury

From Salisbury to Devizes

Anant bank and ditch

Lake
Group.

Scale of Chains.

80 Chains, or 1 Mile

Wilsf.
Grou

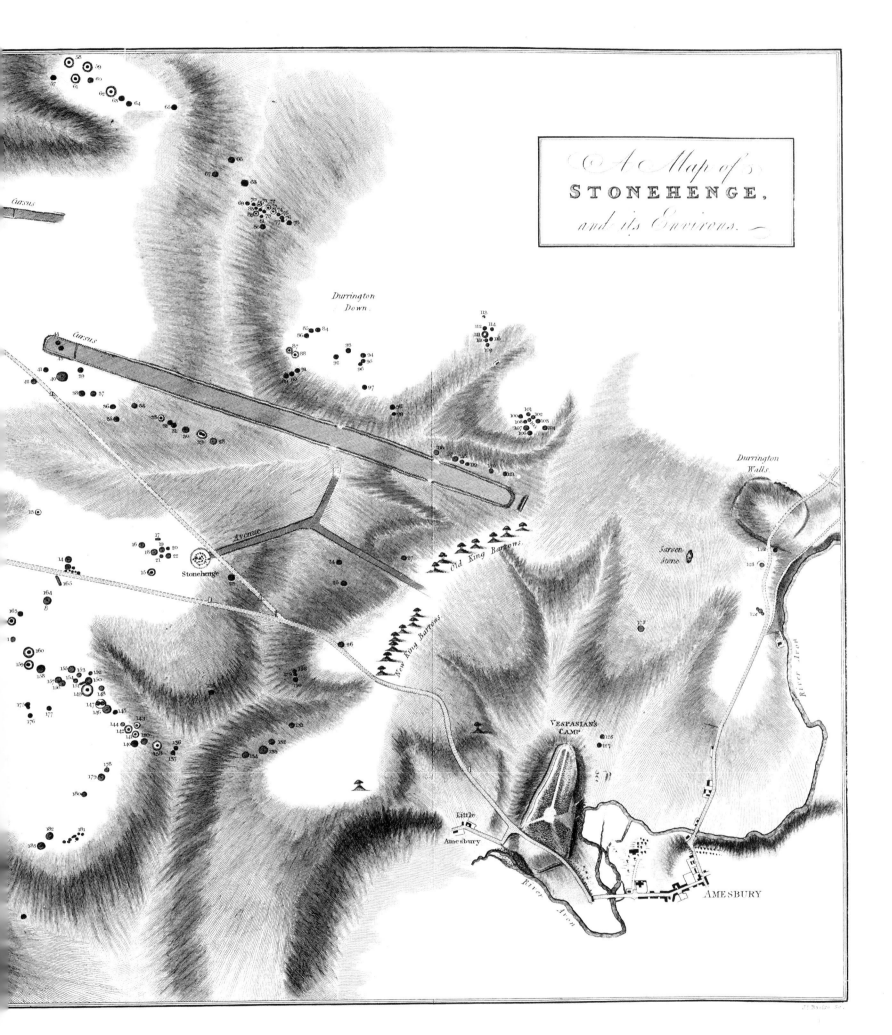

A Map of
STONEHENGE,
and its Environs.

Cursus

Durrington
Down.

Cursus

Avenue

Stonehenge

Old King Barrows.

New King Barrows.

Sarsen
Stone.

Durrington
Walls.

River Avon

Vespasian's
Camp

Little
Amesbury

AMESBURY

River Avon

Published for W. Miller, Albemarle Street, London, Jan.ʸ 1,1811.

The barrow classification devised by Colt Hoare and Cunnington.

BELL BARROW   BOWL BARROW

DRUID BARROW

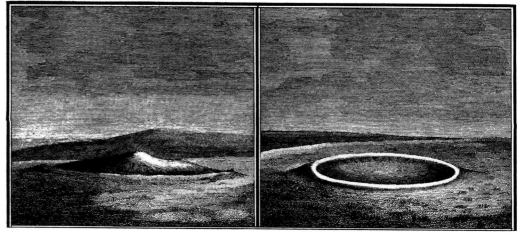

DRUID BARROW   POND BARROW

The arrangements were very simple and were largely a continuation of those that Cunnington had made with Coxe. Colt Hoare, through his landowning contacts, searched for sites to examine, arranged the excavations and provided the necessary finance. As an aristocrat he had no intention of getting his hands dirty. Cunnington was in day-to-day charge, supervising the excavations, collecting finds and making notes. The digging was carried out by an exceptional father-and-son team, the Parkers, who, because they were regularly employed on excavations, developed the ability to distinguish the subtle changes in soils that indicated the proximity of important finds. The team was completed by Philip Crocker, a man of extraordinary abilities as a surveyor, draughtsman, map maker and artist. No-one before had assembled such a talented team of investigators.

Cunnington had already had another look at Stonehenge, digging in the summer of 1802 'at the front of the Altar... to the depth of 5ft or more', where he found what had by this time become familiar artefacts for this site: charred wood, animal bones and 'stags horns'. He also investigated the Slaughter Stone and found a hole underneath that he took to be its original socket, proving that it had once stood upright. But it was barrows that fascinated Cunnington and, sharing his enthusiasm, Colt Hoare soon grew to be 'barrow mad'.

Between 1803 and 1810 Cunnington and his team opened 465 barrows in Wiltshire, nearly 200 of them in the area around Stonehenge. This was Colt Hoare's 'Stonehenge Environs', a landscape within which lay the densest concentration of prehistoric monuments, and particularly of round barrows, in the whole of Wiltshire. The barrows lay in lines along ridge tops, in clusters and in isolation, a varied collection that they classified using terms of which some are still used today. 'Bell' and 'bowl' barrow are still acceptable but 'Druid barrow', a term that is a direct legacy of Stukeley's obsession, has now been replaced with the more descriptive but less romantic 'disc barrow'. Pond barrows seem to have been a bit of a problem; their form was recognised and they were recorded as being components of barrow groups, but beyond that they seem to have been largely ignored.

The 'Stonehenge Environs' was a happy hunting ground for barrow diggers and, under instruction from Colt Hoare, Cunnington dug every barrow that he could. The only ones that were spared were those that lay under growing crops (although there was always a chance of coming back for these at a later date) and the King Barrows, the long meandering line that lies on the ridge to the east of Stonehenge. Frustratingly, they had been planted with trees over 50 years earlier (the trees are clearly shown on the Stonehenge Environs plan) and the landowner refused permission for his valuable timber to be felled. This is consequently the only group of unexcavated barrows within the entire Stonehenge landscape.

So what was the great fascination with round barrows, and why was so much effort put into digging them? What Colt Hoare was interested in, and what Cunnington was charged with recovering, were not the burials that they knew lay under the barrow mounds. These were of no interest; bones could not help them to understand the ancient history of Wiltshire, and so they were invariably returned to the grave, usually with some respect: 'Due reverence has always been paid to the mighty dead; their bones and ashes have been carefully collected and buried in the same tomb.' This does not always seem to have been the case though. Their account of the excavation of one of the Cursus Barrows notes that, while 'throwing out the bones of a skeleton', they found that they would withstand 'being thrown for a considerable distance without breaking'. But what they really wanted were the objects that accompanied the burials: the pottery vessels, the weapons and the ornaments of bronze, amber and occasionally gold. So long barrows which, as they had already proved, contained little but bones and pottery, were no good to them. And there was the added advantage with round barrows that it was much easier to locate the main burial. Almost without exception it lay directly in the centre of the mound and could be reached very efficiently in one of two ways: either by a trench dug right across the mound or, in the case of the larger barrows where this would have involved considerable earth-moving, a shaft dug down from the summit of the mound. The small craters on the tops of many of the larger surviving barrows are the visible evidence of these early excavations. By the standards of modern excavation the work was carried out very rapidly; two or three low barrows could be dealt with in a day, although some of the larger ones took considerably longer.

In the majority of cases, the final act was to deposit a metal token stamped with the words 'Opened by RCH' and the date; a reminder to future excavators that they had been beaten to the most obvious finds.

Cunnington's records are as brief as the excavations were rapid, and his observations are often not as detailed as those made by Stukeley nearly a century earlier. There is a brisk efficiency about references to barrows that have been 'explored by some prior investigator' or 'opened by shepherds'. The rite of burial was usually described, whether cremation or inhumation, and they soon realised that they should expect skeletons with 'legs gathered up according to the primitive custom'. Burials were sometimes missed, most famously on the first attempt at excavating Bush Barrow, and there was obviously also some consideration of investment and return. This is clearly demonstrated by the observation that a barrow 'if more minutely examined, might very probably produce other interments, but from its great width, the operation would be attended with a very heavy expense'.

A cloth bag of Colt Hoare's barrow opening tokens, never used and discovered in a drawer at Stourhead House.

Cunnington's excavation work can, at worst, be seen as the efficient and cost-effective creation of a collection of ancient artefacts to satisfy his wealthy patron. But it was more that this. There was a purpose to it, a 'research design' in modern archaeological terminology, and the way in which it was carried out has left a hugely important legacy. Cunnington's site notes, albeit brief, were linked to the maps and plans drawn up by Philip Crocker on which the individual barrows were numbered. The finds themselves were also carefully numbered and drawn. Cunnington, fortunately for future archaeologists and

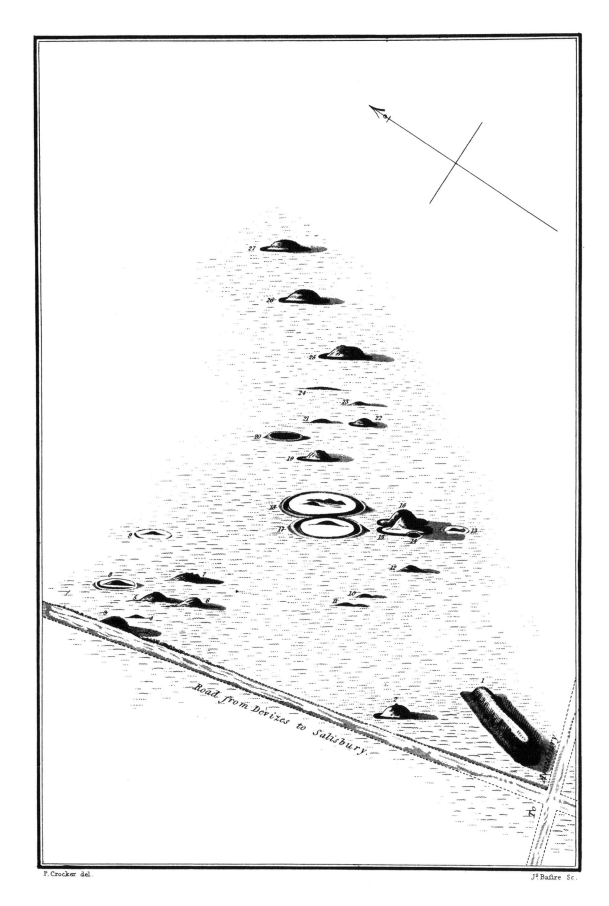

P. Crocker del.

Jᵉ Basire Sc.

GROUP OF BARROWS ON WINTERBOURN STOKE DOWN.

Published for W. Miller, Albemarle Street, London, Janᵧ 1.1811.

The Stonehenge Urn – engraved in *Ancient Wiltshire*.

museum curators, had apparently taken to heart instructions issued to him by the renowned antiquary, Thomas Leman of Bath:

> You will excuse me I am sure when I take the liberty of pointing out to you the necessity of immediately pasting a small piece of paper on to every piece of pottery or coin that you may hereafter find, describing with accuracy the very spot in which you find them.

This means that the objects can be traced from the moment of their discovery. Take one particular pot, found in a barrow close to Stonehenge:

> The tumulus nearest that place produced the largest sepulchral urn we have ever found, it measures fifteen inches in diameter at the top and is 22 ½ inches high; it varies also most decidedly in shape and pattern from all others in our collection; on which account we have distinguished it by the name of the STONEHENGE URN.

We can then follow this pot on its journey from the excavation back to Cunnington's house in Heytesbury. His daughter must have had a firm grip, the pot was not dropped and it joined the growing collection of finds, some mundane and others very special, in what was effectively Cunnington's garden shed. From here it was sent to Colt Hoare at Stourhead where it was drawn by Philip Crocker and, after the sale of the Stourhead collection in 1883, ended up in the collections of the Wiltshire Heritage Museum in Devizes. It is finds like these that give Devizes Museum a better collection of early Bronze Age material than the British Museum,

The antiquary (William Cunnington) and his daughter take the Stonehenge Urn back home to Heytesbury. Miraculously it survived the journey.

though it is ironic to note that, when the purchase of the Stourhead finds was proposed, there were those who wished to know why the museum should wish to acquire such 'rubbish'.

As more barrows were dug, and the collection of well recorded and carefully stored finds continued to grow, Cunnington's understanding of the barrows they came from unfortunately did not seem to grow in the same way. His early confidence that he could predict the contents of a barrow from its shape faded in the light of what he saw as inconsistency and whim on the part of the barrow builders. He came to the conclusion that the ancient Britons 'had no system in regard to the form of the tumulus... but appear to have been influenced by caprice than by established rules'.

Even though at times he must have despaired of ever understanding the barrow builders, there were spectacular finds to lift the spirits. The richest were made in 1808 at Bush Barrow, one of the group that lies along the crest of Normanton Down just to the south of Stonehenge. In the early 18th century William Stukeley singled this barrow out and showed it as it was at the time, crowned with a small fenced enclosure. He does not seem to have attempted to excavate it, so it remained intact, fenced and 'with a rough appearance' until nearly a century later. Then first some farmers and later Cunnington dug into the barrow, neither with any success. Fortunately it was Cunnington rather than the farmers who returned in September 1808, this time with considerable success. This is the published account of the excavation, taken from Colt Hoare's *Ancient Wiltshire*:

Bronze daggers and axe from Bush Barrow, excavated by Cunnington in 1808.

> Our researches were renewed in September, 1808, and were amply repaid for our perseverance and former disappointment. On reaching the floor of the barrow we discovered the skeleton of a stout and tall man lying from south to north: the extreme length of his thigh bone was 20 inches. About 18 inches south of the head, we found several brass rivets intermixed with wood, and some thin bits of brass nearly decomposed. These articles covered a space of 12 inches or more; it is probable, therefore, that they were the mouldered remains of a shield. Near the shoulders lay the fine celt, the lower end of which owes its great preservation to having been originally inserted within a handle of wood. Near the right arm was a large dagger of brass and a spear-head of the same metal, full thirteen inches long and the largest we have ever found, though not so neat in its pattern as some others of an inferior size which have been engraved in our work. These were accompanied by a curious article of gold, which I conceive had originally decorated the case of the dagger. The handle of wood belonging to this instrument, exceeds anything we have yet seen, both in design and execution, and could not be surpassed (if indeed equalled) by the most able workman of modern times. By the annexed engraving, you will immediately recognise the British zigzag, of the modern Vandyke pattern, which was formed with a labour and exactness almost unaccountable, by thousands of gold rivets, smaller than the

Gold lozenges, the 'belt hook' and the 'sceptre' from Bush Barrow.

OPPOSITE
The Bush Barrow finds from *Ancient Wiltshire*. Crocker has captured the delicate decoration on the dagger handle and even the size of the minute gold pins.

smallest pin. The head of the handle, though exhibiting no variety of pattern, was also formed by the same kind of studding. So very minute, indeed, were these pins, that our labourers had thrown out thousands of them with their shovel, and scattered them in every direction, before, by the necessary aid of a magnifying glass, we could discover what they were; but fortunately enough remained attached to the wood to enable us to develop the pattern. Beneath the fingers of the right hand lay a lance head of brass, but so much corroded that it broke into pieces on moving. Immediately over the breast of the skeleton was a large plate of gold, in the form of a lozenge, and measuring 7 inches by 6. It was fixed to a thin piece of wood, over the edges of which the gold was lapped: it is perforated at top and bottom, for the purpose, probably, of fastening it to the dress as a breast-plate. The even surface of this noble ornament is relieved by indented lines, checques and zigzags, following the shape of the outline, and forming lozenge within lozenge, diminishing gradually towards the centre. We next discovered, on the right side of the skeleton, a very curious perforated stone, some wrought articles of bone, many small rings of the same material, and another article of gold. The stone is made out of a fossil mass of tubularia, and polished; rather like an egg form, or as a farmer who was present observed, resembling the top of a large gimlet. It had a wooden handle, which was fixed into the perforation in the centre, and encircled by a neat ornament of brass, part of which still adheres to the stone. As this stone bears no marks of wear or attrition, I can hardly consider it to have been used as a domestic implement, and from the circumstances of its being composed of a mass of sea-worms or little serpents, I think we may not be too fanciful in considering it an article of consequence.

This account, in many ways, encapsulates the approach that was adopted by Cunnington and Colt Hoare. There is little description of the barrow itself, and the skeleton, which gets a passing mention as being 'stout and tall', is assumed to be male. The objects are mostly described in some detail, although 'another article of gold' hardly seems adequate, and more time is spent discussing the perforated stone, perhaps as it is seen as more of a curiosity.

Much time and effort were spent on the acquisition of objects but, despite all that Colt Hoare's wealth and influence could bring to bear on the study of the ancient past, he and Cunnington still struggled to create order from their finds. The antiquarian Leman (the man who had suggested that labelling finds was crucial) suggested that there were three succeeding ages, of stone, bronze and iron, to which artefacts could be assigned. Cunnington countered this with examples of having found objects of all three materials together in the same barrow, although he had realised that burials with iron objects were generally to be found higher up in the barrow, and could therefore be of a later date.

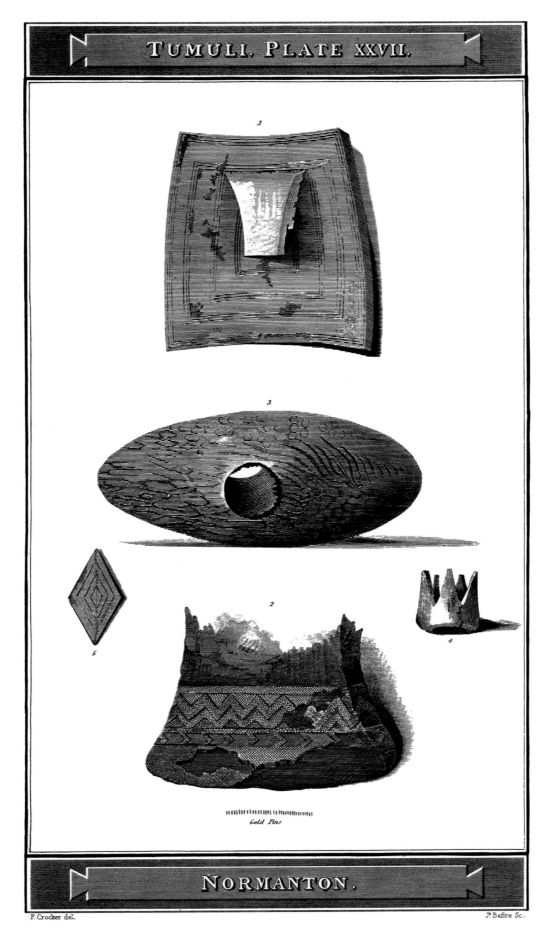

1

3

5

2

4

Gold Pins

P. Crocker del.

J.ª Basire Sc.

Published for W. Miller, Albemarle Street, London, Jan.ʸ 1. 1812.

Crocker

The final account of their explorations in the Stonehenge area and its hundreds of barrows was published in the first of the two huge volumes that make up *The Ancient History of Wiltshire*. Cunnington lived just long enough to see the first parts of *South Wiltshire* published in 1810, with a suitably antiquarian title page and an engraving of his portrait as its frontispiece. Acknowledging his debt to Cunnington's energy and dedication, Colt Hoare dedicated the first volume to his friend and colleague.

Ancient Wiltshire, is it is commonly referred to, is still, along with Cunnington's original notes and correspondence, a valuable resource for today's students of prehistory. It also has a huge visual appeal due to Crocker's maps, his inventive perspective views of barrow cemeteries and his astonishing illustrations of the objects. In their published form, reduced to black-and-white engravings, lines and stipple, they are still fine and objective records of the objects as found. The pottery types are instantly recognisable, even if there is no sense of scale, and bronze daggers are shown complete with fragments of adhering wood and textile. What the engravings do not convey is the extraordinary beauty of the original watercolours in which he captures the hues of the ancient pots and vivid colours of corroded bronze.

Cunnington died in 1810, his life prolonged by his years of active fieldwork. Earlier that year he had dug at Stonehenge for a third and final time, returning to the Slaughter Stone to confirm what he felt from his earlier investigation, that it had once stood upright. And this time he left behind a bottle of port 'out of consideration for future excavators'. But this is effectively the sum total of the contribution that he and Colt Hoare made to the understanding of Stonehenge. There is a substantial section in the *Ancient History of South Wiltshire* devoted to Stonehenge – over 24 pages – well over half of which consists of a reiteration of previous studies and theories. There is, in all fairness, a good contemporary description of the site, with detailed plans and Philip Crocker's fine view of the stones from the west. There are discussions about the component stones, suggestions that the bluestones, referred to as 'unmeaning pigmy pillars of granite', were a later addition and even mention of Druids, although not in Stukeley's obsessive way. There is no disagreement with Stukeley's suggestion that Stonehenge was a 'monument of the Britons', but no great advances in understanding either. Perhaps it is no wonder that the section on Stonehenge ends with the words, in bold letters:

" HOW GRAND! HOW WONDERFUL! HOW INCOMPREHENSIBLE!"

A small Bronze Age vessel from a bell barrow in the Normanton group (thought by an observer at the time to resemble Stonehenge).

A replica of the same vessel commissioned by Colt Hoare from his friend Josiah Wedgwood.

OPPOSITE
Philip Crocker's stunning watercolours (from which engravings were prepared) were the first record of the excavated finds and bring out both delicate decoration and the vibrant colours of decay.

Stonehenge may have been incomprehensible to Colt Hoare, but about the same time that *Ancient Wiltshire* was published ideas developed that helped to create order in the chaos that was the distant past. The Danish antiquary Christian Thomson was the first to have the idea that prehistory could be divided into three

Constable's watercolour, first exhibited in 1836.

ages – of stone, bronze and iron – widely accepted. This was essentially the same structure that Leman had suggested but that Cunnington had rejected – unfortunately, as this way of using materials to structure time would have helped Cunnington and Colt Hoare enormously in ordering and understanding their finds. But at least, in their systematic collecting and prompt publication, they had created a database that could be analysed in the light of this new thinking. In the introduction to *Ancient Wiltshire* Colt Hoare had stated boldly that 'We speak from facts not theory', but now his 'facts' were to be used to support others' theories.

In the first half of the 19th century, as science gradually started to unravel some of Stonehenge's mysteries, its enduring dramatic qualities attracted England's finest landscape painters. Constable made only one visit, sketching a close-up view of the stones on 15th July 1820. He painted two preliminary watercolours, each showing essentially the same view of the stones from the south, but experimenting with additional space and the treatment of the sky. The final watercolour, in Constable's words, of the 'mysterious monument of Stonehenge, standing remote on a bare and boundless heath', was shown at the Royal Academy in 1836. The stones, tumbled and leaning, are still recognisable, but from them now spring two rainbows, arcing up into a turbulent sky.

Turner's watercolour of 1828 is even more dramatic. Stonehenge is now reduced to abstraction: the uprights are far more slender than they are in reality and the setting is only really recognisable from the lintelled stones. Its importance is as a backdrop to a scene of great drama and human tragedy. The tranquillity of Constable's rainbows has been replaced by the deadly power of lightning and in the foreground the shepherd and his flock, which appear time and again as a pastoral motif in Stonehenge paintings, lie dead on the ground while the shepherd's dog howls for its master.

Turner's watercolour – an apocalyptic scene at an abstract Stonehenge.

Stonehenge in 1853 by William Russell Sedgefield – the earliest known photograph.

Just as it had done for centuries, and just as it does to the present day, Stonehenge would continue to attract painters and poets; but in the middle of the 19th century it also began to attract the attention of a new kind of artist, armed not with pencils and brushes but with cameras. Photography, although not by that name, had been possible since as early as 1826, but in England it was not until the 1850s that it became both practical and affordable. With restrictive patents relaxed and costs decreasing, 1853 was the year of liberation for the new art of photography, and it was in that year that the first known photograph of Stonehenge was taken. The picture, now in the Royal Collection, is a close-up of the stones from the west and was taken by William Russell Sedgefield of Devizes. This is our first image of Stonehenge as seen, not through the subjective eyes of an artist, but through the dispassionate lens of a camera. Stonehenge appears as a remote ruin, with the carriage among the stones the only apparent sign of life. The landscape appears bleak, the skyline relieved only by the trees masking the King Barrows on the eastern skyline. This photograph marks the beginning of a change in our perception of Stonehenge, because from this time onwards the camera would document every change, every event and every visitor of note. Stonehenge had lost its privacy.

By the 1860s the new science of prehistory could suggest with some confidence that Stonehenge dated to the Bronze Age. But even in this age of new enlightenment there were still those who found it impossible to accept that a monument of such sophistication could have been built by ancient Britons – except, that is, for the arrangements of bluestones, the 'little central circle of unhewn monoliths', that were considered insignificant enough to have been moved without Roman supervision and know-how. There were also those who refused to let go of

Colonel Sir Henry James of the Ordnance Survey, accompanied by bored minion, at Stonehenge in 1867.

long-standing antiquarian ideas. Colonel Sir Henry James, the Director General of the Ordnance Survey, might be assumed to have been a factual, down-to-earth sort of person, and he was keen to embrace photography as a means of recording ancient monuments. So far so good: but in 1867 he published a book, *Plans and photographs of Stonehenge and of Turusachan in the Island of Lewis with notes relating to the Druids and sketches of cromlechs in Ireland.* It is the second part of this rather lengthy title that gives away his intellectual tendencies. To him 'the construction of this grand work (Stonehenge) has traditionally, and I think rightly, been attributed to the Druids'.

Henry Browne's first guidebook of 1823.

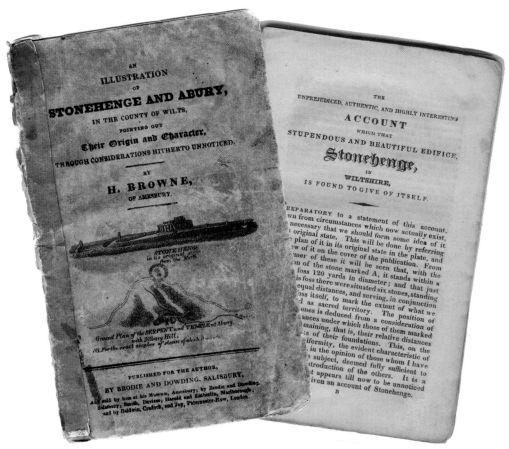

Darwin used fallen and half-buried 'Druidical' stones at Stonehenge to demonstrate the action of earthworms.

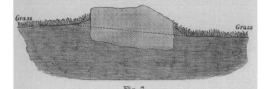

CHAP. III.   UNDERMINED BY WORMS.   159

was thus ascertained, as shown in the accompanying diagram (Fig. 7) on a scale of ½ inch to a foot. The turf-covered border sloped up to the stone on one side to a height of 4 inches, and on the opposite side to only 2½ inches above the general level. A hole was dug on the eastern side, and the base of the stone was here found to lie at a

Fig. 7.

Section through one of the fallen Druidical stones at Stonehenge, showing how much it had sunk into the ground. Scale ½ inch to 1 foot.

depth of 4 inches beneath the general level of the ground, and of 8 inches beneath the top of the sloping turf-covered border.

Sufficient evidence has now been given showing that small objects left on the surface of the land where worms abound soon get buried, and that large stones sink slowly downwards through the same means. Every

Given the confusion that still reigned amongst the intelligentsia even at this comparatively late date, it is hardly surprising that the visitor to Stonehenge should have been presented with a somewhat eccentric explanation of its history. In 1822 Henry Browne became Stonehenge's first official guide and protector, making a precarious living from visitors' tips and responsible for preventing them from hacking off fragments of stone as souvenirs. The problem with Browne's account of Stonehenge was that it was based on already outdated biblical teachings in which the world was created in 4004BC. He was also a catastrophist, a firm believer in the reality of Noah's flood and consequently that Stonehenge was antediluvian, one of the few structures that survived the great inundation. These beliefs continued to be peddled by his son, who took over custodianship of the stones after his father's death in 1839. There was clearly a living to be made: in 1857 the railway reached Salisbury, less than 16km (10 miles) away, and visitor numbers increased, lured by the possibility of a day's excursion to Stonehenge from London.

In June 1877 one of the more distinguished visitors to Stonehenge was Charles Darwin. The great naturalist and author of *On the Origin of Species* was curious not so much about the place itself but about the action of earthworms in burying fallen stones by turning over the soil. This was a subject that had fascinated him in his younger days and he had returned to it in old age. At Stonehenge he was allowed to dig small holes, the results from which appeared in a chapter in his last book, published in 1881, the year of his death: *The Formation of Vegetable Mould, through the Action of Worms.*

In that same year, 1877, the egyptologist and archaeologist Flinders Petrie made an extremely accurate plan of the stones, allocating them all the numbers that are still used and plotting them, he claimed, to the nearest tenth of an inch. The reason for such precision was to try to discover the unit of measurement employed by the original builders, following Stukeley's argument that they were more likely to have designed the structure using whole units rather than fractions. The results were puzzling. According to Petrie, the earthworks and the Station Stones appeared to have been set out using a measure of about 224.8 inches (approximating to ten Phoenician units of 22.51 inches), while the main stone structure used the Roman foot of 11.68 inches. As Petrie was surveying a 4,000-year-old ruin, parts of which had eroded, collapsed, been hacked at by souvenir hunters and even completely disappeared, his precision seems unnecessary and the inconclusive results are hardly surprising.

During the reign of Queen Victoria the visitors who at first arrived at Stonehenge by rail and coach were followed by those who made their way by traction engine, by bicycle and eventually by car. Members of the royal family came to picnic and look extremely bored by the whole experience in the photograph that records their visit in about 1880.

Members of Queen Victoria's family and guests at Stonehenge c.1880.

By the end of the 19th century Stonehenge was in a ruinous state.

But as more visitors wandered among the stones there was increasing concern for their safety and for that of Stonehenge itself. Stonehenge was at this time owned by the Antrobus family of Amesbury, who employed the latest in a long line of custodians to look after the site – William Judd, a photographer who made a good living from taking photographs of visitors. Most pictures taken in the 1880s show his smart caravan, part shelter, part photographic studio, parked close to the stones, and he no doubt continued to try to dissuade visitors from breaking off pieces of the stones to take home as souvenirs.

1882 saw the passing of the Ancient Monuments Act, a piece of legislation that was intended to offer legal protection to some of England's most precious historic sites. Those that were considered to be of national importance were included on a list, or 'schedule', on which Stonehenge naturally appeared. There was now an Inspector of Ancient Monuments too, the celebrated archaeologist Augustus Pitt Rivers, often

The effect that government purchase would have on Stonehenge – the view of the magazine *Punch* in 1899.

HOW STONEHENGE MIGHT BE POPULARISED IF THE GOVERNMENT BOUGHT IT. SUGGESTION GRATIS.

The 1893 guide book published by William A Judd, photographic artist who could supply 'photographs of Stonehenge from 20 different points of view'.

STONEHENGE.

ITS PROBABLE ORIGIN,

AGE,

AND USES.

Edited and compiled from the most authentic sources,

BY

WILLIAM A. JUDD,

MADDINGTON, WILTS,

1893.

PRICE ONE SHILLING.

described as the father of modern archaeology. In the autumn of 1893 he carried out an inspection of Stonehenge and his report, dated 2nd October, outlines the critical state into which it had fallen: 'It is quite certain that sooner or later, more probably soon than later, most of the stones will fall though natural causes. It does not require to be an engineer or an archaeologist, but merely the exercise of a little common sense to see that some of the stones are in the process of slowly falling now. This fact is recognised by the useless and unsightly wooden props that are set up against two of them.'

The only remedy, according to Pitt Rivers, was 'to have the inclining stones brought up to the perpendicular, and the foundations should then be set in cement, concrete or masonry. This would be very expensive, but it would secure the monument to posterity'.

Pitt Rivers' report and its sensible recommendations were endorsed by other influential archaeologists but nothing was done, largely due to the unwillingness of the landowner, Sir Edmund Antrobus, to submit to what he saw as government interference. So Stonehenge would no doubt have remained in this state, crumbling and clearly neglected but beyond the help of the archaeological establishment, had not, at the turn of the century, the predicted collapse taken place.

CHAPTER 5   Restoration and exploration – the early years

Given the state of Stonehenge at the time of the 1900 collapse, it must have been difficult to know where to start with the job of making it stable. An advisory committee was convened, with representatives from the Society of Antiquaries of London, the Society for the Protection of Ancient Monuments and the Wiltshire Archaeological Society. They easily identified which, among Stonehenge's many problems, was the priority: Stone 56, the tallest of the sarsen uprights, was leaning at a perilous angle. This stone was the sole surviving upright of the tallest of the five graduated sarsen trilithons which had collapsed many centuries earlier. There is no record of when or why this earlier collapse occurred, as there was with the trilithon that fell at the end of the 18th century, but even the earliest engravings show only one of its uprights standing and the other leaning inwards at a crazy angle. On more accurate portrayals it is shown resting on one of the elegant upright pillars of the bluestone horseshoe. Stone 56, 40 or more tons of elegantly shaped sarsen, must have tilted gradually over the years; the other option, a sudden fall, would surely have splintered the bluestone pillar and may well have broken the back of the sarsen. But by 1901, despite what appeared to be some sort of precarious equilibrium, there were renewed fears that it could not remain in this position and would soon fall completely, perhaps breaking in the process.

So arrangements were made with Sir Edmund Antrobus to have it straightened. This was to be partly an engineering exercise, supervised by the Wiltshire architect Mr Detmar Blow with the assistance of an engineer, Mr Carruthers. The first stage of the work involved securing the leaning stone in a substantial timber framework or crib. But it had also been accepted that there should be an archaeological component to the work, and that the area around the base of the leaning stone had to be properly excavated. This work was entrusted to Professor William Gowland of the School of Mines at South Kensington, a surprising choice as he was a mining geologist and an expert in early metalworking rather than an archaeologist. He turned out to be the ideal man for the job. Unlike many later excavators at Stonehenge, Gowland restricted his efforts to the task to which he had been appointed and carried it out to the highest standards of the day. He may not have done any actual digging but, unlike many archaeologists of the time, he was on site every day, supervising his workmen and making sure that nothing was dug without his involvement. His methods of retrieving and recording finds were also very advanced. A graduated wooden 'registering frame' was set up around the sides of the excavation which, combined with a numbered vertical rod, enabled the position of every find to be recorded precisely. The soil was removed not in the archaeological layers that were encountered, but in horizontal 'spits' either three or six inches deep. Furthermore, so as to be certain that not even the smallest artefact was missed, all the excavated soil was sieved through meshes of one, half, quarter and one-eighth of an inch. In order to make sure that the archaeologists carried out this meticulous work free from disturbance, Sir Edmund employed a policeman.

The excavation, which was carried out between 18th August and 25th September 1901, was very small, but even such a restricted area had to be dug in sections, each of which was filled with concrete before the next could be dug. As the excavation progressed Stone 56 was winched upright, finally regaining the vertical on 19th

Professor William Gowland, the first 20th-century excavator of Stonehenge.

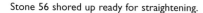

Stone 56 shored up ready for straightening.

Stone 56 returned to the vertical with Gowland's meticulous excavation in progress. One of his workmen digs inside a wooden 'registering frame' while two others sieve for finds.

Gowland's wooden registering frame and vertical rod.

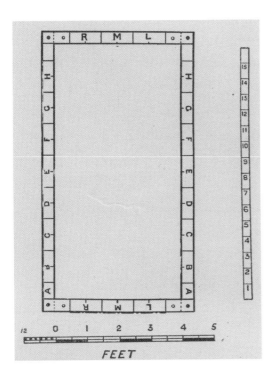

September, after which its concrete setting was completed. Had the other matching upright not been smashed by its fall, then no doubt this and the intact lintel would also have been raised at this time, and the Great Trilithon would have stood complete.

With his work on site finished Gowland then analysed and published his results with exemplary promptness. Despite the limited size of the excavation the results were highly significant. From the eccentric shape of the hole that held Stone 56, Gowland could demonstrate that, contrary to what might have been expected, it had been raised from the inside of the structure. He recovered many sarsen 'mauls', battered round balls that showed how the stones had been worked into their elaborate shapes, and he was also able to suggest that the sarsens and the bluestones were raised at very much the same date. This, he decided, was 'during the latter part of the Neolithic age (the New Stone Age) or the period of transition from stone to bronze, and before metal had passed into general practical use'. Gowland estimated this to be some time around 1800BC (a very good guess for its time), a date that fitted with his idea that Stonehenge, a temple to worship the sun, had been built by 'our rude forefathers'. So at last, Romans, Danes and Druids had been banished by practical archaeological research.

Gowland's excavation, the first at Stonehenge to be conducted using modern archaeological methods, remains even to this day one of the best in the site's long history of investigation. The end product, the straightened-up Stone 56, also provides a very convenient chronological marker, enabling undated photographs to be assigned to either the pre-1900 period (stone leaning) or post-1900 (stone straight).

The controversial 1901 additions to Stonehenge: fence, ticket booth and policeman.

This was the first step in what was to be a protracted programme of restoration at Stonehenge. At the same time, major changes were being made in the way that the site was run. In May 1901 Sir Edmund Antrobus decided to erect a fence around Stonehenge and to charge admission, bringing to an end the somewhat informal arrangements and *ad hoc* custodianship that had been in place for at least 80 years. There was immediate protest by the indignant inhabitants of Amesbury and the surrounding villages, who saw this as the removal of their ancient and inalienable right to visit Stonehenge whenever they liked and free of charge. A mass protest was organised but, as Sir Edmund was within his rights, the fence stayed and within five months 3,770 visitors had paid their shilling entrance fee. £168/10/- may not seem a huge sum, although it rose to nearly £300 *per annum* by 1904, but for the first time Stonehenge had started to make money.

Gowland's work may have been the final nail in the coffin for the idea, current since the 17th century and much promoted by Stukeley in the 18th, that Stonehenge was a Druid temple. But even if the real (prehistoric) Druids had been banished, there were more recent followers of a reinvented druidism who were keen to see Stonehenge as their spiritual home. The Ancient Order of Druids, a secret society with some similarity to Freemasonry, had been founded in 1781 (so was not strictly 'ancient') and flourished during the 19th century. On 24th August 1905 a huge crowd of nearly 1,000 members of the Grand Lodge of the Ancient Order of Druids

STONEHENGE, AS IT WAS AND AS IT IS.
THE ENCLOSURE OF THE ANCIENT MONUMENT.

AS IT WAS.

In 1901 the villagers of Amesbury gathered at Stonehenge to protest against the newly introduced fence and admission charge.

gathered at Stonehenge for a mass ordination. The reporter from *The Star,* sent to cover the event, was singularly unimpressed and wrote that the ceremony was conducted by a 'train load of sham druids' wearing 'calico nightshirts' and 'cotton wool beards'. In his opinion they had invaded the simple majesty of Stonehenge with their 'shoddy mysteries'. Despite this bad press, during 1905 Stonehenge received further visits from a variety of Druid groups (a tendency towards factionalism has persisted to the present day). There was conflict between Druids and landowner, not only over the charges for admission but when one group was caught trying to bury the ashes of its deceased members among the stones.

The mass ordination of Druids in August 1905.

Such small acts of what was regarded at the time as vandalism pale into insignificance when the overall state of Stonehenge is considered. That following year, 1906, saw the first photograph of Stonehenge from the air, an oblique view taken in the autumn from the basket of a Royal Engineers' balloon by 2nd Lt Philip Henry Sharpe. This view, and another vertical view, were published a year later in the journal *Archaeologia*. Both emphasised Stonehenge's neglected and dilapidated state. The custodians' small wooden hut sits close to the Heel Stone by the side of the Amesbury–Devizes road, with a well-worn path leading to the stones. But the rest of the site is scarred by many other tracks that criss-cross the fragile earthworks, showing up as white chalk scars in the downland grass. Worst of all is the major branching route, a byway which crosses the earthwork enclosure in a north–south direction and passes perilously close to the stones.

Moreover, visible within the stones are matchstick-like wooden props holding up some of the surviving but leaning uprights of the sarsen circle. Pitt Rivers had reported two such props when he carried out his inspection in 1893, but only 12 years later there were eight. HM Office of Works, the Government body responsible at that time for ancient monuments, was concerned but powerless. The Ancient

Stonehenge criss-crossed by eroded tracks – the view from an army balloon in 1906.

Canadian troops marching through Stonehenge on their way back to Larkhill Camp in 1915.

Monuments Board had tried to persuade Sir Edmund Antrobus to place Stonehenge in their care, but without success. Their frustrations can be felt in correspondence during 1904:

> One cannot but regret that in this country, unlike several foreign states, there is no legal power to take possession of Stonehenge as a National Monument: paying the owner whatever may be the fair value of his interest in it.

A hand-written note in the margin of this letter simply says 'nothing can be done at present'.

So nothing was done. The proximity of traffic on the byway to the stones is evident in a photograph taken in 1915 of Canadian troops returning to their barracks at Larkhill, less than a mile north of Stonehenge. Here the traffic is only horse-drawn artillery, but the same track was used by lorries and even some of the earliest tanks, prompting more concerned letters from HM Office of Works, this time to the War Office. Surprisingly, even among the horrors of the First World War some notice was taken of these fears for the safety of Stonehenge and the track was diverted further west, well outside the earthwork enclosure, thus preventing any further damage by the 'thoughtless military'. That left the activities of the Royal Artillery, based just to the north at Larkhill, to cause concern. In 1916 the custodian noticed a fresh crack on one of the fallen stones and was in no doubt what had caused it: one of the frequent test explosions of landmines on the Plain, 'near enough to shake his hut and dislodge objects from its shelves'.

A positive air show over Stonehenge. A card sent from Larkhill Camp in 1915 as the horrors of the First World War unfolded.

Yet more military threats to the stability of Stonehenge appeared soon afterwards, this time from the Royal Flying Corps. In 1917 they established a training aerodrome on the crest of Stonehenge Down, the low rise to the west of the stones. As well as a rash of contemporary postcards usually entitled 'Flying at Stonehenge', which show aircraft carefully superimposed on the sky above the stones, this spawned a number of fascinating rumours. One, widespread at the time among both the local population and the military, was that there were plans to demolish Stonehenge as it was a hazard to low-flying aircraft. Failing this, the stones facing the airfield were to be painted white to make them more visible. Another story, perhaps more credible given the excitable nature of military pilots, is that when coming in to land they would swoop low and attempt to 'skim' Stonehenge's lintels with their landing wheels.

Somewhat amazingly Stonehenge survived the First World War intact and by the end of it had a new owner. For years there had been concerns that Stonehenge might fall into commercial hands or, worse still, be sold to some rich American, dismantled and shipped off across the Atlantic. Then in 1915, after the heir to the Antrobus estate had been killed in action and Sir Edmund himself had died, the entire estate was put up for auction at the New Theatre in Salisbury. Stonehenge

Lot 15 – Stonehenge. The 1915 auction catalogue.

Colonel William Hawley – excavator of Stonehenge from 1919 to 1926.

was lot 15 and was bought for £6,600, apparently on impulse, by Cecil Chubb, a local landowner. Nothing changed very much under the new ownership except that admission charges were halved for serving members of the armed forces. But three years later Chubb offered his impulse buy to the nation, which gratefully accepted and rewarded him with a knighthood. Old Sir Edmund would have been furious that Stonehenge had finally fallen into the hands of the very bureaucracy that he hated so much. The gift also thwarted a scheme that was being devised by Flinders Petrie, many years after he had originally surveyed the site; he had decided that Stonehenge was an ancient royal burial place and to prove this had been hoping to buy it from Chubb and carry out an excavation.

Stonehenge was now safely in the hands of the nation, or more precisely the Office of Works, but it was in a far from safe condition. The structural survey that was rapidly carried out confirmed Pitt Rivers' earlier conclusion, that several stones were in imminent danger of collapse. It also seems that the wooden props that he had condemned as both useless and unsightly may actually have been effective in holding up some of the more wildly leaning stones. By 1919 some of these props sported notices requesting the public 'not to disturb the pegs', presumably because this would have resulted in dire consequences not only for Stonehenge but also for those doing the disturbing. A programme of restoration was devised, working on the sound principle that no more should be done than was absolutely necessary and that 'smartening up' Stonehenge should be avoided at all costs. This restrained approach is in stark contrast to some earlier schemes for restoration, one of which involved the complete rebuilding of Stonehenge, no doubt with the use of much concrete, and the tidying up of the area amidst the stones with a nice neat layer of tarmac.

It was obvious that any restoration that involved straightening leaning stones would, as did the work carried out in 1901, require the investigation of any areas of ground to be disturbed. This could only be carried out under the supervision of a suitably qualified archaeologist, so once again the Office of Works turned to the Society of Antiquaries for advice and for a suitable candidate. But the chosen person would not simply be digging holes for engineers: the Antiquaries saw this as part of a far grander research scheme that would eventually involve the excavation of the whole of Stonehenge 'within and including the circular ditch and bank'. So if the restoration was to be modest in its ambitions, the excavation most certainly was not.

The obvious choice for the task was Professor Gowland who had done such a fine job in 1901, but he was too old and infirm so the work was entrusted to Colonel William Hawley, who had originally been intended as his assistant. Hawley seemed suitably qualified: he was ex-army and an experienced archaeologist who had already worked at Old Sarum where he had developed a good relationship with the Office of Works. He was also, very importantly, a respected member of the Society of Antiquaries. Invariably clad in tweed jacket and cap, with a moustache to rival Gowland's, Hawley appeared confident as he started work at Stonehenge, perhaps not realising what a long and at times dispiriting project he had embarked upon.

Health and Safety at work 1919. Lifting the twisted lintel off Stones 6 and 7 in the sarsen circle.

The restoration work began in the autumn of 1919 and tackled what was seen to be the most urgent problem. Stones 6 and 7, uprights of the outer sarsen circle, had both taken on a pronounced lean but in opposite directions; one leant inwards, the other outwards, creating a peculiarly twisted structure (held up with wooden props) on which their lintel was precariously perched. The first stage of the operation was to wrap the lintel in felt for its protection, encase it in a stout wooden crib and remove it with a suitably hefty crane. Clearly, from the evidence of the photograph that records the operation, there were no health and safety regulations in 1919. With the lintel removed, the two uprights were encased in even more massive structures of wood and steel and were then eased upright by means

Easing sarsens back to the vertical using giant screw jacks.

One of Hawley's 'registers' from the 1920 excavation season.

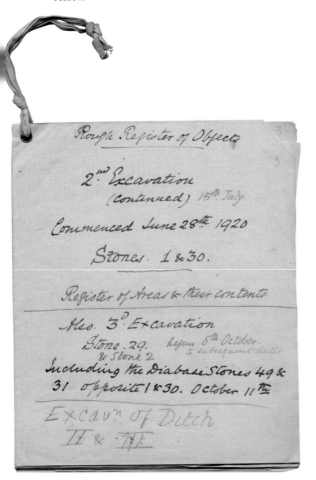

of giant screw jacks. Thick concrete foundations were laid and the lintel set temporarily on its uprights to make sure they were in the right position before they were firmly concreted into place. Finally, on 17th March 1920, the lintel was replaced.

In examining the area around Stones 6 and 7 Hawley used the same methods as Gowland, including a measuring frame. He was also concerned about the recovery of finds and sieved the excavated soil in the same way as his predecessor. The next stones to be dealt with, in 1920, were those of the best surviving section of the outer circle, numbers 29, 30, 1 and 2, still supporting their lintels but leaning outwards. There were further plans to raise both the stone that fell in 1900 and the complete trilithon that collapsed in 1797, but money ran out. So Hawley's restoration work was at an end and it was time for him to start on the second part of his commission, the Society of Antiquaries' research excavation.

In 1920 he started on the first of seven long seasons at Stonehenge that saw him working in all weathers, often alone, from March to November each year. The ditch was his first objective and he tackled it in a series of cuttings, each 26ft (7.9m) long. There was a sound reason for this unusual length, as each cutting could be subdivided crossways, from side to side of the ditch, into alphabetically lettered foot-wide strips (a–z, hence 26ft). Between 1920 and 1926 (with the exception of 1923)

Hawley's excavation of the ditch on the south-eastern side of the enclosure revealed its irregular profile and clear causeways.

Hawley excavated about half of the ditch, in an arc that ran from the south around the eastern side as far as the main north-easterly facing entrance. This arc can be identified today by the 'sharper' profile of the ditch that was never completely backfilled after excavation. Hawley's records are far from comprehensive, but it is possible to reconstruct from them a good idea of the original form of the ditch and the nature of the deposits that filled it.

From previous experience Hawley would have been able to recognise the sequences of deposits that fill chalk-cut ditches if they are simply allowed to silt up naturally over time. Initially rain and wind produce fine silty deposits on the ditch floor, then the first frosts cause the sides to shatter and a 'primary rubble' soon fills the base of the ditch. The process then slows and finer chalk silts accumulate, sometimes interrupted by more humic layers that show where vegetation had established itself. But this was not the sequence that Hawley consistently encountered when he started to excavate his first trenches in the Stonehenge ditch. In some places the ditch had filled naturally, while in others layers of chalk at a high level provided evidence of deliberate backfilling. He also identified small scoops in the soils that filled the ditch, which contained charcoal, animal bone and even cremated human bone.

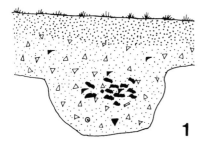

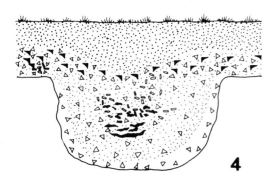

Cross sections of Aubrey Holes 1 (top) and 4, from just south of the enclosure entrance.

But these were the most exciting finds that the ditch contained and on the whole Hawley seems to have been quite disappointed by what he found. As he removed the lower deposits and exposed the floor of the ditch he found antler picks, including at least one heap or 'stack' at the western terminal. There were also animal bones that seemed to have been deliberately placed rather than just thrown in as rubbish. These 'structured deposits' included two ox mandibles (lower jaws) that were found in the ditch terminals flanking the southern entrance, and a complete ox skull placed on the ditch floor. In many of the excavated ditch segments Hawley found a distinct layer of worked flint, the waste material from knapping nodules of flint that were presumably discovered while the ditch was being dug. There was also a small collection of carved chalk objects including perfectly circular balls.

Hawley recorded that the ditch was relatively shallow, with an average depth of between 1.2 and 1.3m (about 4ft) and reaching its maximum of 2.3m (7ft 6in) at its entrance terminal. It was surprisingly irregular in profile, segmented 'like the outline of a string of badly made sausages'. This irregularity, with individual 'bays' separated by 'lateral projections' – spurs of unexcavated chalk that projected into the ditch and sometimes stretched from side to side – puzzled Hawley. His initial thought was that they were 'dwelling places intercommunicating but with some artificial partition between them', but he soon dropped that idea. Despite the animal bones on the floor of the ditch and one place where there had clearly been a fire, Hawley reasoned, quite sensibly, that had people been living in these 'bays' then they would have contained far more 'black refuse, animal bones, pottery and marks of fire'. The alternative was that they were the product of the method of ditch digging, basically a series of elongated pits that would then be broken through to make a continuous, but wobbly, ditch.

1920 was a busy year for Colonel Hawley. He and his assistant R S Newall, a local archaeologist, completed their work on the stones that were to be straightened, began work on the ditch and also embarked on investigating the interior of Stonehenge. This soon produced some exciting results. In his great work *Monumenta Britannica*, published in 1666, the antiquarian John Aubrey had noted a series of slight depressions or 'cavities' just inside the inner edge of the bank. Newall persuaded Hawley that these needed investigation, firstly by probing with an iron bar which quickly proved that Aubrey's observations were correct and that there were buried pits underlying the depressions in the grass. Hawley discovered that there were 56 of them, arranged in a neat circle and spaced between 4.5 and 4.8m (14–15ft) apart. They were initially referred to as X Holes although, in recognition of their original discoverer, their name was later changed to Aubrey Holes. Hawley excavated 27 of them in 1920 and a total of 32 by the end of the 1924 season. They were all roughly circular, although they varied in both depth and profile, and the layers that filled them were also far from consistent. Some revealed hints that they had once held uprights, but whether these uprights were of stone or timber was not at first certain, and nor was it clear whether any timbers had been simply left to rot where they stood or had been removed. More puzzling were the deposits found in the upper fills of the Aubrey Holes, which were similar to those found in the higher levels of the ditch. There were dark soils, charcoal and, once again, cremated human bones.

A glance through Hawley's diaries gives some idea of what he achieved over the years he was working at Stonehenge. As well as the excavation of the ditch and the Aubrey Holes he dug parts of the Avenue close to the enclosure entrance, the ditch around the Heel Stone, the South Barrow and an area around the Slaughter Stone; and then there was the 'general trenching'. This was his method of investigating large areas, an attempt at fulfilling his original brief to excavate Stonehenge in its entirety. It consisted of digging long narrow trenches one at a time, with each one being completed and filled in before the adjacent one was dug. The disadvantage of this method is that the areas investigated, mainly in the north-eastern quadrant of the enclosure, were seen piece by piece and no large areas were ever exposed at any one time. It also seems a little horticultural, digging Stonehenge as if it was an allotment being prepared for potato planting. But even given the limitations of this method his trenches yielded yet more significant discoveries: new stone holes, postholes and, in particular, the two rings of pits that lie immediately and concentric with the outer sarsen circle. These became known as the Y and Z Holes.

It is sometimes hard to understand how Hawley managed to excavate so much. He was far from a young man when he started, he often worked alone, though occasionally he had some assistance from Newall, and as the years went on he was increasingly unwell, troubled by rheumatism and other ailments. As anyone who has visited Salisbury Plain will know very well, the weather can be unpredictable and Hawley was alternately boiled or frozen. Nor can his accommodation have helped his health: at best he had a room in a tumbledown mill a few miles away at Figheldean, where he had to climb a vertical outside ladder to reach his bedroom; at worst he had a wooden shed on site. In the face of all these hardships his achievements seem all the more remarkable.

It seems a sad existence; almost forgotten by those who had at first encouraged his efforts, doggedly carrying on with a scheme that had been so ambitious and was intended to be so high profile. He presented the results of each season's work to the Society of Antiquaries, strictly factual reports that were initially praised for their objectivity then criticised for precisely the same reason. To those who could not grasp the magnitude of Hawley's task he had failed by not providing the answers to the really big Stonehenge questions: who built it, when and, in particular, why? But his work was not entirely inconclusive. Over the years that he dug at Stonehenge he gradually developed ideas about the sequence of construction.

A beautiful polished stone mace-head found with a cremation on the southern side of the enclosure.

He came to the conclusion that there were three stages, the first of which was the ditch and bank, no longer considered as having been lived in but dug for defensive purposes. The idea that the circular earthwork enclosure was the earliest part of Stonehenge was not new – it had first been suggested by Flinders Petrie – but it was Hawley who proved it, using the evidence from his extensive excavations. The ditch also provided evidence for the second stage of construction. Within the layers that filled it he observed some consistent patterns. There was a layer of chalk, quite high up, that he interpreted as spoil from the digging of the Aubrey Holes thrown into the partly silted ditch. Since Hawley considered that the Aubrey Holes had originally held upright stones, this made the second stage a circle of widely spaced stones set close to the inner edge of the bank. Then there was the evidence from the stone chips. The lower levels of the ditch produced few finds and it was only much higher, at the point where the ditch was almost completely silted up, that Hawley encountered chips of both bluestone and sarsen. These were also what formed the bulk of the 'Stonehenge layer', a carpet of stone chips and other debris that he encountered everywhere he dug inside the enclosure. Hawley assumed, quite logically, that this layer was the debris from shaping the central stones and, as its components were only found high in the ditch, that the stone shaping must have taken place some considerable time after the ditch was dug.

So first came the ditch and bank, then the Aubrey Holes. So far so good. But Hawley, like many both before and after him, struggled to make sense of what was left – the central stone structure. Consequently he decided that a third and final stage consisted of all the stones in the centre lumped together and interpreted, in a fairly loose way, as being of 'sentimental or sacred significance'.

By 1926 Hawley had excavated nearly half of Stonehenge, everything that lay on the south-east side of the main axis of the site. He had collected and catalogued the not very spectacular finds and had reburied those he felt could yield no further information. Ten special pits, 'Hawley's Graves', were dug close to his site huts and into them went most of the animal bones, worked flints, stone chips and other bits and pieces. Years later the cremated human bone was also reburied at Stonehenge, Aubrey Hole 7 being considered an appropriate final resting place. Hawley had dutifully written his annual reports, published in the *Antiquaries Journal*, but the final words of the last one showed that Stonehenge had beaten him:

> So very little is known about this place that what I say is mainly conjecture and it is to be hoped that future excavators will be able to throw more light upon it than I have done.

It seemed that Hawley could not win. He had been criticised for failing to provide any interpretation of the results of his work, but those same critics also attacked him when he suggested a sequence of construction for Stonehenge. Later opinion on the subject of Hawley is also divided. In 1925, near the end of his excavations, the President of the Society of Antiquaries praised him for his 'patience and accuracy' that 'would serve as a model in all branches of research'. By 1979 Richard Atkinson, of the next generation of Stonehenge excavators, described Hawley's campaigns as '...one of the most melancholy chapters in the long history of the monument ...'. Again according to Atkinson, '... the regrettable inadequacy in his methods of recording his finds and observations and, one suspects, an insufficient appreciation of the destructive character of excavation *per se* has left for subsequent excavators a most lamentable legacy of doubt and frustration'.

Harsh words, echoed by Christopher Chippindale the author of *Stonehenge Complete*, who considers the Hawley years of 1919 to 1926 nothing short of 'a disaster', the excavations under-resourced and not curtailed, as they should have been, when it was realised that they were going badly wrong. In contrast, Mike Pitts, the author

An aerial photograph taken in the early 1920s shows the excavated Aubrey Holes marked out as white spots and further excavations in progress around the main entrance.

of *Hengeworld,* is inclined to be more charitable, considering that Hawley, for all his faults, gave us the 'underground Stonehenge' of postholes and hitherto unknown pits, as well as the first proof that Stonehenge might have taken longer to build than had previously been thought.

Whether Hawley should be regarded as a hero or a villain will never be resolved, although Stonehenge would probably have been far better served had Gowland been available to carry out the excavations. In this author's opinion it is fortunate that Hawley never completed the job that he had been commissioned to carry out. At least this left half of Stonehenge intact for future archaeologists to explore, even if some of their efforts were not much better.

The guidebook of 1916 was illustrated by Heywood Sumner. This was a great improvement on the versions of the preceding century.

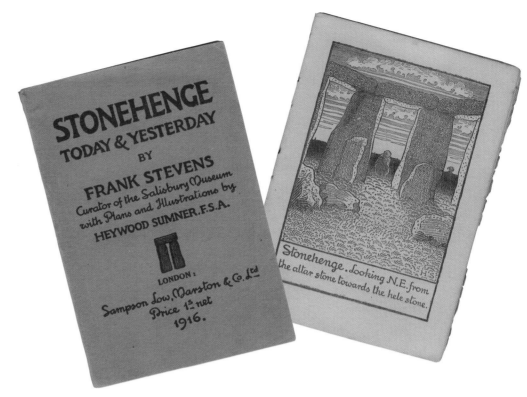

Under polarised light thin slivers of dolerite from Stonehenge appear more like stained-glass windows than geological specimens. These are Thomas's original samples from 1923.

Even before Hawley had embarked upon his campaign of excavations Stonehenge had a new guidebook, *Stonehenge Today and Yesterday*, by Frank Stevens, the Curator of Salisbury Museum. Illustrated by Heywood Sumner's stylish drawings, it confidently stated the date and purpose of this 'weird monument' and was a distinct improvement on Browne's guide of nearly a century earlier. It highlighted some of the major remaining questions, such as where the stones had come from. To a Wiltshire archaeologist the sarsens were easy to understand – local stones that were of interest because of their sheer size and the problem of how they were moved by 'primitive people'. But the 'foreign stones' (bluestones) were a different matter, impossible to match within a hundred miles of Salisbury Plain. A wide range of possible sources was outlined: Kildare in Ireland; Wales; Cornwall; Dartmoor; Shropshire; or Cumberland.

In 1923 this question was tackled scientifically by Dr H H Thomas, a petrologist working for the Geological Survey of Great Britain. He obtained samples of the Stonehenge bluestones from which he prepared thin polished slices that could be viewed using polarised light to reveal the rock's internal structure. These he immediately recognised: they were identical to those from samples he had taken in an area he had previously studied in south-west Wales. Here, in the Preseli Mountains of north Pembrokeshire, close to the coast of the Irish Sea and more than 150 miles from Stonehenge, Thomas found the three main types of Stonehenge bluestone: dolerite, rhyolite and volcanic ash. Many of these rocks break naturally into slabs and pillars, ready-made monoliths waiting to be transported. The source of the stone was no longer in question, leaving only the puzzle of how the bluestones had been transported to Salisbury Plain (*see* chapter 10).

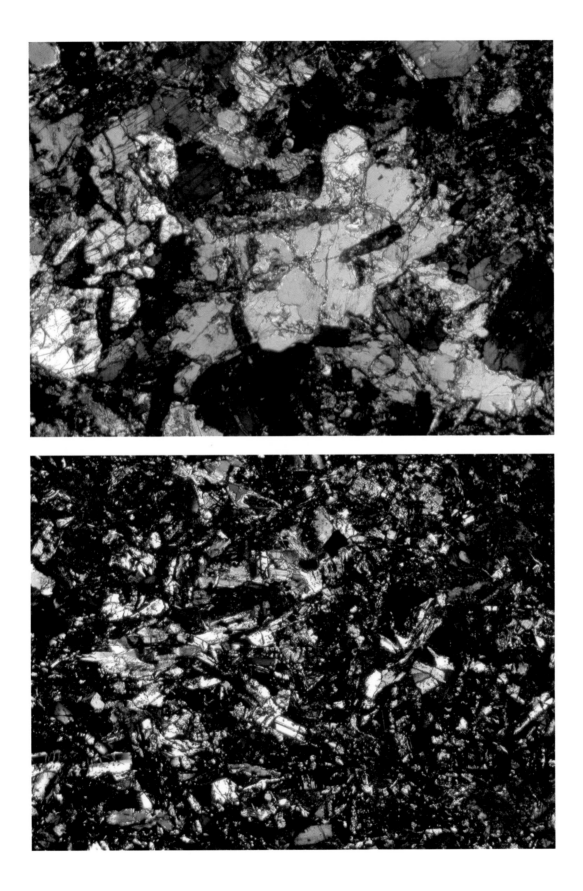

The discovery of Woodhenge. The aerial photograph taken by Squadron Leader Gilbert Insall in 1925 (reproduced upside down in the original excavation report four years later).

There was also an additional bluestone puzzle. In 1934 the archaeologist W E V Young discovered a scatter of bluestone fragments immediately south of the Cursus, close to where it ran into Fargo Wood. Was this where the bluestones were stored, a working site where they were shaped and trimmed, or perhaps even the site of an unknown monument, a bluestone circle? More fragments, discovered in 1947 by J F S Stone, added to the mystery and excavations in 2006, despite finding more fragments of bluestone, still failed to locate the missing 'bluestonehenge'.

The Hawley years, 1919 to 1926, saw changes not only at Stonehenge itself but in the surrounding landscape. Less than 20 years after the stones were first viewed from the air (in this case from a balloon) the skies buzzed with aircraft flying out of a number of nearby military airfields, including the one at Stonehenge Down that lay within sight of the stones. Photographs taken from the air revealed evidence of sites that had been invisible to previous generations of antiquarians and archaeologists. Stukeley had been unable to trace the Avenue beyond the ridge to the east of Stonehenge but now its line could be picked up in growing crops and followed as far as the River Avon at West Amesbury. But the most dramatic discovery was made further up the river, close to the great henge of Durrington Walls. In December 1925 Squadron Leader Gilbert Insall VC MC, based at the nearby Netheravon airfield, was flying over a site that had been described in the early 19th century as a large, flattened 'Druid' barrow. In his own words:

> I was flying a Sopwith Snipe on 12th December 1925, at about 2000ft over Stonehenge, when I noticed a circle with white chalk marks in the centre near Durrington Walls. Stonehenge was visible at the same time and the two sites looked similar from that height.

Plan of Woodhenge from Maud Cunnington's original excavation report of 1929. Note the 'ramped' holes for the larger posts of ring C.

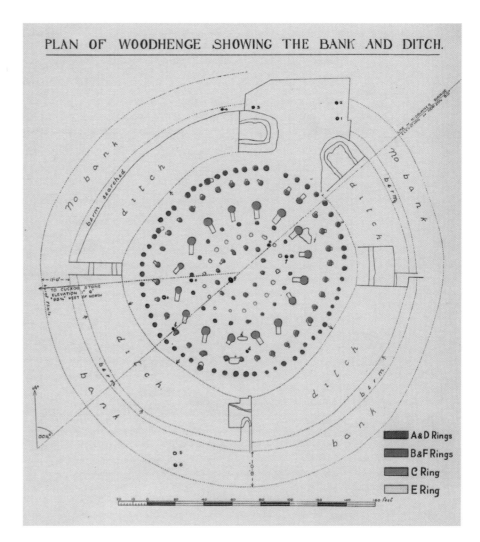

PLAN OF WOODHENGE SHOWING THE BANK AND DITCH.

A & D Rings
B & F Rings
C Ring
E Ring

Over the next few months Insall made a point of flying over it again and again, watching as the crop grew and the marks became clearer. Finally, in July 1926, he photographed the outline of a circular ditched enclosure with a single north-east-facing entrance. Inside it lay what he thought was as many as seven concentric rings of dark spots, perhaps the holes for wooden posts.

The discovery was reported to archaeologist Maud Cunnington, a descendant of Colt Hoare's collaborator who, over the next three years, excavated the entire site. The dark spots that had showed up so clearly in the growing crop represented pits dug into the chalk, 168 holes arranged in six rings (A–F starting from the outside), not seven as had originally been thought. Within the chalk that filled the pits, circular dark spots showed that they had held upright wooden posts that had rotted where they stood. The diameters of the posts varied considerably from ring to ring. The smallest were those of ring E at around 23cm (9in), while the largest were in ring C which were as much as 85cm (nearly 3ft) in diameter. The largest postholes were between 1.75 and 2m (about 6ft) deep and also had one sloping or 'ramped' side, down which the massive oak post would have been slid before being hauled upright.

There were also two holes that appeared to have held stones, now missing, and, in the centre of the site, a burial under a small flint cairn. This contained the skeleton of a young child, about 3½ years old according to the original report, whose skull lay in two halves in the grave. This could simply have resulted from the plates of the skull, unfused in a child of this age, having become separated in the grave. But Maud Cunnington decided that the child's skull had been deliberately split before burial, leading to the assumption that this was evidence of human sacrifice. This question will never be resolved as the skeleton, housed at the Royal College of Surgeons, was destroyed by bombing during the Second World War.

It is hardly surprising that this newly discovered and excavated site soon gained the name 'Woodhenge'. As Insall had noted from the air, there was much similarity between its plan and that of Stonehenge and they even shared the same north-east/south-west orientation. Woodhenge, dated by the distinctive, highly decorated Neolithic pottery that was found in the postholes, was also approximately the same date as Stonehenge. But, unlike Stonehenge, there was nothing but a ground plan, leaving a puzzle as to what it had originally looked like. Cunnington estimated the potential heights of some of the timbers – as much as 6m (20ft) above ground for the tallest – but were they simply free-standing or the components of a huge roofed building? Many reconstructions from the 1940s onwards show a circular building with an open central court, a way of explaining the comparatively large size of the posts of the third ring in from the outside. In practical terms this seems an unlikely explanation, as rainwater would have poured into the centre. It seems more likely that the posts were free-standing, although there is the possibility that they were linked with horizontal timber lintels, echoing the stone arrangements at Stonehenge. They may also have been highly decorated.

But in the end the fully excavated site was displayed in a rather conservative, noncommittal way, with the posts represented by short sections of concrete pipes of appropriate diameter, set upright in the original postholes and with their caps colour-coded according to which ring they were part of. Over the years there has been much criticism of 'concretehenge' but no ideas have been put forward about how to display it better.

By the late 1920s Stonehenge itself was secure in the ownership of the nation and safe from commercial over-exploitation. Its leaning stones had been straightened and stabilised and the excavation trenches backfilled, all left neat and tidy. But the same could not be said for the surrounding landscape, the state of which, increasingly cluttered with buildings, was causing widespread concern. In 1926 the Air Ministry had returned the land on which the Stonehenge aerodrome stood to its original owners, but rather than revert to farmland the airfield buildings then became a pig farm. The Ministry of Works, the guardians of Stonehenge, had built cottages for its custodians in the fork between the A303 and the A344, mirrored across the A344 by the Stonehenge Café. At the time the café was considered to be a 'cheap, flashy little building like the worst type of bungaloid growth', more architecturally suited to a seaside resort than the surroundings of Stonehenge.

The solution to this creeping suburbanisation was found in a national appeal, launched in August 1927. By 1929, with contributions from the public, the aristocracy and the Druids, it had raised sufficient funds for the purchase of 1,500 acres. This land was handed over to the National Trust in order that it should remain undeveloped in the future and the promised tidy-up began. Over the next few years the aerodrome buildings, the cottages and the flashy little café all disappeared, fulfilling the aims of the appeal to 'restore and preserve the open surroundings' of Stonehenge.

What followed was a quiet time in Stonehenge's history. Visitors came, increasingly by car, parked, paid their entrance fee and were free to wander among the stones. Stonehenge sat out another world war during which Winston Churchill paid a brief visit. But in contrast to what happened in the earlier conflict, when negotiations about Stonehenge's safety continued through the war and restoration work began just a year later, this time it was five years before archaeologists once again turned their attention to Stonehenge.

'Fork left for Exeter' down what looks like a narrow lane (actually the A303). The view west towards Stonehenge in the late 1920s.

CHAPTER 6   The recent investigation of Stonehenge

Given the scale of the work that was carried out at Stonehenge between 1919 and 1926 – the excavation of about half of the site and a considerable amount of restoration – it seems surprising that there was enough left to sustain another major campaign. Yet this is precisely what took place at Stonehenge between 1950 and 1964: yet more excavation and restoration that changed the appearance of the stones far more that the work of 30 years earlier.

By 1950 Britain was slowly recovering from the effects of the Second World War and thoughts could turn to less essential subjects, such as archaeology. Colonel Hawley had died, leaving the legacy of his seven years of excavation at Stonehenge – a collection of site notes, unwritten reports and unstudied finds. To the Society of Antiquaries, which had commissioned his original research, the potential that lay within his notes and those neglected finds was clear. So they asked three distinguished scholars to bring the results of Hawley's work to publication. The two major figures in the work that was to follow were Richard Atkinson of the Ashmolean Museum in Oxford, later to be Professor of Archaeology at Cardiff University, and Professor Stuart Piggott of Edinburgh University. Both Atkinson, who was later to be so scathing of Hawley's work, and Piggott had experience of Neolithic ritual sites and were well qualified to tackle Stonehenge. The trio was completed by Dr J F S Stone, a Wiltshire archaeologist who had already excavated in the Stonehenge area, cutting a section across the Cursus in 1947.

With hindsight, perhaps it would have been better for Atkinson, Piggott and Stone to have analysed and published the results of Hawley's work before embarking on any new investigations, but the trio felt from the start that some small-scale excavations were needed in order to answer specific questions.

They made a modest start at Easter 1950 by digging two of the remaining undisturbed Aubrey Holes on the south-western side of the enclosure. These two pits, A31 and A32, confirmed what Hawley had observed, that there was little consistency in their size, their shape or the deposits that filled them. The larger of the pair, A32, contained fragments of sarsen, bluestone, animal bone, flint and antler, as well as cremated human bone and charcoal. Of all these finds charcoal would seem to be of least interest, but two years later it was precisely this humble material that was featured in a *Daily Telegraph* article of 12th May 1952: 'Stonehenge charcoal find. Radioactivity test' announced the result of the first radiocarbon date to be obtained for an archaeological site anywhere in the world. The technique of radiocarbon dating was brand new, pioneered by Professor Willard Libby of the University of Chicago. And the date? – 1848BC plus or minus a substantial margin of 275 years. By present-day standards this is woefully vague, dating Aubrey Hole 32 to somewhere between 2123 and 1573BC. But in 1952 this was hugely important, as it was the first time that Stonehenge or any other site had been given an actual date rather than being described as 'Neolithic' or 'early Bronze Age'. It remains the only radiocarbon date available for an Aubrey Hole.

In 1953 a trench on the south-western side of the site examined a Y Hole and the adjacent Z Hole. Hawley, on the basis of the 'sharp' edges of many of the Y and Z

FROM THE TOP
Richard Atkinson, Stuart Piggott and J F S Stone.

The stump of a curious ridged bluestone (Stone 66), partially uncovered by R S Newall in 1950. It lies half underneath the fallen sarsen upright of the Great Trilithon.

Holes that he had excavated, had concluded that they had never held upright stones. Atkinson, who had already established himself as the leader of the trio of archaeologists and its spokesman, came to the same conclusion.

The rest of that season's excavations concentrated on examining the Avenue. Cuttings were made through its ditches and banks close to the Heel Stone (the ditch surrounding which was also examined) and also at its 'elbow', the point downslope from Stonehenge where it makes an abrupt change of direction and heads off eastwards towards the King Barrow Ridge. Trenches were also dug here to test the idea, believed by both Stukeley and Colt Hoare, that the Avenue branched at this point. The results of this investigation were inconclusive.

Even if 1953 was not a particularly spectacular year for excavation results one remarkable discovery was made, not by digging but through simple observation. Atkinson was a keen and prolific photographer and is credited with having taken many of the large number of photographs from this era, even when he himself appears in the image. One of the tasks for 1953 was a photographic survey of the stones and on a July afternoon, waiting for the raking light to pick out details of the 17th-century graffiti carved on Stone 53, one of the trilithon uprights, Atkinson noted something different. In contrast to the sharp, chisel-carved names there were softer outlines of what appeared to be prehistoric axe blades and a dagger. Over the summer more and more axe carvings were found, until the total stood at over 40, all on upright sarsens of the trilithons and the outer circle. Although there was no way of directly dating these carvings, they clearly represented typical Irish middle Bronze Age flat axes with a tapering butt and a broad cutting edge, dateable in mainland Britain to around 1500BC.

The dagger carving was a bit more of a problem. The weapon represented was elaborate, with a slender blade that curved outwards into a guard, a short handle and a pronounced pommel. Unlike the axes, this was not a form that could easily be matched in Britain, or in fact in northern Europe. The closest match appeared to be in the royal shaft graves of Mycenae in Greece, a similar date to the axes and once again leaving open the possibility of foreign influence at play in the building of Stonehenge.

Atkinson's 1953 photograph of the dagger and the axe – the first carvings to be discovered.

The discovery of the carvings in 1953 was undoubtedly of great importance. The stones were not only exotic in origin, smoothed and shaped, but could now be seen to have been decorated. What is extraordinary is that this decoration was not spotted earlier. There had been suggestions as early as 1893 that there could be carvings on the stones and there are photographs from this era that clearly (albeit with hindsight) show the dagger and axes on Stone 53, the place where they were eventually first spotted.

In 1954 Atkinson and his colleagues returned to Stonehenge itself, excavating a total of seven trenches, four of which were dug through the ditch, bank and counterscarp, concentrating on an area just to the north-west of the entrance. This was their first look at the sequence of ditch deposits, with which they must have

1954 – excavation of the eastern side of the bluestone circle showing below-ground stumps.

been familiar from Hawley's notes, drawings and photographs. Unfortunately, at the point where they chose to excavate the ditch there was one highly significant variation in this sequence. Atkinson described the finds from the ditch, noting the importance of a handful of scraps of bluestone. The lowest level at which they were found in the 1954 cutting was not far from the base of the ditch, just above silts that Atkinson estimated could have accumulated in around 50 years. On the basis of this evidence, which had not been found in earlier ditch cuttings, he deduced that the bluestones were on site 'when the ditch was only partly silted, and hence at an early stage in the sequence of construction'. This is entirely logical but when John Evans re-excavated this cutting in 1978 as part of a study of the environment of Stonehenge, the reason for this anomaly became apparent. The 1954 cutting had clipped the edge of a Beaker period grave (described in more detail later in this chapter) cut down from a high level in the silted-up ditch. The bluestone fragments that had been used as evidence that these stones were on site so early were not from the lower ditch silts but from the filling of the much later grave.

The 1954 ditch excavation seems to have confused rather than clarified the overall interpretation of Stonehenge but the season's remaining trenches, all of which lay on the line of the bluestone circle, were far more informative. One trench, which examined a segment of the circle between Stones 32 and 33, revealed five additional stones

The enigmatic Q and R Holes – as discovered and 'restored'.

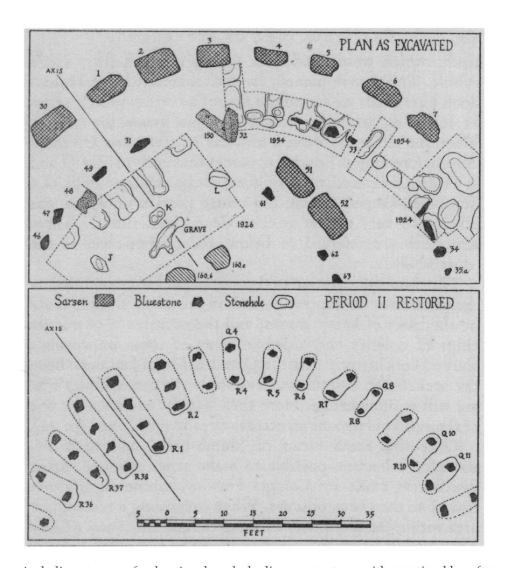

including stumps of volcanic ash, a dark olive-green stone with a noticeably softer texture than the other types of bluestone. This softer texture presumably accounts for the fact that there are no pillars of this stone surviving above ground. These additional stones demonstrated that the pillars of the bluestone circle were closer set than had been originally suggested, and that the overall number of stones in this setting was perhaps as many as 57, not 40 as was previously thought. But the most significant find was of an entirely new series of holes, invisible on the surface and not previously recognised in excavation. The first holes appeared between the bluestone circle and the sarsen circle, rather irregular in shape and filled with tightly packed dirty chalk. These were named the Q Holes, from the antiquarian John Aubrey's frequent use of the phrase '*quaere quot*' ('enquire how many') in the margins of his working manuscripts. Then a corresponding series of holes with an identical filling was found just inside the bluestone circle. These were designated R Holes. But then it was realised that there was a physical link between these two apparently separate arcs of holes: the Q and R Holes formed the ends of a series of short trenches described as a 'dumb bells', each with a centre section filled with very tightly packed clean chalk rubble.

Moreover, when the bases of the Q and R Holes were examined in detail not only did they show the impressions of stones but there were minute chips of bluestone embedded in the soft chalk. This was proof of bluestone settings predating the existing circle and horseshoe, a pattern that fitted nicely with the new evidence from the ditch.

Having discovered this new series of stone settings there remained the problem of how to interpret it. Looking back through Hawley's records it was clear that he had unwittingly found and excavated parts of these 'dumb bells'. Adding this evidence to the new findings produced a wide arc of at least 12 pairs of Q and R Holes which, if extended round at the same spacing, would have consisted of 38 pairs of stone holes. Unfortunately, subsequent excavations would fail to locate a continuation of this original arc, leaving the Q and R Holes as a bluestone enigma, clearly early in the overall sequence of construction but of unfathomable form.

The final element of the bluestone settings that was examined in 1954 was a single fallen pillar lying on the southern side of the outer circle. Stone 36 had long been recognised as something unusual. In 1929 Hawley's former assistant Newall, assisted by the Rev George Engelheart, dug under it and felt, although did not see, mortice holes that showed it to have originally been a lintel. Atkinson felt that the stone deserved a more thorough examination so it was hoisted up on a block and tackle and turned on its side. The true elegance of the stone was now revealed, shaped according to Atkinson by people who clearly possessed not only manual skill but a feeling for form and design. Its basic shape was a prism but its subtleties inspired him to an almost poetic description: 'not a true prism, for all the edges are slightly curved, and all the surfaces except the base gently rounded, so that the outlines are softened, and the stone takes on a cushioned quality which belies the unyielding hardness of the material'.

Cleaning up Stone 36, the beautiful bluestone lintel revealed by excavation in 1954.

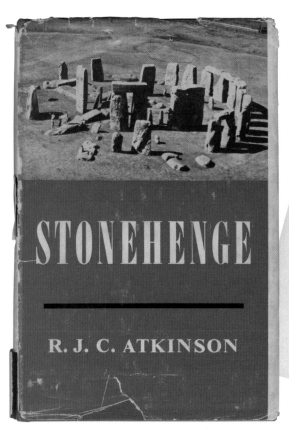

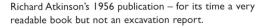

Richard Atkinson's 1956 publication – for its time a very readable book but not an excavation report.

Apart from the sheer aesthetic qualities of Stone 36 it posed some interesting questions. It was the second bluestone lintel to be identified and there were the uprights to go with them, pillars in the bluestone horseshoe that showed signs of having originally had tenons. So Atkinson could suggest a phase of 'tooled bluestones' which must, as there were now two lintels, have included at least two miniature trilithons. The remarkable Stone 36 also provided evidence that this was not a short-lived structure. One of its mortice holes was surrounded by a shallow depression, presumably a carefully worked seating for the upright on which it sat, and within this hollow the surface of the stone appeared worn, even polished. This did not appear to be deliberate but more the result of friction, perhaps caused by the expansion and contraction of the touching stones. But such a polish would only develop very slowly, suggesting that these stones must have stood as trilithons for many years.

1954 had been a highly successful season and Atkinson, as the lead archaeologist within the team, felt that there was now enough information available to go into print, and by the time that excavation resumed in 1956, *Stonehenge* had been published. This was a book not for archaeologists but for the ordinary reader, 'authoritative, vigorously written and pleasingly produced', and was instantly popular, going to a second impression by August of that year. In it Atkinson describes the sequence of construction and the dates of the various phases, based on the results of the first three seasons of the excavations that started in 1950. His sequence, which was to remain the accepted truth for nearly 40 years, is as follows.

OPPOSITE
The sequence of construction suggested by Atkinson as a result of his excavations in the 1950s.

Stonehenge I consisted of the ditch, the bank and the Aubrey Holes, now described as 'ritual pits dug for some religious or ceremonial purpose'. 'Ritual' is a very convenient term for the prehistorian, meaning in reality that he or she has no idea for what purpose the structure or deposit in question was originally intended. The only stones allocated to this early stage of construction are the Heel Stone and the two stones in the entrance (the Slaughter Stone and its missing pair). Also close to the entrance, four postholes near the Heel Stone and rows of posts on the entrance causeway represent the timber elements of this phase.

The double bluestone circle in the newly discovered Q and R Holes appears in Atkinson's Stonehenge II, along with the ditch around the Heel Stone and possibly two additional stones in Holes B and C that lay between the enclosure entrance and the Heel Stone. The Avenue is also considered to belong to this phase, and is suggested as having been constructed as a processional way up which the bluestones were hauled on the last stage of their journey from Wales. Despite having earlier dismissed the many postholes discovered by both Hawley and his own team as being impossible to interpret, Atkinson notes that any timber structure from the first phase must have been dismantled or destroyed before the bluestones arrived.

The third and final stage has echoes of Hawley's similar lumping together of all the remaining central stone structures, but Atkinson refines his sequence, dividing it into three sub-phases.

Stonehenge IIIa, according to Atkinson, involves a complete rebuilding of the monument and is a purely sarsen phase, including the five trilithons, the outer circle with its 30 uprights, the Slaughter Stone and its pair and the four Station Stones. A logical sequence of construction is proposed, starting with the trilithons, working outwards and ending with the peripheral stones. There is some doubt expressed as to whether the Station Stones, which unlike all the other stones in this phase are largely unworked, belong here or should be seen as part of the earlier monument.

This left four elements to be placed in their correct order in the overall sequence: the present bluestone circle, the present bluestone horseshoe, the assumed setting of dressed bluestones and the Y and Z Holes. By playing games with the numbers of bluestones and available stone holes, Atkinson came to the conclusion that his second sub-phase, Stonehenge IIIb, included two of these elements, one being some sort of structure, of unknown layout or function, that incorporated the dressed bluestones. Here too were the Y and Z Holes, apparently intended to receive the 60 bluestones left over after 22 of them had been selected for the dressed bluestone structure.

The final reorganisation of the bluestones came in Stonehenge IIIc when the setting of dressed stones was dismantled and attempts were made to remove any traces of jointing. The stones were then set up in the present arrangements: simple pillars laid out in a circle and a horseshoe.

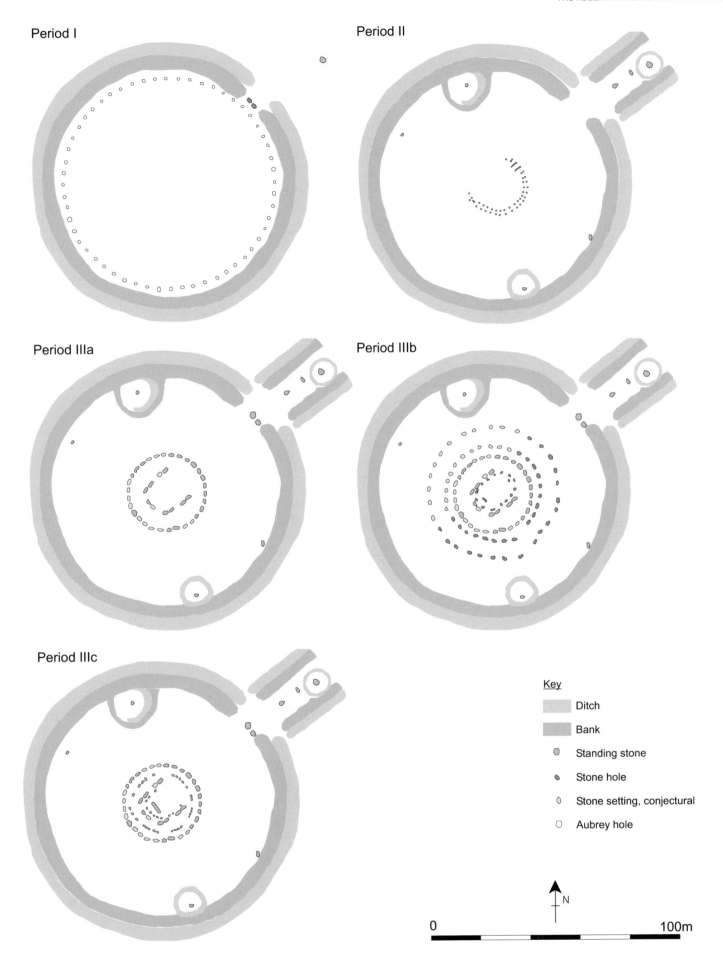

Period I

Period II

Period IIIa

Period IIIb

Period IIIc

Key

Ditch

Bank

Standing stone

Stone hole

Stone setting, conjectural

Aubrey hole

N

0   100m

The ruins of the sarsen trilithon that collapsed in 1797. Lying in the foreground is the fallen lintel of the Great Trilithon.

OPPOSITE
The start of the engineering works in the spring of 1958. The crane is just about to lift an upright of the sarsen circle that has fallen inwards.

Atkinson also suggested dates for his phases, using the evidence from the admittedly small number of finds, backed up by the single rather vague radiocarbon date obtained from an Aubrey Hole. Stonehenge I lay in the later part of the Neolithic, between 1900 and 1700BC; Stonehenge II, associated with Beaker pottery, dated to some time between 1700 and 1550BC; while Stonehenge III was completed around 1500BC.

Despite having apparently sorted out the sequence and dating of Stonehenge, the ambitions of the project continued to grow and in 1956 permission was sought from the Ministry of Works for far more extensive excavations. The new excavations were intended to refine the sequence by providing supporting evidence, with all the results published in a full excavation report. These ambitions seem slightly at odds with Stuart Piggott's statement, in a letter to *The Times* of September 1956, of the principles that guided their investigations at Stonehenge: 'At all times during the recent excavations of the site, the paramount necessity of restricting the excavated areas to the minimum has been in our minds, and we have been very conscious of the need to leave for future generations of archaeologists the opportunity of checking our own work.'

Permission was forthcoming, and in 1956 there was more work on the Avenue, cuttings through the ditches that surround the Heel Stone and one of the Station Stones and the re-excavation of two of Hawley's old trenches. Work was also started on an area close to the base of the trilithon that had collapsed in 1797. This year's proceedings were enlivened by the discovery, on 3rd July, of an unexploded 13-pound shell, dismissed as 'quite harmless' by the army personnel who were called in to deal with it.

But even as these excavations were taking place plans were being drawn up for further restoration work, on a scale not seen before. What was planned was far from minimal, would involve the excavation of one of the largest and most complex areas of the site to date and would radically change the physical face of Stonehenge.

The photograph taken in 1955 from high in the interior of Stonehenge shows the aftermath of a series of major collapses. In the foreground is the lintel from the Great Trilithon that had fallen into the centre of the site centuries earlier. Beyond the three upright bluestones are two now recumbent sarsens, the uprights of the trilithon that collapsed outwards in 1797. Its lintel, on which one of the mortice holes can be seen, lies beyond, half buried under a broken lintel from the outer circle. This and one of its uprights fell in 1900, leaving the remaining upright slightly askew. What was now being proposed was the re-erection of virtually everything shown in this photograph with the exception of the lintel of the Great Trilithon. The two bluestones to the right were to be removed and replaced and the uprights of the sarsen circle were to be reset and straightened before the repaired lintel was replaced. But most ambitiously, the entire trilithon, perhaps as much as 70 or 80 tons of collapsed sarsen, was to stand again. The total cost of this ambitious scheme was estimated as £8,500.

TRI-LIFT FOR STONEHENGE —BUT NO FAKING

STONEHENGE is to be back as it was 300 years ago.

Work which starts this week on re-erecting the great trilithon — three-stone arch-way — should be finished in three or four months, announced the Minister of, Works, Mr. Hugh Molson, in the Commons yesterday.

Stonehenge, however, will not be seen as the Ancient Britons knew it. Many stones knocked down by the Romans are to be left on the ground.

"We have no intention of faking Stonehenge," Mr. Molson assured M.P.s.

Fifteen men and a 70-ton crane will do in a few months what it took 150 Ancient Britons with crude ropes and levers an inestimable time.

In position

The crane will lift the two upright stones—each weighing between 45 and 50 tons. Then a back into position. Then a smashed lintel will be repaired and replaced.

It was the discovery of carvings on one of the fallen stones which prompted the decision to lift them. It was felt that sightseers — 200.000 visit Stonehenge every year— might rub away marks by standing on them.

This work was scheduled to start in the spring of 1957, but the sheer scale of the project, the engineering requirements as well as the archaeological considerations, meant that it was postponed until the following year. A tight schedule was drawn up. Four weeks of preparation were to start on 24th February, followed by five weeks for the removal of stones, during which the archaeologists would start work. Six weeks were then allowed for the replacement of stones, to be completed by 9th June, leaving two weeks for the contractors to finish their work and 'leave site perfect' in time for the summer solstice on 21st June. Fortunately this whole project is extremely well documented in a series of fascinating photographs.

Atkinson and Piggott duly started in late March 1958, working inside a fenced-off quadrant of the interior and alongside the engineers who were to remove the stones. Some of the smaller ones could be shifted comparatively easily, although the first lifts were not entirely without incident. One photograph shows Stone 22 from the sarsen circle, which fell inwards in 1900, ready for lifting, trussed up in a steel frame and with the crane standing by. The uprights that flank it have been provided with some token protection, more it seems to prevent cosmetic damage, but not enough to save one of them from receiving a hefty clout when Stone 22 slewed on lifting. The blow was not at the time considered enough to have destabilised it, but it does seem more than coincidence that this same stone, number 23, fell over without warning in March 1963.

The two uprights of the fallen trilithon posed even more of a problem. Each weighed about 40 tons, the largest of the sarsens to be moved in recent times, and they were not this time simply to be winched upright from a leaning position but required lifting clear of the working area. The first stage of the archaeological work was to free the stones from the ground in which they were very firmly embedded. Trenches were dug alongside them, cutting through the 'Stonehenge layer' with its eclectic mix of stone chips, ancient flint tools and broken Victorian lemonade bottles. 'Tide marks' on the exposed sides of the stones showed the considerable depth to which they had sunk. Brave diggers (not Atkinson or Piggott – they supervised from the surface) then tunnelled beneath the stones so that steel hawsers could be passed through for the lift. At this stage there were clearly concerns about the integrity of the two massive stones: had their fall caused undetected fractures that could spell disaster when they were subjected to the strains of the lift? Their surfaces were examined in minute detail and they were even x-rayed, the public being warned to stay clear by small signs saying 'Danger Radio-Active'.

Meanwhile the enormous construction camp grew in the background. Huts were built, as well as offices, stores, a mess room and ablutions; there was even a dormitory, perhaps in anticipation of night shifts towards the end of the project. The surface of the site inside the enclosure was covered in protective 'airstrip' matting and, within the area designated as the 'stone park', additional ground protection was provided by railway sleepers.

Stones 57 and 58 were removed successfully, encased in massive steel cradles and lifted using the Brabazon crane, a monster borrowed from the nearby RAF station at Boscombe Down. Originally built to lift the prototype of the Bristol Brabazon plane in the event that it crash-landed, this crane, capable of lifting 60 tons, was the only one available that could move the sarsens. Their removal now presented Atkinson and Piggott with a unique opportunity: a large area totally undisturbed by previous excavators. In terms of adding to the understanding of the sequence of construction it could not have been better placed. Within their trench they knew that at the very least they would find a segment of the bluestone horseshoe, the setting for an entire trilithon, an arc of the bluestone circle and part of the sarsen circle. There was also the possibility of more evidence for the enigmatic Q and R Hole structure and confirmation of whether or not it was a complete circle. So, in the comparatively short time allocated before the engineers returned, all the archaeological deposits were removed down to the level of the bedrock. The chalk surface that was exposed looked like a lunar landscape, pitted and cratered with the expected and the unexpected, a vivid testimony to Stonehenge's long and complex history of construction.

Burrowing under Stone 57 in order to insert lifting cables. Note the feet just visible in the tunnel and, in the foreground, the heaped up debris from the 'Stonehenge layer'.

Planning the area excavated in 1958 as part of 'Operation Trilithon'. The complexity of the below-ground archaeology is evident from the pitted and cratered surface of the chalk.

In the photographs taken of this area towards the end of its excavation, Atkinson, cigarette-holder permanently in mouth, takes measurements, while Piggott, renowned for his draughtsmanship and rarely without his woolly hat, draws the plans. The holes for Stones 57 and 58 can be easily recognised, both surprisingly shallow considering what they had supported for so long. The drystone-wall-like structure at the rear of Hole 58 is part of the packing that fixed the stone in position once it had been hauled upright. Anything would do for the packing: left-over chalk, fragments of sarsen and bluestone, even broken antler picks, all tightly rammed in.

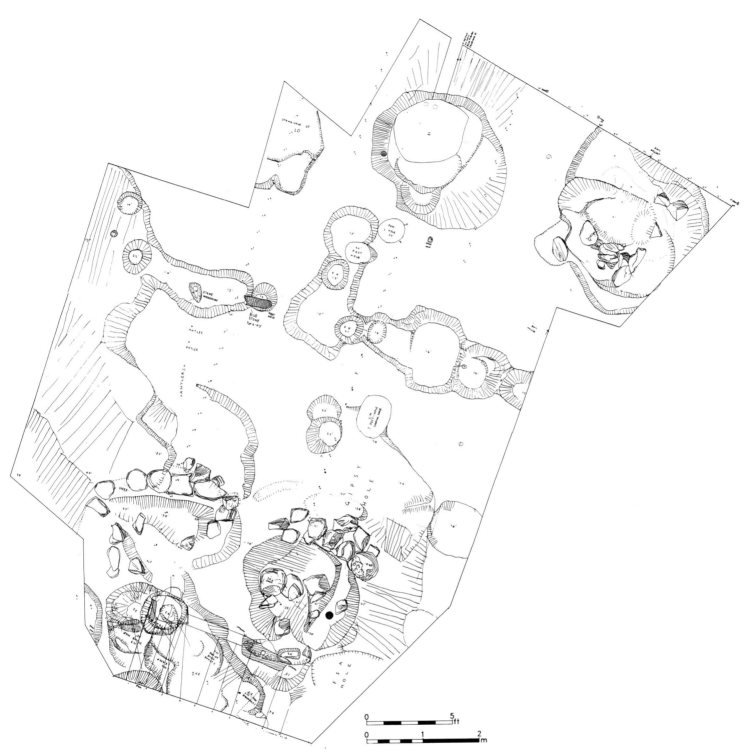

The plan drawn by Stuart Piggot of the Operation Trilithon excavation area. The plan is orientated the same way as the preceding photograph.

Piggott's plan presents, in graphic form and in much greater detail, what photographs can only hint at. Beyond the recognisable holes for sarsens and bluestones there are terraces in the chalk, scoops and hollows, and the small and enigmatic pits that may have held either stones or wooden posts. Some relationships can be seen between different parts of the overall plan, a stone hole maybe perhaps cutting through a posthole, but much of the key to understanding the complexity demonstrated by the plan lay in the layers above the chalk, and of these we have little record.

Replacing the lintel on the restored trilithon with the 'Brabazon crane' capable, according to its sign, of lifting 60 tons.

Prior to being filled with concrete the eroded hole in Stone 60 was large enough to provide shelter in bad weather.

The excavation was completed on time and the engineers, under the supervision of Mr Bailey, the senior architect, moved back in. The photographs indicate that night shifts became necessary in order to keep the project on schedule, but eventually the sarsens returned and were set back in their original position, no longer in pits packed with rubble and chalk but set in a solid bed of concrete. The final stage of Operation Trilithon, as it is described in some of the works files, was the replacement of the lintel on the newly erected uprights. This was a delicate operation, again carried out using the Brabazon crane, and one that nearly ended in disaster. An inexperienced operator, lowering the lintel, lost control of the descending stone and only the insertion of a piece of metal into the mechanism saved Atkinson from being crushed.

Operation Trilithon was the largest single engineering operation in Stonehenge's extensive restoration, but it was not the last. In 1959 work was carried out on Stone 60, the sole surviving upright of another fallen trilithon. This trilithon could not be fully restored, as Stone 60 was the only component that survived in one piece,

A dramatic night-time image of the newly restored trilithon.

albeit with a hole near its base big enough for several people to shelter in during bad weather. The stone was straightened and the hole filled with concrete, the neatness of which, compared to the wonderfully organic shapes of many of the sarsens, still puzzles visitors to the site. In this same year Stones 4 and 5 in the outer circle were also straightened.

There was then a pause until the severe winter of 1963 when Stone 23 in the outer circle (the one that had been heavily nudged during the 1958 restorations) unexpectedly fell over. It was re-erected during May and June 1964 and at the same time the opportunity was taken to straighten four more uprights. These were Stones 27 and 28 in the outer sarsen circle and the two uprights (Stones 53 and 54) of one of the intact trilithons. These were the final stones to be reset, completing a protracted restoration that had started with Gowland's straightening of Stone 56 in 1901. At that time there had seemed two very different options for Stonehenge:

The end of restoration in 1964 – Atkinson checks the final position of Stone 53 before it is lowered into its new concrete setting.

either complete restoration or complete collapse. Fortunately, what happened sporadically over the next 63 years was neither of these options but a process of what can be regarded as cosmetic dentistry on a large scale in which stones were straightened up, repaired, had their cavities filled and were scrubbed clean. The end result was neither a pile of inexplicable rubble nor a concrete monstrosity, but the restored ruin that we see today.

In the 1964 photograph of Stone 53 dangling above its newly prepared concrete setting, Richard Atkinson is clearly in charge. Observed by Mr Bailey of the Ministry of Works, he checks the final position of the stone with a plumb bob while, in the background, Stuart Piggott looks on. It was Atkinson who had published *Stonehenge* in 1956 and it was Atkinson who now took on the responsibility for the analysis and publication of the findings from the excavations he had carried out with Stuart Piggott and initially with J F S Stone.

Despite what this advertisement implies, picnicking at Stonehenge was officially discouraged.

Throughout what can perhaps best be described as the 'Atkinson years', between 1950 and 1964, the experience enjoyed by visitors to Stonehenge had remained essentially unchanged since the time when the first fence and turnstile were introduced in 1901. Visitor numbers increased annually, and now most people turned up in private cars which could be parked either in the official, if fairly basic, car park by the side of the A344 or on the verges of the nearby track. Once the admission fee had been paid access was unrestricted; the stones were there to be enjoyed and there was soft grass to picnic on in the summer, even though this was officially discouraged as food scraps apparently encouraged mice and rats.

One of the custodians' less enjoyable jobs (especially in the snow) – cleaning graffiti off the stones.

As Stonehenge became not only more popular but also more accessible, the number of visitors increased to such an extent that their feet wore away the grass around the stones and the bare dusty earth of dry summer days became a swamp in wet weather. The solution, an echo of the Victorian idea of a neat layer of asphalt, was to replace the grass with something more durable. Early in 1963 up came the grass and down went a layer of clinker from Melksham gasworks, which was rolled down and topped off with Breedon gravel. This surface certainly solved the problems that had arisen with the eroded grass but now Stonehenge looked like any other ancient monument, its stones lost in a sea of uniform, sterile Ministry of Works gravel. The gravel also made its own problems, clinging to the soles of visitors' shoes and eroding the fallen stones that they then walked over. On windy days it flew around, grit-blasting stones and visitors' ankles alike. This was far from an ideal solution.

This era also saw the return of graffiti to Stonehenge, but whereas visitors in the 18th and 19th centuries had come armed with hammers, chisels and patience to cut their neat inscriptions, it was now paint that appeared on the stones. The fence that surrounded Stonehenge at this time was little more than a token gesture, intended mainly to ensure that daytime visitors paid their entrance fees. It certainly failed to deter a number of nocturnal 'artists' who, starting in 1959, found the newly

There is no evidence for Elvis ever having visited Stonehenge

restored stones an irresistible canvas. On 28th March that year daubs included names accompanied by footprints, lines and circles, followed by further messages on the night of 31st October – Halloween. These graffiti, including the apparently insincere 'we are sorry', were thought to be the work of the 'bearded types' who had turned up during the previous evening hoping for something to happen. The pattern was repeated throughout the 1950s and 1960s, the stones painted with messages of support for pirate radio stations, New Forest ponies, football clubs and the Campaign for Nuclear Disarmament. The most persistent offenders appear to have been university students who daubed with such regularity that questions were raised in Parliament about how Stonehenge could be better protected. The Ministry of Works also took the unusual step of writing to all colleges and universities noting that Stonehenge 'appears to offer an irresistible attraction to those responsible for Rag Week stunts' and asking if they could kindly stop their students painting it. By the late 1960s students appeared to have got the message, one of the last incidents, in April 1968, being attributed to the author's old university (but prior to his student days).

1968 saw the opening of a pedestrian underpass, enabling visitors to walk below the A344 rather than risking life and limb crossing the road. By 1973 even the old car park had gone, along with the north–south track that had long acted as an overspill parking area. In their place was a much bigger car park, together with a new custodian's office, shop and toilets. In earlier years toilets had not been thought a necessity as it was considered that visitors had the whole of Salisbury Plain as an outdoor facility. Thankfully attitudes had changed.

These improvements to the safety and comfort of Stonehenge's many visitors also resulted in new and important archaeological discoveries. In 1966 and 1967 the husband-and-wife team of Faith and Lance Vatcher excavated the area of the new car park to the north of the A344 and also the smaller area on the southern, Stonehenge side of the A344 that was to be disturbed by the construction of the underpass tunnel and ramp. In the car park, about 200m (656ft) from Stonehenge, they found three large pits, between 1.5 and 2m (5–6ft 6in) in diameter and about 1.3m (just over 4ft) deep. All showed clear evidence that they had once held large wooden posts around 0.75m (about 2ft 6in) in diameter, some of which had been held upright in their pits using wooden wedges. As the pits contained nothing in the way of finds except a single piece of burnt bone and quantities of charcoal, it was assumed that they must belong to the Age of Stonehenge, most likely to some time within the later part of the Neolithic period. But the charcoal was unusual, identified as all being pine, a species that was thought not to grow on the chalk and that certainly should not have been around during the later Neolithic. Two radiocarbon dates explained why the posts were of such an unusual timber: they dated not to the Neolithic but to the Mesolithic, the Middle Stone Age. To these three pits, the position of which is marked out by large concrete spots in the car park, can be added a fourth, discovered about 100m (330ft) to the east in 1988, just behind the ticket office. This pit, which despite having no clear impression of a post may originally have been dug to contain one, also contained little in the way of finds except pine charcoal. Three more radiocarbon dates fixed its construction firmly in the Mesolithic period, between

NO ACCESS
TO STONE CIRCLE

PLEASE NOTE
Because of damage to the
monument visitors are not
now permitted to enter the
stone circle but can view it
only from a distance.

1978 marked the end of unrestricted access to the centre of Stonehenge.

9,000 and 10,000 years ago and at least 4,000 years before any construction work started at Stonehenge. The function of these remarkable pits and the posts that they held still remain one of the greatest puzzles of the Stonehenge landscape.

On the opposite side of the A344 the Vatchers made another unexpected discovery. Within the area stripped of topsoil lay a 10m (33ft) length of ditch, running south-west/north-east and ending in a rounded terminal before it reached the edge of the road. The ditch turned out to be deep, sharply 'V'-profiled and to contain, in its lower levels, the clear impressions of over 20 closely-set wooden posts between 25 and 40cm (10–16in) in diameter. These were clearly the remains of a substantial timber palisade, the posts of which seemed to have been left to rot where they stood. But even more surprising was the skeleton of a young adult male found crouched in a small grave cut into the upper levels of the ditch terminal, and so clearly of a much later date. There was, and still is, no direct dating for what became known as the 'palisade' or 'gate' ditch. The human skeleton provided the only samples for radiocarbon dating and turned out to have been buried at some time between the 8th and the 5th centuries BC, during the Iron Age. The palisade itself can only be dated by comparison with other similar structures, of which there are two obvious examples in Wessex: at Mount Pleasant near Dorchester in Dorset and at West Kennet near Avebury in north Wiltshire. Both are firmly dated to the later Neolithic, between 2500 and 2000BC, so it is reasonable to assume that the palisade ditch must be contemporary with the stone building phase at Stonehenge. How it functioned is more difficult to say. It can be seen on aerial photographs stretching off to the south-west; perhaps when first built it was a great timber barrier, helping to define Stonehenge's sacred precinct.

1977 was to be the last year of unrestricted access to the centre of Stonehenge and the freedom to wander among the stones. The gravel that had seemed such a neat and visitor-proof solution in 1963 had not been an unqualified success and, as visitor numbers continued to climb, it was decided that the damage to the stones was unacceptable. But if the gravel had to go then so did the visitors. On 15th March 1978 signs went up explaining that visitors were no longer allowed inside the stone circle but could view it 'only from a distance'. This was not a popular move and the 'SOS' (Save Our Stonehenge) campaign was launched with the aim of changing official minds and restoring unrestricted access. The campaign failed, the gravel was replaced by grass and shortly afterwards the line of the old eroded track that loops through the western side of the earthwork enclosure was surfaced in order to allow visitors a closer look at the stones.

1978 also saw more investigation at Stonehenge itself when John Evans returned to re-excavate a trench originally dug across the ditch by Atkinson in 1954. This cutting was located just north-west of the main entrance. John Evans' interest was in recovering from the layers that filled the ditch the land snails that would provide clues to the natural environment in which Stonehenge was built and developed. But there was an unexpected twist to the investigation. Part of the section – the vertical slice through the layers of chalk and soil that filled the ditch – collapsed to reveal human foot and leg bones. Evans decided to investigate further

The skeleton of the Beaker period Stonehenge Archer discovered by John Evans in the Stonehenge ditch in 1978.

and found a grave, cut into the chalky ditch silts and containing the skeleton of a young man lying on his side with knees bent. Some parts of the skeleton had clearly been disturbed and there was a gap in the spine but all the bones were present, even if not all in the right place. It seems likely that some animal, a rabbit or badger perhaps, had burrowed through the skeleton at some time, giving it a rather jumbled appearance.

Next to the lower forearm the excavators found a flat plate of fine-grained stone, each end of which had been drilled with a single neat hole. This was instantly recognised as an archer's wrist guard, designed to protect the arm from the sting of the bow string and part of the package of equipment introduced along with the first Beaker pots. This person did not have a Beaker, but he did have several finely worked barbed-and-tanged flint arrowheads, some with their tips broken off.

Mike Pitts' roadside trench of 1979. Expanded foam fills the newly discovered stone hole 97.

The wrist guard and arrowheads suggested that the young man was an archer, buried with his most precious possessions. Only later did it emerge that the tips of the flint arrowheads were embedded in his bones and that, far from being placed with him in the grave, the arrows were the cause of his death. The discovery of this grave also helps to explain why Atkinson found chips of bluestone so unusually low down in the ditch fill in this cutting in 1954. The bluestone fragments were not in the ditch silts but were part of the fill of the grave, which had been dug down through the almost completely filled-up ditch at a much later date.

The story of the recent investigation of Stonehenge and its immediate surroundings ends in 1979, just one year after the discovery of the 'Stonehenge Archer'. Mike Pitts, at that time curator of the museum at Avebury, was called in to avert what could have been an archaeological disaster when the GPO decided to lay a new telephone cable alongside the A344. For some reason this was not communicated to the archaeological authorities, with the result that the trench-digging machine was stopped only inches from the ditch surrounding the Heel Stone. That it was stopped was, in itself important, but of far greater significance was that when the trench-digging resumed, this time by archaeologists, a new stone hole was discovered. Its chalk base was crushed, showing that it had, at some time, held a stone. The Heel Stone (96) had a new companion, Stone 97 – an extraordinary discovery to be made in 1979 after centuries of study at Stonehenge might have led to the conclusion that there was nothing more of any significance to be found.

More excavation on the side of the A344 in the following year revealed a hearth and a stoneworking floor that, because of the restricted area over which the stone debris was found, is suggested by Mike Pitts as having been inside a building of some form. The results of these new discoveries were promptly analysed and published in 1982.

It was now over 30 years since Atkinson and his colleagues started the excavations at Stonehenge that were to result in the 'definitive' publication of all excavations since 1919, and 18 years since their last investigation. So, while the archaeological world carried on waiting for Atkinson to publish his report, attention turned to Stonehenge's remarkable prehistoric landscape.

PRESS PASS HOLDERS AND DRUIDS ONLY

The sign that went up over the entrance to the access tunnel each summer solstice during the 1980s.

CHAPTER 7   A growing understanding of the landscape

In the first half of the 20th century, as Stonehenge underwent the first of its major campaigns of restoration and investigation, the surrounding landscape remained largely unchanged. There were, of course, modern intrusions like the airfield and the short-lived cottages and café, but on the whole fields that had been cultivated for centuries continued under the plough and long-established downland grass continued to be grazed by flocks of sheep. There seemed little danger that the fears expressed by William Long in 1876, that in the future we would have to 'look for Stonehenge in a field of turnips', would be realised.

All this was to change during the Second World War. In the drive to maximise food production huge areas of ancient grassland were ploughed up with little regard for the fragile ancient sites they contained. The conversion of grassland to arable was sometimes carried out using fearsome machines like the Gyrotiller, a giant rotavator, the blades of which minced soil, chalk, rabbits, bushes and anything else that got in the way. So by the time excavation restarted at Stonehenge in 1950 the face of the surrounding landscape had changed irreversibly. Many sites, particularly lower, more vulnerable round barrows, had disappeared completely and their identity and location would re-emerge only in the form of cropmarks or soilmarks on aerial photographs. Other sites were still recognisable, but the process of gradual erosion had now started and each autumn ploughing would see them further eroded until they too had effectively disappeared.

Disc barrows of the Wilsford group showing up as bare soil marks in a ploughed field. More barrows lie in the adjacent woodland.

Decorated Neolithic chalk plaques from a pit on the King Barrow Ridge.

During the 1950s and 1960s the response to this gradual destruction by ploughing was weak. Even in the case of Scheduled Ancient Monuments (recognised as being of national importance) it was generally not considered possible to remove them from cultivation. The alternative was excavation, to 'rescue' them from further damage – 'preservation by record' in the terminology of modern commercial archaeology. As a result these two decades saw a spate of rescue excavations carried out within the Stonehenge landscape, with Ministry of Works contract archaeologists digging ploughed barrow after ploughed barrow. In most cases the results were predictable: the modern archaeologists had been beaten to the central burial by Stukeley or Cunnington, the pots and bronzes were gone and just the bones remained. But what these excavations demonstrated most clearly was that there was more to a barrow than just the central burial. The old method of digging a pit in the centre of the mound in order to locate the main burial revealed little about the structure of the barrow whereas total excavation, using the quadrant method, could show the whole sequence of construction. This method involved the excavation of two opposing quarters, or quadrants, which would provide two vertical slices, or sections, at right angles to each other, through the whole mound. Excavation was completed by removing the remaining two quadrants. Examining barrows in this way often produced additional burials, either under the mound and therefore contemporary with the central burial, or in a secondary position, within and around the barrow mound and ditch. These demonstrated that many barrows were not just simply for one person but could be a focus for burial, perhaps of an ancestral group, for some considerable time.

1962 – excavation in progress near the base of the remarkable Wilsford Shaft.

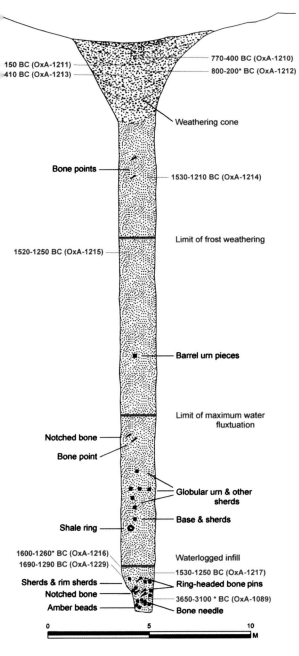

150 BC (OxA-1211)
410 BC (OxA-1213)

770-400 BC (OxA-1210)
800-200* BC (OxA-1212)

Weathering cone

Bone points

1530-1210 BC (OxA-1214)

Limit of frost weathering

1520-1250 BC (OxA-1215)

Barrel urn pieces

Limit of maximum water fluxtuation

Notched bone
Bone point

Globular urn & other sherds

Base & sherds

Shale ring

1600-1260* BC (OxA-1216)
1690-1290 BC (OxA-1229)

Waterlogged infill

1530-1250 BC (OxA-1217)

Sherds & rim sherds
Notched bone
Amber beads

Ring-headed bone pins
3650-3100 * BC (OxA-1089)
Bone needle

0   5   10
M

Cross section of the Wilsford Shaft.

There were, though, some far more surprising discoveries. In the summer of 1960 Edwina Proudfoot set out to investigate the remains of three barrows on Normanton Down to the south-west of Stonehenge. Two were quite straightforward bowl barrows but the third was more unusual: a pond barrow, the bank of which had been bulldozed into the hollow by the farmer on the grounds that, if a cow were to fall in 'it would be trapped and die'. It was assumed that the excavation would not take long but after several weeks' digging what was revealed was not a shallow hollow but a huge conical pit, at the base of which was a narrow cylindrical shaft. By the end of the 1960 season this had reached a depth of more than 18m (60ft). By the end of the 1961 season a further 6m (20ft) of fill had been removed, and the bottom of the shaft was finally encountered in the third season of excavation in 1962. This was at a depth of around 30m (100ft), by which time excavation could only be carried out with the aid of mechanical hoists and closed-circuit television.

This was the Wilsford Shaft, an extraordinary feat of prehistoric engineering which Paul Ashbee, who had taken over the excavation, considered to be some form of ritual structure. So, as the lower fills were reached and waterlogged deposits were first encountered, there were high hopes of spectacular finds. In reality what emerged from the gooey mud at the bottom of the shaft were more mundane objects: animal bones and pottery, together with organic finds, rare on chalkland sites but preserved by the wet conditions. These included fragments of rope and wooden buckets, wool, dung and the remains of insects, pollen, beetles, plant fibres and moss. After considerable delay, the report of this amazing excavation finally appeared in 1989. The lower waterlogged fills of the shaft appear to have accumulated in the middle of the Bronze Age, some time around 1500BC, but there is one very puzzling radiocarbon date, from the lowest of all the samples, that suggests that it may have been dug nearly 2,000 years earlier, in the early Neolithic period. Its function too is open to question and the report shows two entirely different opinions. Paul Ashbee, the original excavator whose background was firmly in the archaeology of ceremonial sites, still saw it as a ritual shaft, perhaps a means of communicating with the beings of the underworld. In contrast Martin Bell, an environmental archaeologist brought in to study the wide range of waterlogged remains, came to a more practical conclusion. On the evidence that the shaft reached down to the water table and contained the remains of rope and buckets, he suggested that it was a well.

It was not just the effects of ploughing that resulted in new discoveries during the 1960s; a spate of road improvements played a considerable part too. To the east of Stonehenge a swathe of the Avenue was excavated before the A303 was 'improved' as far as the King Barrow Ridge. Late Neolithic pits were discovered that contained, as well as the more usual finds, decorated chalk plaques – rare examples of prehistoric art. To the west, improvements to the junction of the A303 and the Salisbury to Devizes road, adjacent to the Winterbourne Stoke Crossroads barrows, revealed the remains of a late Bronze Age village dating to around 1000BC. Defined on one side by a 'stockade trench', there were at least three small circular round houses, each with a south-facing porch. But the largest road excavation, and by far the most important, was carried out by Geoff Wainwright in 1967.

Geoff Wainwright's huge 1968 excavation at Durrington Walls. Beyond the post pits of the southern circle lies the massive ditch.

A late Neolithic Grooved Ware pot from Durrington Walls.

Durrington Walls, the giant henge lying close to the west bank of the River Avon to the north-east of Stonehenge, would have remained a huge enigma if it had not been for the decision in the mid-1960s to straighten the road that ran through the centre of the enclosure. There were protests by archaeologists who felt that such vandalism should not even be considered, but they were overruled and the road was allowed to go ahead on condition that it was preceded by a full-scale investigation. Over two seasons, in an excavation of unprecedented scale, archaeologist Geoff Wainwright stripped the entire road corridor down to the

Peter Dunn's reconstruction of the southern circle at Durrington Walls.

natural chalk. This was a huge area, over 760m (850yd) long and up to 40m (45yd) wide. A 34m (37yd) length of ditch was emptied, and at this point in the circuit was shown to be up to 6m (20ft) deep and varying in width from around 7m (23ft) at its base to nearly 18m (60ft) at the top. The 57 fragments of antler picks found clustered together on the ditch floor, the only digging tools available to the Neolithic builders, were a strong reminder of their motivation and perseverance.

Inside the enclosure the second season of excavation revealed the remains of two circles of timber posts. The larger of the two emerged as a confusing mass of postholes just inside the south-eastern entrance of the enclosure. Initially it consisted of five rings of comparatively small but deeply set posts with a separate line, often referred to as a façade, on its south-eastern side shielding them from the adjacent gap in the ditch and bank. This structure was then replaced by one with six rings, the outermost nearly 40m (133ft) in diameter within which the largest posts were nearly 1m (over 3ft) in diameter and set in postholes 2.5m (8ft) deep.

Finely worked flint arrowheads of a distinctively late Neolithic type from Durrington Walls.

OPPOSITE
Sacrificed on the altar of fashion? A wonderful image from a 1970 *Vogue* photo-shoot by the celebrated fashion photographer Norman Parkinson.

A second circle lay about 120m (131 yards) north, but whereas the southern circle had been protected from the effects of ploughing by a deep accumulation of soil, this one was badly damaged. The surviving evidence shows a square central setting of four large posts surrounded by a ring of smaller posts about 14.5m (48ft) in diameter. This circle also had a façade of close-set posts and was approached from the south by an avenue of upright timbers. These circles, like that at Woodhenge, are difficult to interpret. The posts may have been free-standing or may equally have been components of roofed buildings. Whatever form they took, the circles were undeniably the focus for the use and disposal of large quantities of animal bones, perhaps suggesting feasting, and of the distinctive and highly decorated late Neolithic pottery known as Grooved Ware. Radiocarbon dates suggest that Durrington Walls was built and used at about the same time that the stones arrived at Stonehenge, around 2500BC.

What had taken place at Durrington Walls between 1967 and 1968 was excavation on an industrial scale, witnessed by the volume of finds that Salisbury Museum found itself having to store. There were over 3,300 sherds of pottery, 8,500 animal bones, huge quantities of flint tools and working debris and 316 red-deer antlers. The Durrington excavations had offended some members of the archaeological establishment, but Geoff Wainwright's bold approach was exactly what was required and the rapid publication of the results silenced the remaining critics. Field archaeology would never be quite the same again.

Excavation is one way to build up an understanding of a landscape but though digging provides considerable detail it generally focuses on a very specific location. To paint a broader picture requires methods of archaeological survey that are extensive rather than intensive. The value of aerial photographs in providing an overview of past land use and settlement had been obvious since the days of pioneering aviation, and spectacular discoveries like Woodhenge had served only to emphasise their potential. Since those early days the Stonehenge area had been a magnet for aerial archaeologists as, even if there were no new discoveries to be photographed, Stonehenge itself was always there, imposing and photogenic. The result was that by the early 1970s thousands of aerial photographs had been taken of the Stonehenge area, many held in the collections of the National Monuments Record (NMR) or Cambridge University Air Photo Library (CUAP). Those taken between the two world wars, many collected by O G S Crawford while he was the Archaeological Officer of the Ordnance Survey, were of particular value in showing the downland landscape prior to the great changes of the 1940s.

The purpose of aerial survey is to record evidence of past human activity. Field boundaries, roads and railways are all part of the human impact on the landscape, but these are usually all well documented and shown on modern maps. What aerial archaeology seeks are the more subtle traces of undocumented activity: the straight ditch that shows evidence of an ancient boundary; the circular mark that represents the location of a levelled round barrow; the rectangular scatter of brick and tile that marks the position of a Roman building. These will show up as marks in the bare soil of ploughed fields, as shadows in grassland under a low light or as

AERIAL PHOTOGRAPHY

In 1906 Stonehenge was the first archaeological site in the UK to be photographed from the air – but from a balloon, not a plane. Since then aerial photography has developed into a powerful tool for understanding sites and wider landscapes.

Patterns are always easier to understand when viewed from above. For example, the pattern on a carpet will seem much clearer when viewed while standing up rather than lying down. In the same way, aerial photography can be very useful in showing the layout of sites that exist on the ground only as shallow earthworks or the low foundations of buildings, especially when photographed in low, slanting winter light. This produces shadows that can highlight even the shallowest surface features. A dusting of snow, or even partial flooding, can also help to accentuate poorly defined remains.

In areas that are regularly cultivated and where there are no surviving surface indications of ancient sites, the view from above can reveal buried remains at varying times during the annual agricultural cycle.

Soil marks can appear after ploughing: infilled ditches often contain darker soils while those over banks or mounds are often stonier and lighter in colour, contrasting with the surrounding undisturbed soils.

Crop marks reveal buried archaeological sites as a result of the differential growth of crops over ditches, pits and walls. Crops growing over a silted or infilled ditch will grow taller and stronger as their roots can penetrate deeper and obtain more moisture and nutrients. Conversely, over a buried wall the crop will be comparatively stunted and as a result will also tend to ripen earlier. These contrasts are visible at different stages in the growth cycle. A buried ditch, for example, may first show as a darker green mark in a field of lighter green wheat or barley, then vanish as the rest of the crop germinates. As the crop ripens those crops over the ditch will 'turn' slightly later, giving a green mark in a generally yellow field and eventually, as the rest of the field begins to fade, they will appear yellow on a brown background. Factors such as the underlying geology and recent rainfall can affect how crops will grow and in certain circumstances can produce 'reverse' marks where ditches appear yellow on a green background. Also, different crops react in different ways.

Parch marks can appear in grassland under conditions of extreme drought when the grass growing over both ditches and buried walls will wither and turn yellow while other areas still remain comparatively green.

No single photograph will ever provide the complete picture of a site. To understand as much as possible sites need to be photographed regularly under varying soil and crop conditions.

Photographing the marks produced by shadows or in bare soil, growing crops or parched grass, creates a record; but that record is only of any use if the information is plotted onto maps at an appropriate scale and made widely available. English Heritage's National Monuments Record in Swindon holds the largest collection of aerial photographs in Britain: over 600,000 images that can be consulted by the public.

Since the early 1990s English Heritage has been carrying out the National Mapping Programme (NMP), a systematic programme of mapping and recording archaeological features visible on aerial photographs. The aim of the NMP is to enhance the understanding of past human settlement, by providing primary information and synthesis for all archaeological sites and landscapes from the Neolithic period to the 20th century.

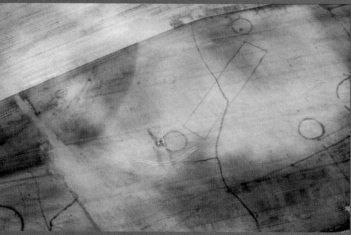

Warborough, Oxfordshire. Cursus and ring ditches in a growing crop. The field to the right is at a more advanced stage of growth and the colour contrast is not as strong. (NMR 23088-00)

Goodwood Park, West Sussex. Enclosures and ditches showing up as parch marks in summer grass. (NMR 15380-33)

OPPOSITE TOP
Green Down, Oxfordshire. Irregular prehistoric 'Celtic' fields showing up as contrasting soil marks in a ploughed landscape. (NMR 21035-21)

OPPOSITE BOTTOM
Barnack, Peterborough. Initial crop growth is much stronger over the buried ditches providing a strong colour contrast. (NMR 21048-33)

contrasts in colour and height in growing crops. The processes that produce these marks are complex, depending on soil type, moisture, light and vegetation, and the marks themselves are of little use, even when captured on photographs, unless they can be mapped and analysed.

This was the task that was undertaken for the Stonehenge area by the Royal Commission on the Historical Monuments of England (more usually known as the RCHME). Partly to coincide with the publication of a report on the future of Stonehenge, the RCHME undertook the plotting and analysis of all the aerial data from its surrounding landscape. The title of their 1979 publication, *Stonehenge and its Environs*, was a direct reference to Colt Hoare and the first reliable map of the area published nearly 180 years earlier in his *Ancient Wiltshire*. Three fold-out maps accompany this publication. One shows the distribution of barrows by type, indicating once again why Colt Hoare and others who were 'barrow mad' had been so attracted to the Stonehenge environs. Another shows historic and present land-use, a stark reminder of how little ancient grassland remained in the late 20th century, and also helping to explain why more sites in the western half of the study area survive as earthworks. The reason was clear once the extent of 19th-century cultivation was plotted. It lay in a broad swathe along the west bank of the River Avon, in the open fields of the villages of Lake, Wilsford, Normanton and West Amesbury. But the most interesting map is simply titled 'General map of monuments'.

On this are all the known sites, the henges large and small, the two cursus monuments and the hundreds of barrows that make up the landscape of prehistoric ceremony and burial. But for the first time, teased out from the aerial photographs, there are the subtle traces of everyday life: acres of small irregular fields, miles of boundary ditches parcelling up the landscape and even the occasional small ditched enclosure that hints at a place of human habitation. These fields, ditches and enclosures cannot be dated, and indeed it is likely that they belong to a period after the end of Stonehenge's active life, but for the first time evidence of everyday prehistoric life had been recorded within the Stonehenge landscape.

The RCHME publication went further than just lists and maps of monuments. It analysed the mass of data, both new and old, and it made recommendations. Some were quite specific: the investigation, by means of geophysical survey or small-scale excavation, of key sites that remained undated or of uncertain function. There was also growing concern about the long-term survival of what had been clearly demonstrated as a complex, highly fragile and, in places, eroding archaeological landscape. English Heritage immediately responded, commissioning Wessex Archaeology, based nearby in Salisbury, to undertake a second, more intensive survey of the Stonehenge landscape. The Stonehenge Environs Project, just one of a number of landscape surveys carried out in the Wessex region in the early 1980s, was intended to take the RCHME's results one stage further. Aerial survey was to be backed up with fieldwork on the ground and, where appropriate, by geophysical survey and excavation. The aim was not simply to develop a better understanding of the landscape, although this research was clearly important, but to work out ways in which sites of all types could be managed and preserved for the future.

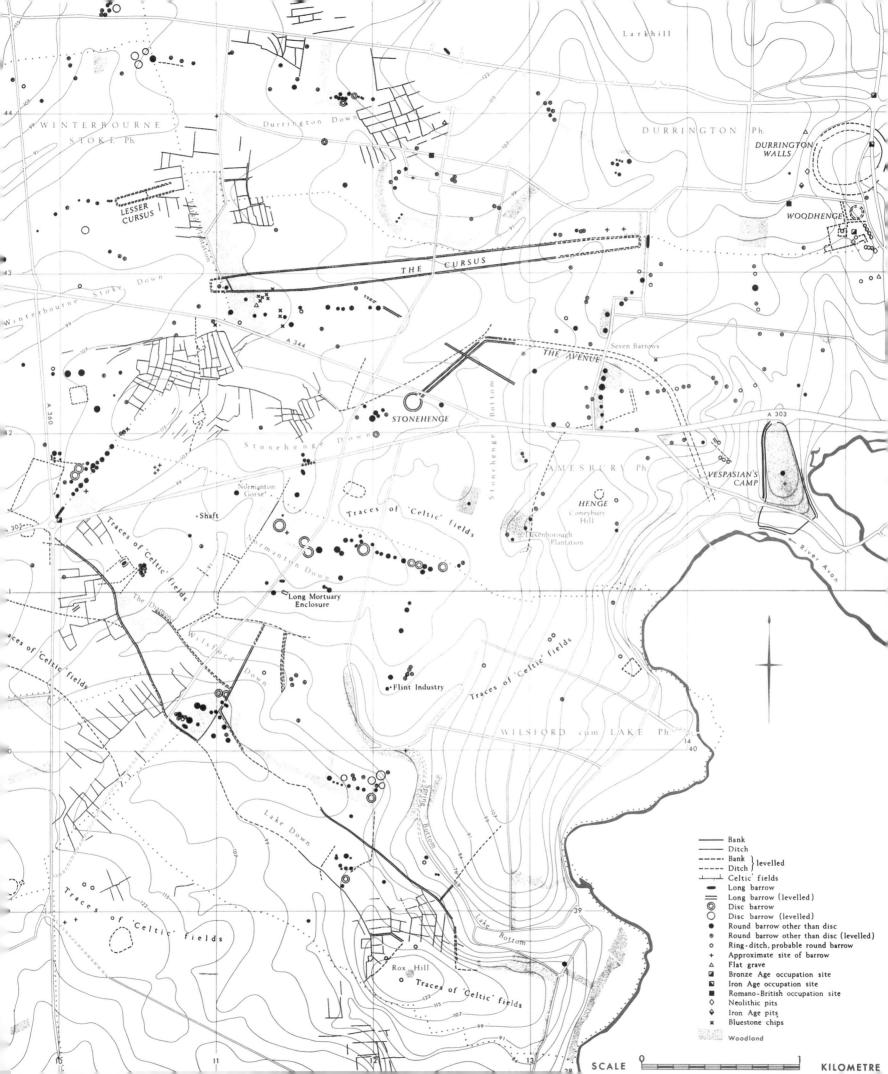

LARKHILL

WINTERBOURNE STOKE Ph.

Durrington Down

DURRINGTON Ph.

DURRINGTON WALLS

LESSER CURSUS

WOODHENGE

THE CURSUS

Winterbourne Stoke Down

A 344

THE AVENUE

Seven Barrows

STONEHENGE

A 303

Stonehenge Down

Stonehenge Bottom

AMESBURY Ph.

VESPASIAN'S CAMP

Normanton Gorse

HENGE
Coneybury Hill

· Shaft

Traces of 'Celtic' fields

Gravenborough Plantation

Traces of 'Celtic' fields

Normanton Down

Long Mortuary Enclosure

River Avon

The Diamond

Wilsford Down

· Flint Industry

Traces of 'Celtic' fields

WILSFORD cum LAKE Ph.

14
40

Lake Down

Spring Bottom

Traces of 'Celtic' fields

Lake Bottom

39

Rox Hill

Traces of 'Celtic' fields

Traces of 'Celtic' fields

——— Bank
——— Ditch
- - - - Bank ⎫ levelled
- - - - Ditch ⎭
┴┬┴ 'Celtic' fields
▬ Long barrow
≣ Long barrow (levelled)
◉ Disc barrow
◯ Disc barrow (levelled)
● Round barrow other than disc
⊙ Round barrow other than disc (levelled)
○ Ring-ditch, probable round barrow
+ Approximate site of barrow
△ Flat grave
◪ Bronze Age occupation site
◩ Iron Age occupation site
■ Romano-British occupation site
◇ Neolithic pits
⬠ Iron Age pits
✕ Bluestone chips

▒ Woodland

SCALE

KILOMETRE

In 1980 I was invited to direct the Stonehenge Environs Project. This was every prehistoric archaeologist's dream, and so it was with great excitement that I started the first excavation in the autumn of that year. This was one of the RCHME's specific recommendations – the partial excavation of what was thought to be a small henge on Coneybury Hill, to the south-east of Stonehenge. Aerial photographs showed an oval mark with a central dark splodge (a term much used by aerial archaeologists). So was it a henge and if so what had survived the centuries of ploughing?

Coneybury was investigated with great care. The site was surveyed in detail to produce a contour map that would show up even the subtlest traces of surviving earthworks. Geophysical and geochemical surveys were carried out to detect not only the more obvious buried ditches or pits but traces of enhanced magnetic or chemical signals within the soil itself, signals that could point to areas of human activity. Only after all this preparatory work did excavation start. But even then the agricultural topsoil was treated as an integral part of the site and excavated not with a machine, as Wainwright had done at Durrington Walls, but by hand, in a grid of 1m squares, and mostly sieved. This meant that all finds were recovered but the painstaking procedures slowed the excavation down to a snail's pace.

Coneybury was, as had been thought, a small henge with a deep, steep-sided ditch. Inside the ditched enclosure there was nothing as striking as Woodhenge's circles of postholes, just a central cluster of large pits, some containing Grooved Ware pottery, that may represent the type of four-post structure seen in the centre of Durrington's northern circle. There were also hints of a circle of small posts running concentrically with the inner edge of the ditch and, most remarkably, hundreds of small holes made where sharpened wooden stakes had been banged into the hard chalk. These fragile traces had only survived because the interior of the site had been deliberately terraced back into the slight hill slope where an accumulation of soil (the 'splodge' visible on the aerial photographs) had protected it from the effects of ploughing. This was exactly the sort of information that the project had been designed to produce.

Most sites have their surprises, and Coneybury's lay outside the henge itself. The magnetometer survey had produced a very strong localised signal from just outside the enclosure entrance. We couldn't resist investigating it. The Coneybury Anomaly was a big pit, nearly 2m (6ft 6in) in diameter and 1.25m (4ft) deep, and the bottom 30 or 40cm (just over 1ft) of dark ashy soil contained a huge collection of pottery, animal bones and flint tools, not of later Neolithic date but much earlier. The henge, on the basis of a single radiocarbon date, was constructed around 2700BC, whereas the Anomaly was dug and filled over a thousand years earlier, during the earlier part of the Neolithic. The 1,744 pieces of pottery represent at least 39 simple, round-bottomed pots of varying sizes. Over 2,000 animal bones were from both domesticated and wild animals, mainly cattle and pig, with a few sheep, both red and roe deer and, reflecting the proximity of the River Avon, brown trout and beaver. What was deliberately dumped in this huge pit appears to be the rubbish left over from either one very big feast or a whole series of smaller ones, very similar to the deposits found carefully placed in the ditches of causewayed

Environmental archaeologist Martin Bell taking soil samples for snail analysis from the ditch of Coneybury Henge in 1980.

The rich deposit of bone, flint and pottery on the bottom of the Coneybury Anomaly – an early Neolithic feasting pit.

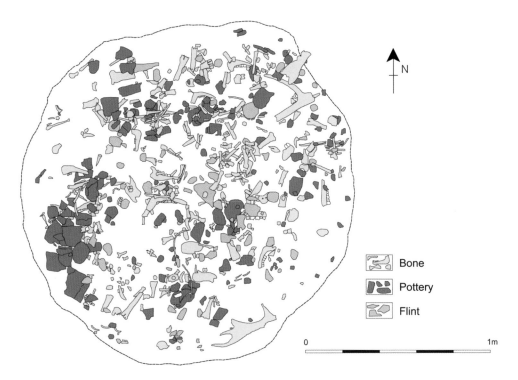

Bone

Pottery

Flint

0   1m

enclosures at this time. This may be more than just the disposal of 'rubbish' – it may have been a way of commemorating an event. Whatever the reason for their disposal, the contents of the pit offer a unique snapshot of life before Stonehenge, when the first farmers and herders were still using all the resources and food that the wild world could offer.

It was now time to start the field survey. In introducing fields and farms into the landscape, the RCHME survey begged the question: did people actually live close to Stonehenge while it was being built and used? Answering this question was not easy. There were no clues from southern England about what Neolithic settlements or houses looked like at that time, so how could we know what to look for? Any buildings were going to be of wood so their decay would leave little trace; and on top of that, most of the landscape, with the exception of small areas of grassland looked after by the National Trust or English Heritage, was ploughed on an annual basis. What was needed was a way of exploiting these destructive processes, so we set out into the bare, windswept, winter fields, scouring the surface not for traces of eroded earthworks but for the rubbish left behind by our ancestors.

Everyday life generates rubbish. Today we throw out paper, glass, plastic, tin cans, cardboard and food waste, which all end up being recycled, incinerated or dumped into large holes in the ground. Prehistoric rubbish – broken pots, broken or worn-out stone tools along with any food waste that couldn't be fed to animals or made into something useful – was disposed of far more simply. As the imperative was to get it out of the house it was either piled up somewhere convenient, forming a midden, or was scattered nearby, sometimes on arable fields where the organic components acted as fertiliser.

GEOPHYSICAL SURVEY

Geophysical survey allows archaeologists to detect buried remains without digging. It helps with the analysis and interpretation of sites, as well as pinpointing where to excavate.

There are several different methods of investigation, each appropriate to answering particular questions. These methods are all under constant development and refinement.

Magnetometer survey is the most widely used geophysical survey technique and uses instruments such as the fluxgate gradiometer that detect subtle differences in the local magnetic field. Closely spaced readings are collected continuously which means that large areas can be covered in a relatively short time.

The magnetometer produces a higher reading when a buried pit or ditch has a different magnetic response from that of the surrounding soil. Archaeological remains such as kilns, hearths and furnaces can be detected as the clay has been magnetically enhanced by burning. Ditches and pits can also be located when they have silted up with more magnetic topsoil.

Caesium magnetometers are much more sensitive instruments than standard fluxgate gradiometers.and can detect weaker signals or signals from a greater depth.

Magnetometer sensors are usually carried but better results can be obtained if they are securely mounted on a cart to reduce up and down movement.

Earth resistivity survey is a popular method of geophysical survey particularly for finding buried buildings or stones. Electrodes are inserted into the ground at regular intervals across a site, introducing an electrical current. The resistance to this current is measured and will vary according to changes in soil moisture or porosity. Walls usually have a high resistance while ditches filled with moist soil tend to have a low resistance.

This method can be slow and laborious as until recently the surveyor had to 'prod' the electrode frame across the site. A new wheeled device promises to speed the process up considerably.

Ground penetrating radar (GPR) can provide information on the depth and three-dimensional shape of buried structures like building foundations. GPR sends a short pulse of radio frequency energy into the ground and records the time and amplitude of echoes reflected from buried features. Reflections from deeper remains take longer to reach the surface and allow the depth of burial to be estimated.

Closely-spaced lines of GPR data can be used, after computer processing, to produce a series of highly detailed horizontal 'time slices' through a site. GPR systems are very flexible and can be operated over a range of different surfaces, for instance through tarmac roads and concrete, to help reveal the underlying archaeology. Within standing buildings, GPR may be the only practical geophysical technique to apply.

Caesium magnetometer plot of an Iron Age round house at Flint Farm, Hampshire.

The strange non-magnetic caesium magnetometer cart used by English Heritage's geophysics team.

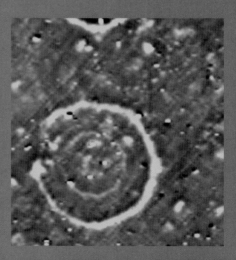

A selection of flint tools for cutting, scraping and piercing collected from ploughed fields during the Stonehenge Environs Project.

So in general terms, if you can find the rubbish it might give you a clue about where people were living. So what we were looking for within the ploughed parts of the Stonehenge landscape were the more solid elements of this prehistoric rubbish. Pottery of Neolithic and Bronze Age date is usually badly-fired, soft and can be totally destroyed by ploughing and the action of frost. In contrast stone tools, mainly of flint, together with the debris produced in their manufacture, are basically indestructible. It was these that would provide the initial clues to what people were doing in the landscape at the time of Stonehenge.

Although the collection of artefacts from ploughed fields ('flinting') had been going on for centuries, by the 20th century 'fieldwalking' or 'surface collection' (a more scientific sounding term) had become an accepted method of extensive and non-destructive survey. Finds were now recorded precisely, within subdivisions of 100m by 100m squares based on the National Grid.

Fieldwalking unfortunately has to be carried out in winter when the fields are bare and is therefore usually an extremely cold and wet exercise. Over four such freezing winters we scoured a total of 302.5 hectares (7,52.5 acres): 39 fields identified with names like Sewage Works or Bunnies' Playground. This labour produced 102,175 pieces of worked flint, representing all stages in the process from flint mining through the manufacture of tools to their use and eventual disposal. Flint came from surface workings (the only proper mines that are known from the Stonehenge area are shallow ones near Durrington Walls), which showed up as clusters of large rejected cores, hammer stones and the rough flakes removed from the outer surface of natural flint nodules. The flakes that represent the next stage of working, smaller and with less of the outer cortex (skin) still remaining, are more difficult to characterise. They may just be waste material, discarded in the process of shaping a core for a specific purpose, 'blanks' intended to be further worked into tools like scrapers or knives, or alternatively may have been used without further modification as simple yet effective cutting tools. The next stage of the process was to modify flakes or cores to produce recognisable tools: axes, arrowheads of a variety of shapes, scrapers for removing fat from hides, knives, piercers and other tools of elaborate shape but uncertain function. These finished objects are the most useful elements of the whole collection. Not only can they often be more precisely dated, but clusters of them hint at the places where people actually lived.

The most striking of these tool sites lay on the King Barrow Ridge to the east of Stonehenge. But was this the last, eroded trace of a settlement from the time of Stonehenge? We tried to find out by using all the techniques we had used at Coneybury Henge: looking for magnetic soils that might point to ancient hearths, and enhanced phosphate levels that could indicate the presence of what can perhaps best be described as muck heaps. The next stage was excavation.

At first glance the results might not seem too exciting – just lots more flint tools, burnt flint and fragments of sarsen. But some of the signals from the geophysical survey did turn out to be from small pits cut into the chalk. These contained the sort of finds that would not have survived ploughing: fragments of pottery and the bones of cattle, pig and a few sheep and roe deer, the sort of rubbish that would be expected close to where people were living. But what were they living in? There were no signs of substantial post-built houses of the sort that are found perhaps 1,000 years or more later – nothing but clusters of small round stakeholes. These could obviously be of a much later date but in the light of what turned up at Durrington Walls over 20 years later – small rectangular stake-walled and chalk-floored houses – perhaps our few stakeholes were indeed traces of the buildings that we had been keenly searching for. It's just that we didn't recognise them.

The summer excavations were a delight. On the King Barrow Ridge in 1983 we camped next to the site, cooked in a portacabin and carried out our ablutions at a nearby cattle trough. All this and a fabulous view west over Stonehenge. What more could any archaeologist want?

English Heritage funded the bulk of the Stonehenge Environs Project, the field survey and the excavation of ploughed sites. But such sites were never going to

A younger version of the author excavating early Neolithic pits close to Robin Hood's Ball causewayed enclosure in 1984.

provide very much environmental evidence; that required better preserved sites with ancient soils buried beneath upstanding banks. So surviving earthwork sites like the Cursus and its associated long barrow, a peculiar Beaker period earthwork known as the North Kite and several sites around Robin Hood's Ball were also investigated. Thanks to this work, many of these specific sites were dated for the first time, and the evidence from the soils within their ditches and from under their banks helped to build the first picture of the changing environment through Stonehenge's long history. Since it was published in 1990 this picture has been added to and refined by Mike Allen of Wessex Archaeology, so what follows is our current understanding of the Stonehenge landscape in prehistoric times.

It is hard to imagine a landscape of dense ancient woodland, interspersed with areas of lighter woodland containing oak and hazel, but this was the natural environment of the Wessex chalkland before any human modification. All this changed during the fourth millennium BC, in the early Neolithic, when the first piecemeal woodland clearance took place. The extent of this early clearance is uncertain, but it did result in open areas large enough to allow grassland to be established and maintained, probably by grazing cattle. There is also some evidence for small-scale cereal cultivation even at this early date. From this time onwards, the pattern of woodland clearance and the 'mosaic' of different types of land use that this creates move inevitably towards a more open landscape. There are episodes of woodland regeneration during the later part of the Neolithic but these seem to be localised and short-lived, with the result that by the beginning of the Bronze Age Stonehenge is surrounded by well established open grassland, grazed now by sheep as well as cattle. Mike Allen has suggested that at this time there may also be an increase in cereal cultivation, 'an economy to support the stones', but there is very little firm evidence for this either in the form of surviving grains or in the development of more regular and established fields.

What is certain is that the 'mosaic' of different types of land use would not have been static. Clearings would have been established and then perhaps abandoned to become overgrown with scrub, while grassland and arable fields may have been rotated in the same way that they were in more recent times, with grazing animals replenishing the fertility of the thin chalk soils. All our environmental evidence provides is a snapshot of specific locations at specific times; the more snapshots the clearer the picture, but the bigger picture may always be a little blurred.

The SEP added another layer of information to the increasingly complex prehistoric landscape, demonstrating that the surroundings of Stonehenge were not just for burial and ceremony but that people lived and worked there as well. Since the report was published in 1990 more fieldwork and excavations have been carried out in order to assess the potential impact on the archaeology of various road improvement and visitor centre schemes. But despite this more recent work, the broad picture of land use and environmental development painted by the SEP has remained essentially unaltered.

ENVIRONMENTAL EVIDENCE

Almost all human activity – clearing woodland for farming, felling trees to construct a timber circle or introducing grazing animals – will have an impact on the natural environment. This impact can be measured, at a local or at a much wider scale, by using any one of a number of environmental indicators.

The effects of pollen are well known to hay fever sufferers: at certain times of the year plants and trees release vast quantities of pollen grains that drift with the wind to settle often at some distance from their place of release. Pollen grains are very robust and can survive for long periods preserved in waterlogged or acidic soils. These are unfortunately scarce in the Stonehenge area, but pollen evidence has come from the waterlogged deposits at the base of the Wilsford Shaft and from samples taken from the Avon valley. Pollen paints a broad picture of the vegetation from the surrounding area, and will give an indication of the percentage of grassland, woodland and arable fields.

There are many species of land snail, and while some are described as catholic in their preferences for habitat (in other words, not bothered about where they live) there are others that are considerably more choosy. Some prefer short grazed grassland, others deep woodland leaf litter, while some frequent broken ground and therefore like the margins of cultivated fields. Fortunately the shells of such creatures survive well in the chalky alkaline soils that surround Stonehenge, particularly where they are protected from

mechanical damage. Ideal places to find useful collections of snails are in soils buried beneath barrow mounds or banks or in the layers of soil that gradually accumulate in ditches. The snails from a sequence of layers, from the bottom to the top of a ditch for example, can show changes in the local environment over a long period of time. Where many such sequences can be obtained from a study area, as is the case with the Stonehenge landscape, they can be overlapped to provide a broader picture of landscape change through time.

Animal bones are also good indicators of environment. The ratio of wild to domesticated species can show the sort of economy that was being practised which will reflect the degree to which the natural vegetation had been modified. Domesticated animals may require a specific type of land use; sheep, for example, suggest open grassland while pigs will happily forage within woodland.

Plant remains can also provide valuable evidence, from charcoals that demonstrate the types of trees that were being used for construction or fuel to the charred grains and husks that provide the only direct evidence for cereal cultivation.

Salisbury Plain is not ideal for the preservation of some types of environmental evidence, but snails, animal bones and the occasional deposits that contain either plant remains or pollen combine to provide one of the more complete environmental sequences from the British chalk.

Obtaining environmental samples by coring river-valley sediments.

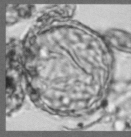
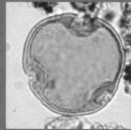

Pollen: from top *Ulmus* (Elm) and *Tilia* (Lime)

Discus rotundatus (left) is a shade-loving snail species while *Pupilla muscorum* prefers more open country.

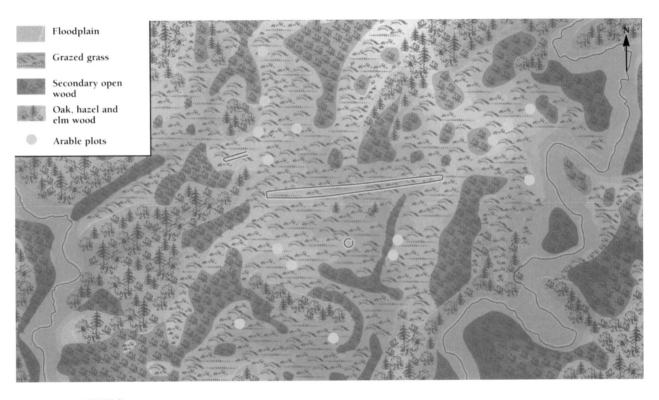

The Stonehenge landscape around 3000BC.

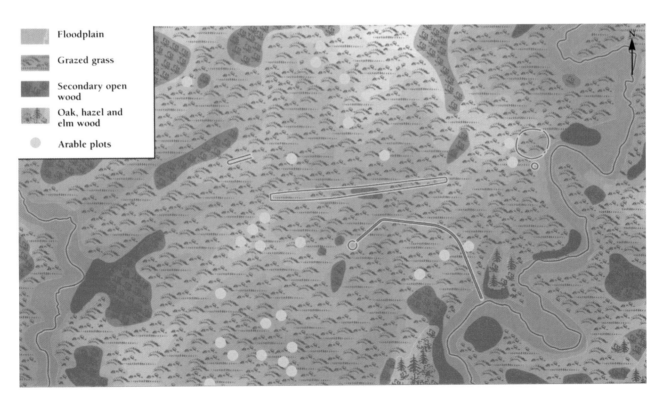

The Stonehenge landscape around 2300BC.

Lidar picks out the low earthworks of the western end of the Stonehenge Cursus as it passes through Fargo Wood.

The flinty surface of the newly discovered Durrington Walls 'Avenue'.

Encircled by large timber posts the remains of a small rectangular house were discovered inside Durrington Walls in 2006.

What has changed is the way in which the landscape is investigated and interpreted. The extensive use of the now wide range of geophysical survey techniques has in some areas revealed the buried archaeology that neither aerial photography nor fieldwalking could reveal. In addition, the entire Stonehenge area has recently been the subject of a lidar (light detection and ranging) survey. This uses a pulsed laser beam mounted in a plane which accurately measures between 20,000 and 100,000 points per second to build up a highly accurate, high-resolution model of the ground surface. The survey discovered entirely new sites and extended the known limits of many others, particularly field systems that had previously been plotted from aerial photographs. The lidar also demonstrated that some sites that had previously been thought to have been entirely levelled by ploughing, for example the Lesser Cursus, still survive as slight earthworks.

The accurate digital terrain models that can be produced from lidar data allow modern features such as trees and buildings to be stripped away, effectively creating a virtual prehistoric landscape. This allows the identification of 'viewsheds' showing, for example, which other monuments are visible from Stonehenge itself and perhaps hinting at the thought processes behind the laying out of the landscape. Some of the phyical relationships between sites are very obvious and can easily be seen on the ground. Stonehenge itself sits at the centre of a 'bowl' ringed by low ridges that are capped with the visible mounds of round barrows. But beyond this obvious observation, numerous interpretations of this 'sacred geography' have appeared in recent years, using the subtleties of the gently rolling terrain, the contents of the individual barrows, decoration on pottery and

individual experience to try to understand the minds of the Stonehenge people. As there is no such thing as certainty or proof for any of these interpretations, this will continue to be a rich area of debate for years to come.

Perhaps the greatest changes in our understanding of the landscape in the near future will come from the Stonehenge Riverside Project, a major new investigation that started in 2003 with a reassessment of Durrington Walls, the giant henge on the bank of the River Avon to the north-east of Stonehenge.

Even given the scale of Geoff Wainwright's excavations in 1967, Durrington Walls remained, until recently, largely unexplored and not fully understood. In 2003 geophysical survey identified two new entrances to the henge, both with what have been described as 'crab claw' ends to their ditches (one end sticking outwards and the other inwards). One entrance, later blocked up, faces north, the other, on the south side, faces Woodhenge.

In 2004 one of the major discoveries was an avenue running out from the downslope entrance towards the nearby river. The avenue consisted of a central roadway, its 15m (50ft) wide surface 'metalled' with small flint cobbles and flanked on either side by a gulley and an external bank. A pit that originally held a large stone was cut through the metalling. This surfaced roadway, justifiably claimed to be the earliest in Europe, runs in through the entrance of the henge towards the southern circle which recent excavations suggest may all have been built at one time rather than in two distinct phases. Its alignment can be interpreted as either south-east, running out of the henge in the direction of the mid-winter sunrise, or north-west, heading into the henge in the direction of sunset at the summer solstice.

Within the henge, buried beneath deep deposits of hill-wash soil, the investigation of one of the circular features that showed up on geophysical survey has revealed a deep ditch about 30m (100ft) in diameter with an entrance that is flanked by a closely set pair of posts. Julian Thomas, the excavator of this part of the site, would like to see these as evidence of a 'tridendron' – a wooden version of the trilithons that are found at Stonehenge. In the centre of this large ditched enclosure, and in the centre of a smaller example that lies close by, were the remains of small rectangular houses, each with a floor of packed chalk and a large central hearth. Beyond this chalk floor were traces of walls made of stakes, a flimsy contrast to the massive timbers found in the northern and southern circles and elsewhere.

So what were these houses? Julian Thomas sees them and the ditches and large postholes that surround them as shrines, whereas Mike Parker Pearson sees them originally as houses of the living that then became 'monumentalised', perhaps on the death of their owners and occupiers.

The remains of similar houses were found flanking the roadway just outside the south-eastern entrance and here there seems to be no question that they were purely domestic. They lay close to middens (rubbish heaps) containing huge

The rectangular chalk floor and central hearth of a small late Neolithic house. Part of a more extensive 'village' excavated just outside Durrington Walls in 2006.

quantities of animal bones, particularly pig, the classic feasting animal. The 'sex pit', containing flint nodules which, with imagination, could be seen as representations of male and female genitalia, may indicate another preoccupation, this time with cycles of fertility, birth and death. But amongst all these archaeological riches it was the domestic houses that most impressed me, perhaps because this was what we had spent so long looking for and had so comprehensively failed to find.

Each of the six houses that had been either completely or partially revealed by the end of the 2006 season of excavation consisted of a rectangular white patch of what can best be described as chalk 'plaster', obtained by digging small quarry pits into a layer of chalk marl close to the houses. These are the main floors, varying in size up to about 4m (13ft) by 5m (16ft), each with a central oval hearth and worn beautifully smooth by the trample of feet. It was not possible to resist the temptation to remove shoes and socks and (with the permission of the site director) walk around on one of the floors, with the spine-tingling realisation that I was treading in the footsteps of those who had built the great henge at Durrington and perhaps even Stonehenge itself.

The houses clearly extended beyond the rectangular chalk floors. Traces of walls, built of small stakes that would originally have been daubed in mud and straw, were found at a distance of about 1m (3ft) beyond the limits of the chalk. This suggests that the floored area with its central hearth was surrounded by wooden structures, perhaps benches on which the occupiers slept or some other form of furniture. If this is the case, then these are simply wooden versions of the stone houses found at settlements such as Scara Brae in Orkney.

Durrington Walls has already yielded much new information and will be even better understood when the huge quantities of bone, pottery and stone are analysed and new radiocarbon dates are available. Already it appears that the actual earthwork, the ditch and bank, may be the last part of the complex to be built. Quite what its functions were may not be so easy to resolve.

As chapter 12 will show, throughout the Neolithic and the earlier part of the Bronze Age, while Stonehenge itself became more complex and elaborate, so too did its surrounding landscape. But even as new fieldwork and excavation, along with new ways of looking at the past, gradually enhanced our understanding of this landscape, nothing was happening to develop our understanding of Stonehenge itself. In a repeat of what had happened in the 1920s, the results of all the excavations of the 1950s and 1960s remained unanalysed and unreported. When the results of the Stonehenge Environs Project were published in 1990, the sequence of Stonehenge's construction, first outlined by Atkinson in 1956, still had to be taken on trust, even though it was unsupported by any published archaeological data. All this was to change in the 1990s, when Stonehenge would finally give up some more of its secrets.

The Neolithic village of Scara Brae in Orkney: the houses at Durrington Walls appear to be timber versions of these stone-built structures.

CHAPTER 8   The analysis of Stonehenge

Earlier chapters have described the excavations that took place at Stonehenge during the 20th century: three campaigns in which about half of the entire site within the earthwork enclosure was investigated. Gowland started on a small scale in 1901, followed by Hawley between 1919 and 1926 and finally, between 1950 and 1964, there were the major excavations carried out by Atkinson, Piggott and (initially) Stone. All these excavations produced significant new information and potentially increased the understanding of Stonehenge.

But to be of any real value, the results of an excavation need to be widely publicised and all the data need to be accessible to other researchers. Excavation by its very nature is destructive: evidence in the ground is dug away, finds are removed from their contexts, samples are scattered to a variety of experts and laboratories for post-excavation analysis. The whole process must be meticulously recorded while it is going on, and those records and the finds must be carefully stored and preserved in a full archive housed somewhere accessible like a museum. Only then can an

Key

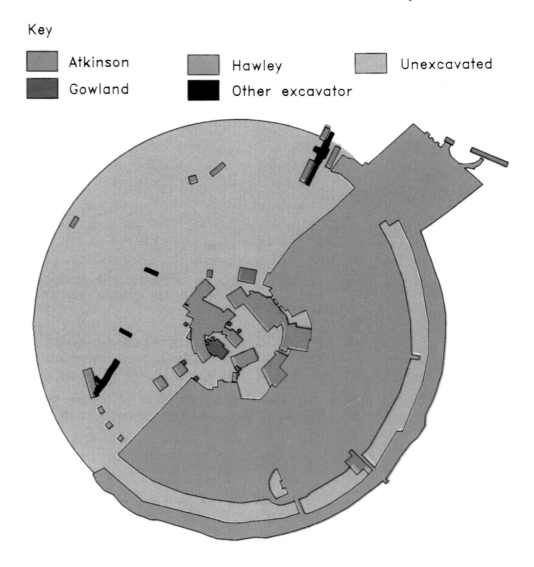

The extent of 20th-century excavations at Stonehenge.

Excavation and reconstruction at Stonehenge in the 1960s.

excavation report be prepared and conclusions drawn; and this full record allows later researchers to re-examine and reinterpret the findings in the knowledge that they are in full possession of all the available data.

This is a fundamental responsibility for all those who embark on excavation. Indeed, in 1946, just before he started work at Stonehenge, Atkinson himself described the failure of archaeologists to publish their results as 'a crime against science' – a strong statement by someone who has been described by an eminent 21st-century archaeologist (with an exemplary publication record) as 'a serial offender'.

By the mid-1980s, 20 years after the end of the last excavation at Stonehenge, only the results of Gowland's work in 1901 had been published (very promptly, in 1902). Hawley had prepared basic annual reports for the Society of Antiquaries, but they contained little analysis and when he finished his work, halfway through the soul-destroying task of attempting, almost single-handedly, to excavate the whole of Stonehenge, no attempt was made to bring his findings together. Atkinson, Piggott and Stone's declared priority was to report on these earlier excavations but as they became increasingly involved in their own excavation project their clarification of Hawley's work seems to have been conveniently put to one side. It is a sad fact that for many years the only account of their excavations and the conclusions they had reached was Atkinson's 1956 *Stonehenge*. This was undeniably popular, and an easily digestible explanation, for a non-scholarly audience, of the sequence of construction that Atkinson believed he had teased out of the complex ruin. But it was not an excavation report, even of those first few years of investigation. Unfortunately it had to suffice for many years – it was in print until 1979 – and the unavailability of the primary data meant that the Stonehenge sequence it outlined was unchallengeable.

Marcus Stone died in 1957 and by the mid-1980s Stuart Piggott had retired. The site records were all with Richard Atkinson in Cardiff while the majority of the finds were housed in the Salisbury and South Wiltshire Museum. A series of dedicated research assistants still worked on the archive, creating order where none had existed, and at intervals Atkinson made promises that the report was well on the way and would be with the publishers in the near future. Eventually it was realised that the passage of time and Atkinson's failing health would prevent this ever happening. So in 1993 Wessex Archaeology, still based in Salisbury but now a much larger archaeological company, was given a monumental task by English Heritage. They were first to bring together all of the finds and records, and from them create an organised and useable archive capable of being analysed and interpreted. They were then to use this to prepare a report for publication. The work started in April 1993 and was completed in December 1994, enabling the publication in the following year of the long awaited *Stonehenge in its landscape: 20th-century excavations.*

At 618 large pages this is a volume for the serious student of Stonehenge, its bulk due largely to its presentation of much of the available factual evidence. This includes detailed descriptions of the individual cuttings that were excavated, the plans and photographs that make up the reassembled site record and details of all the finds. This evidence, everything that we have from the 20th-century excavations, forms the basis for our current understanding of Stonehenge and presents it with no preconceptions. Everything in this report had to be based on facts and on a large number of new and more reliable radiocarbon dates.

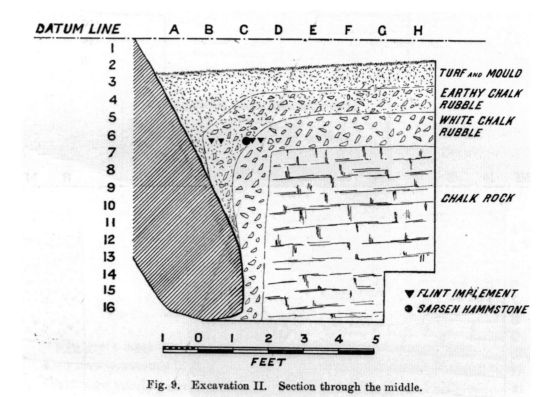

The published cross-section drawing of the hole containing Stone 56, excavated by Gowland in 1901.

Fig. 9.   Excavation II.   Section through the middle.

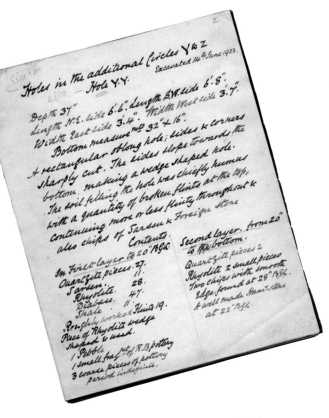

Hawley's notes on the excavation of Y and Z Holes in 1923

The team working on this mammoth project faced major difficulties. Trying to unravel the sequence of events that took place several thousand years ago at a site as complex as Stonehenge would not be easy even if the excavations that had provided the evidence were recent and carried out to the highest possible standards. The reality was that they were dealing with records of a very varying standard indeed.

Gowland emerges with distinction: the non-archaeologist who, in 1901, conducted a meticulously organised investigation and promptly published the results which were, considering the limited size of the excavation, highly informative.

Hawley was working in the 1920s and his excavation methods, even if some of them now seem rather agricultural, were generally good for the time, as was the quality of his records. There are site diaries, written in a straightforward way and including useful information about work carried out, the numbers of finds and details of layers encountered, as well as observations about the weather and visitors. There are drawings, mainly plans with a few cross-sections, and a number of photographs. The bulk of the finds considered to be important were eventually deposited in the Salisbury and South Wiltshire Museum, with samples presented to other collections including the British Museum, the Ashmolean and the university museums at Oxford and Cambridge. Unimportant finds, assumed to include much of the flint and stone together with animal bones, were reburied in 'Hawley's Graves', a series of ten pits dug close to the site office. More 'excess' bone, including the cremated human bone from the Aubrey Holes and the ditch and bank of the enclosure, was reburied in 1935 in the already emptied Aubrey Hole 7.

'No written site records have been found from the 1950–1964 excavations and it seems that none were produced.'

So starts the description of the archive of the most recent excavations. It goes on to explain that some of the original site drawings are no longer available and that the photographic archive of 2,096 black-and-white negatives is unaccompanied by any documentation explaining what each photograph shows. A final problem arises from the finds: those from a whole season (1959) appear to be missing, and card indexes of finds prepared after the excavations do not match up with the artefacts that survive in Salisbury Museum. It became increasingly clear that Atkinson's records, which were justifiably assumed to include written notes, drawings and photographs, were inadequate. It is quite frankly a disgrace that Stonehenge, a site of huge and undeniable importance that had been demonstrated to possess complex below-ground archaeology, should have been recorded so badly as late as the 1950s and 1960s.

But this was all the evidence that was available and, considering its shortcomings, it is remarkable that such a coherent account of Stonehenge has emerged. The creation of a systematic and useable archive, in which artefacts were reunited with the records of the trenches from which they had been excavated so many years before, meant that observations could be made about the sequence of construction. The main task was to place in order the individual elements that make up the

Picks of red-deer antler used to excavate the ditch and the stone holes.

whole monument: the enclosure, the circles and horseshoes of bluestone and sarsen and the peripheral elements such as the Station Stones, Heel Stone, Aubrey Holes and the Avenue.

For the densely crowded central structures, the researchers were looking for 'relationships': evidence for one structure being cut through another which could therefore demonstrate a sequence of events. For example, in digging a hole to erect a sarsen, the chalk from the hole may well have been spread out and trampled down to form a hard surface. If this surface was then cut through by the hole for another stone, for example a bluestone, then it is clear that the bluestone has to have been erected after the sarsen. This 'relative chronology' shows the order in which events happened but gives no indication of the time that has elapsed between the events. The bluestone could have been erected hours, weeks, decades or even centuries after the sarsen.

A number of such relationships could be identified from the site records. Many had already been used by Atkinson to construct his sequence but as a matter of course these were reassessed and some were found to be unconvincing. Where there were ambiguities, sometimes a common-sense approach helped. It seems unlikely, for example, that the outer sarsen circle was completed before the five great sarsen trilithons were set up. If it had been, access would have been severely restricted.

The sequence that emerged from these analyses and reassessments was then combined with the results from a new and extensive programme of radiocarbon dating. Huge advances had been made in dating technology since Libby's pioneering work in the early 1950s. Not only were dates potentially far more accurate but far smaller samples were required, meaning that multiple dates could be obtained for key events without the destruction of all the available sample material. Dating Stonehenge might have been considered a comparatively simple task with the hundreds of potential samples of bone and antler to choose from, but in fact there were few from this large collection that fulfilled the necessary requirements. All those from disturbed or mixed deposits were rejected, as were those where there was doubt about where the sample had actually come from. Those that remained were closely scrutinised to make sure that they really would date a specific event or structure.

For example, a complete human skeleton where all the bones are in the correct place (articulated) can be assumed to represent the burial, soon after death, of a corpse complete with all its soft tissue. A sample of bone from such a skeleton would therefore date the time of the person's death and burial. In contrast, a collection of jumbled (disarticulated) human bones, even if all the components of the skeleton are present, could represent the surviving remains of a body that had originally been buried many years earlier and later moved or disturbed. So while a sample from these bones would still date the time of the person's death, it would not necessarily date the time when he or she was finally buried.

In the search for suitable samples it would seem reasonable to assume that an antler pick found at the base of a ditch would have been used to dig that ditch and could therefore be used to date its original excavation. Likewise, animal bones from the same location, perhaps the remains of feasts or celebratory offerings, might also be assumed to date to that time. But it was found that in places the ditch diggers had buried not fresh bones but some that were as much as 300 years old.

As already noted, of all the fragments of antler from Stonehenge there is only one that, without any doubt, could be used to date the excavation of the hole in which it was found: embedded in the side of the hole that held Stone 9, one of the uprights of the outer sarsen circle, was the tip of an antler pick. This cannot have been deposited at a later date and cannot have been from an old antler as they become brittle with age. It must have been broken off at the precise time the hole was dug.

It is the peripheral elements of Stonehenge that cause the greatest problems. Most of them are isolated from other structures and there are therefore no relationships that can be used to suggest their place in the sequence of construction. Most of them have also failed to provide any dateable finds or any suitable samples for radiocarbon dating so they are, in effect, 'floating' in the overall sequence. But on the whole they have a logical place, often convincingly argued by the authors of the recent analysis, and so here they will be allocated to their suggested dates and positions.

What now follows is the current interpretation of the sequence of construction at Stonehenge. It is explained in some detail, using the key arguments that are more fully presented in *Stonehenge in its landscape*, which also provides the phases and dates that are used here. However, since its publication in 1995 there have been some small, but important, developments. The dating of the first Stonehenge has been refined and, more fundamentally, doubts have been cast on the dating of the first sarsen structures. This will be discussed below in more detail but, if the sarsen trilithons were erected much earlier than has previously been suggested, then all the events described below in phases 1, 2 and the first part of 3 must fit into a far narrower time bracket.

Common sense suggests that the sarsen circle must have been completed after the five great trilithons had been raised.

The first Stonehenge. Digging the ditch and building the bank must have been a communal effort drawing in workers from a wide area.

Phase 1: The construction of the ditch and bank, the digging of the Aubrey Holes and their use as postholes

Even the earliest antiquarians assumed that the ditch and bank were the earliest elements of the overall structure of Stonehenge, and this appeared to be confirmed by Colonel Hawley's extensive investigation of the ditch. The evidence for its early date lay in the absence of any stone fragments in its lowest fills, which meant that these layers must have accumulated before any stones, whether bluestone or sarsen, had arrived on site. This assumption has now been confirmed by a series of radiocarbon dates from antlers placed on the ditch floor shortly after it was dug. These date the digging of the ditch to between 3000 and 2920BC. Alex Bayliss, English Heritage's scientific dating expert, achieved this remarkable precision by combining the individual dates to narrow down the margins of error that are a part of any radiocarbon determination.

Any ditch dug into chalk will rapidly start to fill up through a process of natural erosion. Frost and rain will crumble the sides resulting in what is known as a 'primary rubble' – lumps of chalk interleaved with streaks of darker soil that come from the eroding turf and topsoil. But at Stonehenge several things seem to have happened even before these deposits formed. Antlers were placed on the ditch floor, some of which appear to have been casually discarded – the abandoned tools of the ditch diggers – while others were in small heaps or stacks – deliberate 'special' deposits. There were also smooth chalk balls and perforated chalk objects, and in each of the terminals of the southern entrance was a carefully placed ox jaw. Among the objects found on the ditch floor there seems to be a clear distinction between functional tools, represented by the new antlers, and non-functional but special objects represented by the 'antique' bones, objects that were already ancient when buried.

More mundane activities are suggested by the layer of 'foot trampled mud' and the quantities of worked-flint debris seen in places on the ditch floor. The worked flint may well be the result of the ditch diggers simply testing any flint nodules found in the course of their efforts to see if they contained any useable raw material.

Neither of the banks, the inner more substantial one and the smaller counterscarp, have been examined enough to reveal whether or not they cover traces of any sort of activities or structures that predate the enclosure. The counterscarp, in the limited trenches that have investigated it, appears to incorporate quantities of flint, interpreted somewhat fancifully by Hawley as a firm bedding for a quickset hedge to fence off the first Stonehenge.

The excavation of the Aubrey Holes and their first use, most probably to hold upright timbers, is considered to be part of this first phase of construction. There are good reasons for assuming this, despite the absence of radiocarbon dating evidence. Once again, the lack of stone in their lower fills is important, suggesting that they were dug before stone arrived on site. If they did, as is suggested, hold wooden posts, then this too would place them early in the sequence of Stonehenge's development in which wooden uprights have always been considered to be earlier than those of stone. There is also a matter of geometry. The centre point of the circle of Aubrey Holes is almost identical with that of the ditch and bank, which implies that they were constructed at the same time. It would also have been very difficult to lay out the circle with such precision had there been any substantial obstructions (such as large upright timbers or stones) in the centre of the enclosure.

Environmental evidence from the first Stonehenge, from the lowest fills of the ditch and from beneath the bank, indicates that it was constructed in an open, grazed grassland landscape.

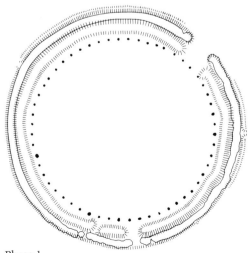

Phase 1

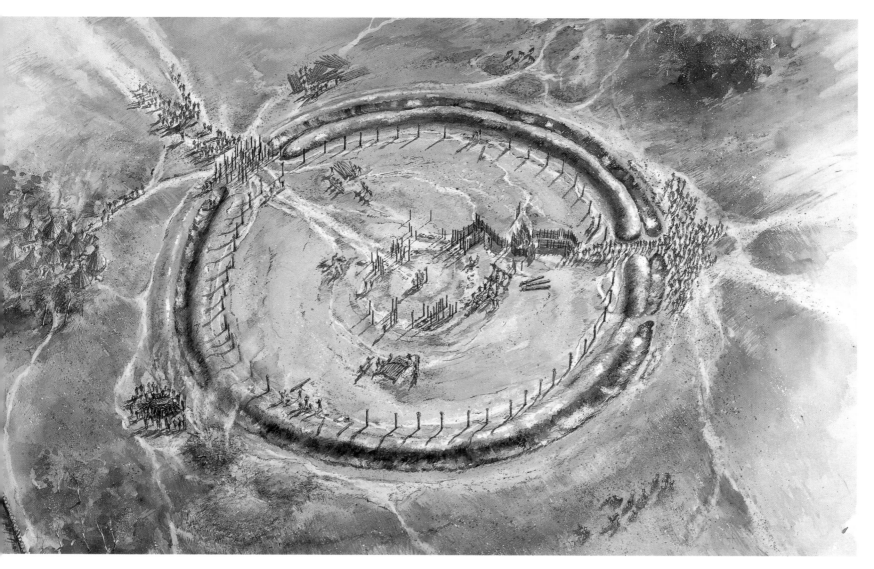

In Phase 2 timber structures were built and decayed, and for a while Stonehenge became a place of burial.

Phase 2: The partial filling of the ditch, the use of the Aubrey Holes and the ditch as a cremation cemetery, and the 'timber' phase

This is a particularly difficult phase both to characterise and to date, including as it does a range of 'pre-stone' structures and activities of which none has been independently dated. The date range suggested in *Stonehenge in its landscape* is between 2900BC (after the ditch was dug) and 2400BC, but it is most likely that this phase was over much earlier, almost certainly before 2600BC. Once again, the absence of stone fragments is crucial evidence through which to assign events to this phase.

So what did happen in Phase 2, captioned in *Stonehenge in its landscape* as 'A change of emphasis'? The ditch continued to fill up, either with natural silts or with deposits of chalk that suggest that in places it was deliberately backfilled. Atkinson suggested that the backfilling around the main north-easterly entrance was in order to realign the enclosure and create a conceptual link with the Avenue that he saw initiated at this time. It now seems that the backfilling here was simply part of a wider phenomenon that occurred in many places around the ditch circuit. It has also been argued that some of the chalk found in the ditch is spoil from digging the Aubrey Holes, which would place their initial use slightly later than is usually assumed. In either case, small cuts were then made into the top of the ditch fill into which pottery, animal bone and in some cases cremated human bones were placed. These cremations are unusual, in that they are not the burnt bones from whole bodies but handfuls of bone placed in shallow scoops.

Similar deposits of cremated bone were found in the upper fills of many Aubrey Holes, which by now had lost their wooden posts. These were perhaps deliberately withdrawn rather than being left to rot, creating hollows into which the cremations were placed, some accompanied by bone skewer pins and one by a most unusual ceramic object. As Hawley arranged for the cremated bone he had found to be reburied, only one cremation deposit, from the ditch, has been available for examination by specialists. This contained around 1.5kg (over 3lb) of well-cremated bone, most of the bones that could be expected to be recoverable from a funeral pyre. The bones are of a young adult female and include a fragment of vertebra showing signs of blue-green staining. This is usually taken to indicate the presence of copper alloy, although this would be unusually early for the occurrence of metal if the cremations are as early in the Stonehenge sequence as suggested. Although this cremation was 'clean', containing no ash or charcoal from the funeral pyre, Hawley noted others that did contain pyre material, perhaps suggesting that the act of cremation took place quite close to where the remains were eventually buried.

It seems reasonable to assume that the cremations found in the ditch and in the upper fills of some of the Aubrey Holes are all part of the same activity from a time at which Stonehenge took on the role of cemetery. This is a rare form of burial during this part of the Neolithic period, with the only other really convincing example coming from Dorchester-on Thames where bone skewer pins were also found in a cremation cemetery of a similar date.

Within Phase 2 this leaves the 'wooden Stonehenge' to explain: the interpretation of the hundreds of scattered postholes, mainly from Hawley's excavations, that scholars from many disciplines have struggled to shuffle into coherent patterns and structures. Their date is uncertain: one is cut by a Y Hole and occasional examples can be shown to be earlier than stone holes. None has been radiocarbon dated and they are almost without exception devoid of finds. Because they represent long-vanished timber structures the assumption is that they must lie early in the overall sequence. There is also a tendency to assume that they must all have fulfilled the same broad function, whereas they may be the remains of a variety of activities carried out over a long time span.

Their distribution obviously reflects the areas that have been excavated and many more must remain in the unexplored parts of the site, too small to be detected by currently available methods of geophysical prospecting. There are three identifiable

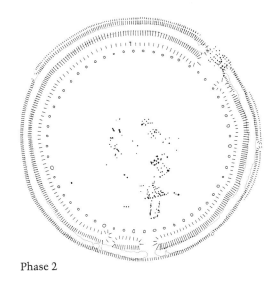

Phase 2

'zones' or clusters: on the main north-easterly entrance causeway, outside the stones on the southern side of the enclosure and, the most difficult to interpret, amongst the central cluster of stones.

On the main entrance causeway Hawley found over 50 postholes of varying size and shape, and recognised that many more had been lost due to the erosion caused by a medieval and modern track running through the enclosure entrance. Hawley considered that some of the larger holes had originally held stones, although it is now considered more likely that they all held upright timbers. There appear to be three elements in the overall plan: lines of posts running side to side across the entrance causeway, lines running parallel to the sides of the causeway, and a diagonal line of larger posts. There is a symmetry within this layout, which offers the possibility that the posts are part of a complex timber entrance, a form of façade incorporating two narrow corridors. But this hypothetical structure fits uneasily with the plan of the ditch and bank and suggests that they are not part of the same layout.

There are alternative interpretations. The posts may have been part of a reinforcing structure laid out over the vulnerable entrance causeway at the time when the huge sarsens were dragged in. But if this was when the postholes were dug, surely at least some of them would have contained chips of stone. Countering this practical suggestion is the interpretation of the posts as markers to record astronomical observations as part of the surveying process, to make sure the stones were raised in their correct positions. This interpretation is discussed in chapter 11.

The second group, on the southern side of the enclosure between the sarsen circle and the bank, has been interpreted as the remains of a passageway from the southern entrance into the interior.

The remaining postholes are those that were found amongst the central stone settings, patterns fragmented by later construction work on a huge scale and incomplete owing to large areas still being unexcavated. *Stonehenge in its landscape* presents the data, noting that this is the first time that the entire posthole pattern has been assembled for scrutiny and also that they may represent a 'complicated structure'. But there is a strong possibility that not all of the posts in this area were raised at the same time and for the same purpose. Atkinson suggests that some had a practical application as components of temporary scaffolding and supports used while stones were being raised. Scholars have nevertheless never stopped trying to construct circular structures out of the scatter of posts – an obvious configuration for the centre of a circular enclosure. Atkinson himself hints at the possibility of a roofed timber building, while more recently Aubrey Burl describes something with 'two concentric rings of sturdy timber uprights, held firmly by ring beams across their tops, supporting a pitched and thatched roof'. The evidence for such a structure is at best tenuous and the question of what, if anything, apart from scaffolding, stood in the centre of Stonehenge before the stones arrived may never be resolved. Perhaps the last word should be left to the computer which, by selecting three postholes of similar size and depth from the hundreds available, was able to generate six plausible circles ranging in diameter from 10–60m (33–200ft).

Stonehenge transformed – the arrival of the first stones.

Phase 3: The stone monument

Within this simple phrase – 'the stone monument' – lie most of the more obvious elements of what we recognise as Stonehenge: the stones themselves, both central and peripheral. Enormous effort was expended over as much as a millennium to build the greatest structure of its age, but this long timescale and the complexity of what was built mean that this broad phase has to be broken down into more manageable subdivisions. These have been labelled phases 3i–3vi.

Phase 3i
Phase 3i starts with a pivotal moment in the history of Stonehenge – the arrival of the first stones – the bluestones from Preseli – initially set up in the enigmatic Q and R Holes. These holes, first identified by Atkinson in 1954 (although Hawley had previously excavated some without recognising their significance), formed the ends of a series of pits shaped like dumb bells, the linking hollow generally filled with

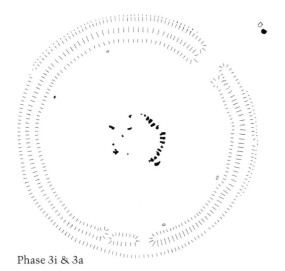

Phase 3i & 3a

tightly packed clean chalk rubble. Although now all empty, some had clearly held upright stones, as the chalk at their bases bore clear rounded impressions and chips of bluestone were found in the soils that filled them. On the basis of Atkinson's descriptions, the Q and R Holes seem very similar in both their shape and their fills. Their layout, however, is puzzling. An arc of dumb bells, some more convincing than others, lies on the eastern and northern sides of the interior, roughly on the same line as the bluestone circle. This arc looks like part of a circular arrangement, but excavations on its projected western side produced not a neat continuation, but a single isolated pit.

There are no reliable radiocarbon dates from any of the Q or R Holes, but they always cut, and are therefore later than, the postholes. They must also be the earliest stone settings, as R38 is cut by the hole for Stone 49 of the bluestone circle and Q4 is cut by the hole for Stone 3 of the sarsen circle.

There is, in addition, the puzzle of the 'crescentic feature', a banana-shaped trench that may originally have held three upright stones and is considered to date to this phase, as may the Altar Stone, the only non-Preseli stone from this phase.

The arrival of the bluestones initiates a long-running and complicated debate. Leaving aside the question of how they got to Stonehenge (which will be examined in chapter 10), there are the questions of just how many stones there were in total and how they can be accounted for prior to being placed in their final settings. On the basis that the Q and R Holes represent part of what must have been a complete double circle of stone holes, Atkinson decided that this original setting had consisted of 82 stones. This was the foundation on which he based all his subsequent calculations of which stones went into which holes but, as it now seems that the Q and R Hole circles were not complete, there must have been considerably fewer stones than this in the first setting. Nonetheless, this is where the puzzle starts, with this first stone structure, perhaps comparatively short-lived but certainly dismantled and its component bluestones apparently removed from the site.

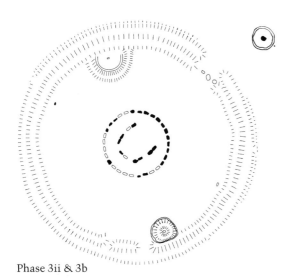

Phase 3ii & 3b

Phase 3ii
With the centre of the enclosure once again empty, the scale of construction moved up a gear with the arrival of the much bigger sarsens in phase 3ii. There are strong similarities in the construction of the circle and the horseshoe of trilithons, both of which have shaped stones, lintels and elaborate carved joints. But the sequence in which they were built is not easy to determine. Because the two structures are physically separate there are no relationships between them, and radiocarbon dates initially seem to suggest that, if anything, the circle was slightly earlier than the horseshoe. But building the trilithons after the completion of the outer circle does not work from a practical point of view.

The dating of these structures, a crucial stage in Stonehenge's development, relies on just four radiocarbon dates. One came from a stone hole of the outer circle (2620–2480BC) and another from one of the trilithons (2850–2400BC). The other

Phase 3ii saw the construction of Stonehenge's most recognisable features – the sarsen circle and the five giant trilithons.

two, which when combined give a date of 2440–2100BC, came from under what Atkinson described as a ramp built for the erection of Stone 56. Atkinson always maintained that this stone, the sole surviving upright of the Great Trilithon and the one straightened by Gowland in 1901, was raised to its original upright position by means of a sloping ramp that lay to its north-west. This has always seemed an odd interpretation as it would have meant that the stone, weighing over 40 tons, had to be raised up on its narrow edge and dropped sideways into its hole. But for many years Atkinson's interpretation was accepted, as were the slightly later radiocarbon dates produced by antlers from beneath it.

However, the function of this 'ramp' and its association with the raising of Stone 56 have recently been questioned and, if the dates from it are rejected, then the dating of the sarsen trilithons – and by implication of phase 3ii – could go back to as early as 2600–2500BC. This would have the effect of squashing all of the earlier structures described above into a reduced time bracket of as little as 300 years.

Stonehenge complete at the winter solstice. By around 2000BC the stones had been rearranged for the last time and the main entrance was approached by the earthworks of the Avenue.

Phase 3iii – the 'dressed bluestone' phase

This is perhaps the most nebulous of the defined phases and, indeed, is described by the authors of *Stonehenge in its landscape* as 'a term of convenience rather than a... real, coherent and separate stage in the development of the monument'. It correlates with Atkinson's phase IIIb, his 'dressed bluestone setting', and is a way of expressing the suggestion that, after their removal from the Q and R Holes and prior to their final arrangement, some elaborately shaped bluestones stood not as simple pillars but in far more complex arrangements. Both lintels and uprights with tenons provide evidence for miniature trilithons which appear to have stood for long enough for the friction of stone on stone to create visible wear on the underside of one of the lintels. In addition, Stones 66 and 68 may have fitted together as a tongue-and-grooved pair, a composite stone.

So there may have been a separate bluestone structure, which may have been raised at broadly the same time as the sarsen structures, or there is always the possibility that these elaborate stones stood elsewhere, perhaps not even within Stonehenge. Phase 3iii is likely to remain a mystery.

Phase 3iv – the bluestone circle and oval
Phase 3v – the bluestone circle and horseshoe
These phases mark a major reorganisation of the stone settings in the interior of Stonehenge and the reappearance of the remaining bluestones, assuming that the majority had been stored elsewhere during the preceding phase. For the sake of simplicity it is best to consider these two phases together, as 3v simply marks a small modification of the arrangements that appear in 3iv.

Of the two arrangements, the one that remains the same throughout, but which today appears the most fragmentary, is the bluestone circle that lies just inside the sarsen circle. Excavations have demonstrated that its stone holes in places cut those of the sarsen circle so it is the later structure, confirmed by two radiocarbon dates of 2480–2140BC and 2290–2030BC. The construction of the bluestone circle, which has been described as being 'ragged' in appearance, is in places very unusual, with stones, many of which are missing, set within a continuous trench rather than in individual stone holes.

The other major bluestone arrangement started off as an oval, lying inside the sarsen horseshoe and reflecting its shape except for being closed off on its north-eastern side by an arc of stones. This structure, which has a far more precise layout than that of the bluestone circle, incorporates larger and more finely worked stones, including tall pillars of the 'dressed bluestone' phase, now with their tenons removed. Once again the bluestone structure can be shown to be later than the one of sarsen that it mirrors, and a single radiocarbon date of 2280–1940BC confirms this and shows that both bluestone structures, circle and oval, were most probably constructed at the same time. This oval was later modified (in phase 3v) by the removal of an arc of four or five stones to leave the horseshoe that can be seen today – and the puzzle of what happened to the bluestones that were removed at this point: were they redistributed in the bluestone circle or taken elsewhere?

The majority of the structures that are found around the main north-easterly entrance to the earthwork enclosure, with the exception of the postholes for timber uprights that have already been described, belong in phase 3. Stone hole E, one of the two that flank the now fallen Slaughter Stone, has been radiocarbon dated to between 2480 and 2200BC, firmly within phase 3 and most probably after the construction of the sarsen circle. But this is as much as can be said for these stones, and for those that stood in holes B and C, despite the complex patterns of removal and rearrangement that have been suggested (but will not be discussed here). This leaves what is happening around the Heel Stone where, due to the proximity of a number of ditches, banks and stone holes, it is possible to work out a sequence of events. These events have been placed in yet another series of sub-phases of phase 3, this time allocated alphabetical suffixes.

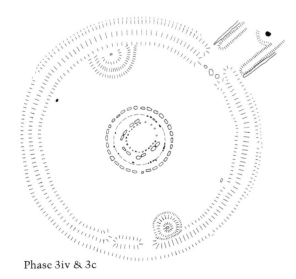

Phase 3iv & 3c

The complicated sequence of earthworks, stone holes and timber settings around the main entrance to the Stonehenge enclosure.

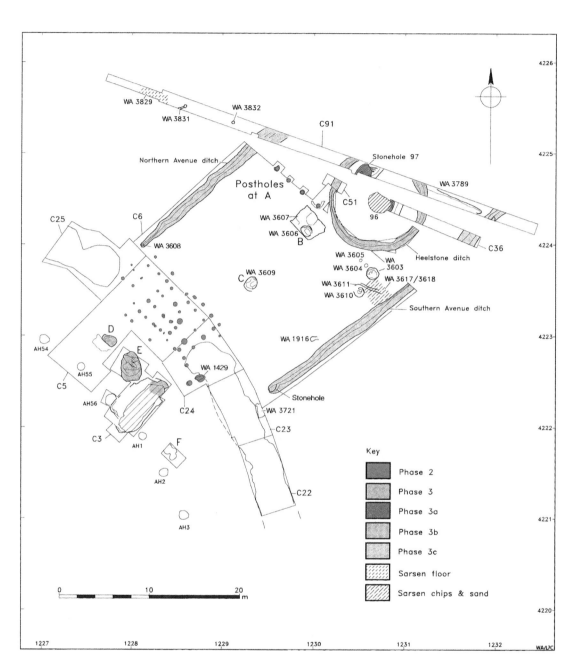

Phase 3a starts with the digging of stone hole 97, the one discovered by Mike Pitts on the roadside verge in 1997. From the clear impression on its base this hole once held a stone, but it is uncertain whether it stood in a pair with the Heel Stone or stood in isolation and was later moved to become what is now known as the Heel Stone. The former seems more likely as the pair of stones would have stood exactly astride the main axis of the enclosure.

Phase 3b is the digging of a circular ditch around the Heel Stone, a ditch that would also have encircled Stone 97 if it was standing as part of the pair. The similarity of this ditch to those that surround two of the Station Stones (the North and South Barrows) leads to the conclusion that these events are connected and happened at the same time.

Phase 3c is the construction of the Avenue, which clearly belongs here as the tail of its bank overlies the partly silted-up Heel Stone ditch. Atkinson suggested that the Avenue was constructed in two distinct stages and over a long period of time, ending in the later part of the Bronze Age. This idea was based on four radiocarbon dates that fell into neat pairs: two early dates from the straight section close to Stonehenge and two late dates from nearer the River Avon. The recent report 'wonders whether this was an example of archaeological testing of the data coming to a halt as soon as a result was obtained which agreed with the prevalent theory'. What is now clear is that the late dates should be regarded with great suspicion (one was a 'bulked' sample of three separate bones and inevitably unreliable), and that on the basis of new dates the Avenue appears not only to belong to Phase 3 but to have been built in one go.

This is the effective end of the construction of the stone monument, resulting in the arrangements of ditches, banks, sarsen and bluestone that can still be seen today, albeit in a ruined and fragmentary state. But it was not the end of all construction; there was a postscript.

Phase 3vi – the Y and Z Holes
It has always been assumed that because these oblong pits, that lie in two circles outside the sarsen circle, are similar in shape and overall plan, they must belong to the same phase of activity. Hawley observed that Y Holes tended to cut, and were therefore later than, postholes of Phase 2, and that in two places Z Holes cut through ramps that had been built to help raise stones of the sarsen circle. They therefore seemed to be late in the overall sequence of construction, but quite how late has been the subject of much speculation. The absence of Z Hole 8 in its assumed position has been used as an argument to suggest that Stone 8 of the outer circle had already fallen by the time the Z Holes were dug. On the basis of pottery found by Hawley, Atkinson originally suggested that the holes were dug in the Iron Age (after 800BC), but after excavating some himself revised this to his Phase IIIb, about 1500–1400BC. This date is not far off that of around 1600BC suggested by more recent radiocarbon dates, but his idea that they had been dug (but never used) for a double stone setting of 60 bluestones does not stand up quite so well.

The Y and Z Holes clearly never held upright stones. Whether they were ever intended to cannot be determined, but what is certain is that they represent the last major phase in the long and complicated development of Stonehenge.

So, having described what Stonehenge is, how it was investigated and what we have learned from these investigations, there still remain three great questions, the answers to which may not lie within the masses of archaeological data and finds that now reside in Salisbury and South Wiltshire Museum. The first of these is: who built Stonehenge?

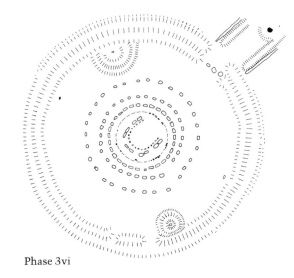

Phase 3vi

CHAPTER 9   **Who built Stonehenge?**

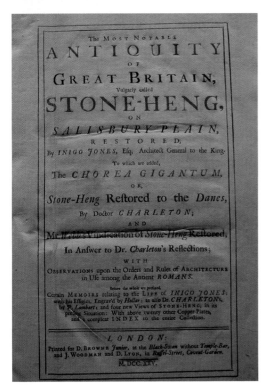

During the 17th and 18th centuries opinion was divided as to whether Stonehenge had been built by Romans or Danes.

OPPOSITE
18th-century graffiti.

Leaving aside the opinions of those who saw Stonehenge as some sort of peculiar and elaborate natural rock formation and those that see it as the product of extra-terrestrial forces, Stonehenge is generally accepted as being the product of human ingenuity and effort. So the question that has been asked for centuries, ever since Stonehenge became a curiosity to medieval historians, is 'who built it?'

As chapter 3 outlined, suggestions have been many and varied. The Romans were strong candidates, an obvious choice due to Stonehenge's supposed affinities with classical architecture, but Danes, Saxons and Phoenicians all had their supporters. Even the Myceneans were briefly considered after the discovery of the dagger carving in the 1950s. In many ways it is not surprising that the architects and builders of such a sophisticated structure were sought amongst more 'civilised' cultures and it took a long time, and many struggles with preconceptions of savagery and barbarism, for 'Ancient Britons' to be acknowledged as the builders of Stonehenge.

> 'As for their manner of living, the Britons were then a savage and barbarous people, knowing no use at all of garments.'

This was Inigo Jones's view of the builders and, although attitudes have become more enlightened, even today the term 'prehistoric' can, in some minds, still conjure up images of something primitive, even bestial. Revealing the reconstructed three-dimensional face of a late Iron Age man to the villagers of Bleadon in Somerset, the place of his burial, provoked genuine surprise that he looked like 'us'. Many had expected that this prehistoric man would be somehow ape-like, with knuckles dragging on the ground, rather than someone who, if cleaned up and in modern clothes, could clearly have walked down the main street of the village without arousing any comment.

The prehistoric people who built and used Stonehenge were modern humans, *homo sapiens*, whose Mesolithic hunter-gatherer ancestors had been true Europeans, living on what was part of the European mainland until rising sea levels finally flooded the Channel and cut Britain off in about 7000BC. From this time onwards the inhabitants of Britain and Ireland, while clearly not immune from continental influence, developed their own insular culture. During the Neolithic period this included building monuments that are uniquely British.

So who were the people that built Stonehenge and what has modern science told us about their lives? There are no written descriptions of physical characteristics, health and life expectancy, no anthropological observations to be made about everyday life, relationships, society and status. What we know about them has to come from the analysis of their physical remains and the tools, pots, ornaments, weapons and food remains that make up the surviving evidence of their everyday lives. Experimentation can also help to understand the meaning of these clues, as can anthropology, the study of contemporary people who are living an essentially prehistoric way of life.

One of the superb disc barrows in the Winterbourne Stoke Crossroads group.

In attempting to reconstruct the lives of those who built Stonehenge there are problems with the evidence available. In order to be able to analyse human remains, the bodies need to have been disposed of in a manner that allows the survival of the more robust parts, usually just the bones, so they can be recognised and recovered at a later date. Fortunately the Wessex chalk provides ideal conditions for the survival of bone, in contrast to the acidic soils of uplands like Dartmoor where bone is eaten away and quickly vanishes. But even where bones do survive, graves need to be marked in order to be recognisable, and from the early Neolithic onwards this marking was normally done with mounds of stone or earth. Even early archaeologists recognised that the barrow mounds of varying shape that dot the British Isles consistently covered human burials of widely differing types. Long mounds often contained jumbled collections of bones, representing the remains of many people, whilst round mounds were built for individuals whose bodies or cremated remains were buried together with a wide range of offerings. But these pioneers also recognised that such burial sites were simply the tip of the iceberg, the graves of important people, singled out by birth, status or wealth, or perhaps by a combination of all three, to be given a special type of burial.

This extract from *A tour in search of Chalk* by 'a pedestrian', a wonderfully amusing modern work written in the style of an early 19th century topographical diary, puts it admirably: 'To study the contents of the barrows of South Wiltshire, and to build a history of the ancient peoples from this research, is to mislead in the same manner as to take a foreigner on a tour of our grand country houses and estates and inform them that this is how all Englishmen live. Within these barrows are surely the ancient Kings and Queens, Dukes and baronets and it is to these conspicuous tombs that all antiquaries are inexorably drawn.'

On the whole, therefore, this is the evidence that we have to work with – the burials not perhaps of 'Kings and Queens' but of an elite. We can study them, but we need to do so with an awareness that the ordinary people, the real builders of Stonehenge, remain unseen and anonymous. So what happened to their bodies when they died?

There is a range of options. They could have been disposed of in ways that would have left no trace: exposed to the elements and to carrion birds and scavenging animals that would have eaten the flesh and scattered the bones. They could have been tossed into the River Avon to float downstream, decay and disperse. Or they could have been buried in very much the same way as their more significant contemporaries but with less ceremony, unaccompanied by elaborate grave goods and without a covering mound. The cemeteries of obvious burial mounds that are such a prominent feature of the Stonehenge landscape may be surrounded with unmarked graves. This was indeed demonstrated in 1983 by the excavation of a small barrow to the north of Stonehenge.

This barrow, on Durrington Down, was the only burial site to be excavated as part of the Stonehenge Environs Project and was chosen because fragments of Bronze Age pottery had been found on the eroded mound, suggesting that urns containing cremations were being damaged by ploughing. Surprisingly, the central burial was intact, undisturbed by 19th-century barrow diggers. Within a deep chalk-cut grave lay the crouched skeleton of a child, about eight years old, buried with nothing more than a straight smoothed piece of deer antler, perhaps a favourite toy. In the corner of the same grave was a heap of cremated human bone, the remains of another child aged between five and ten. So the barrow, which most probably dates to some time just before 2000BC, was built for the burial of two children, an indication that in this case status came not with age or achieved wealth and power, but with birth.

But burials and other funerary rites on this site did not end with the construction of the small flinty barrow mound. On the edge of it, in a deep pit, was another skeleton, this one of a man aged between 35 and 45, tightly crouched and covered with flints. In the same area was a shallow pit containing the cremated remains of three individuals, two adults and a juvenile, while scatters of cremated bone representing at least two other adults were found in the plough soil. All this shows clearly that the barrow, built for the burial of two special children, then became a focus for a whole range of subsequent burials. The only reason, however, that these people were found was because their remains had been buried with care in a place that had recognisable associations with death and burial.

The barrow on Durrington Down shows the variety of ways in which the dead were treated, a variety that can be seen at Stonehenge itself which, although not strictly a funerary site, does have its fair share of burials. The cremated human remains that were buried in the tops of the Aubrey Holes and in the bank and ditch some time around 2800BC are extremely rare examples of burials from this time. In fact there is only one comparable cemetery from this period, at Dorchester-on-Thames in Oxfordshire.

An important Bronze Age child – buried in a deep grave beneath a barrow just to the north of Stonehenge.

The Beaker 'package' that first appeared around 2400BC
– new types of pottery and archery equipment but
above all the first metalwork to be found in Britain.

Obviously these two cemeteries do not represent the entire population of southern England at this time, so what happened to everyone else? If cremation was the preferred rite of disposal then Stonehenge and Dorchester seem to be exceptional in that the burnt bones were collected from the pyre and carefully buried. In most other cases the bones may simply have been left where they were burnt or collected and scattered so that they are now irrecoverable. One major frustration with Stonehenge is that the cremated remains that were found in the 1920s, the key to the lives of the early builders, lie jumbled together in Aubrey Hole 7 where they were reburied in the 1930s.

So at the time when these rare cremations took place there is a real gap in the wider burial record, several hundred years during which we have no idea about how the dead were disposed of. Before this we have the communal and anonymous burials in the long barrows, variations on a theme that is found all over Britain and Ireland. And then later, the gap ends with the first 'Beaker' burials in around 2400BC, a complete change in practice in which individual, recognisable people were buried alone with the trappings of their wealth: the decorated pots, bronze weapons and ornaments that so attracted early archaeologists.

Both groups of burials, however, those that predate Stonehenge and those that took place during or immediately after its great period of construction, provide clues to understanding the lives of the Stonehenge builders. This comparatively small sample would have been much bigger, and the results more meaningful, if the excavators at the time of the great 19th-century boom in round barrow exploration had collected human remains as well as artefacts – although, as has already been emphasised, these people are unlikely to represent a true cross-section of society. They were an elite, who may consequently have been better fed, led easier lives and therefore lived longer.

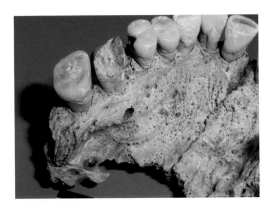

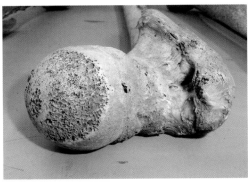

TOP
Painful tooth decay (caries) and a hole marking the
position of an abscess.

BOTTOM
Pitting like this indicates joint disease and would have
resulted in a stiff and painful hip.

The story starts in the Neolithic, a time from which Charlotte Roberts and Margaret Cox found 772 individuals when they carried out their recent examination of all the available burials from this period in Britain and Ireland. The remains of these 772 people represent a population that has been estimated as rising to perhaps 50,000 by the end of the Neolithic.

So what were our Neolithic ancestors like? The men were between 162cm (5ft 4in) and 177cm (5ft 9½in) tall, averaging out at around 165cm (5ft 5in). The range for women was between 151 and 161cm (4ft 11in to 5ft 4in), giving an average height of 157cm (5ft 2in). These heights are essentially the same as those recorded for the preceding Mesolithic population and suggest that the introduction of agriculture did not have any profound effect on nutrition. Logically, it would seem that agriculture must have provided more benefits than those offered by a hunter-gatherer economy, but as far as human health is concerned it has been called 'a backward tumble', for several reasons. Even semi-permanent housing, where the people returned to the same location on a seasonal basis, would have meant the accumulation of refuse, and where there is refuse there are vermin. Crop cultivation could lead to a less varied diet, and living in close proximity to domesticated animals could result in the transmission of infectious diseases such as tuberculosis, anthrax and brucellosis. There is, however, no direct evidence for any of these infections.

What does emerge from the Neolithic skeletons is a picture that is familiar throughout the past, of joint disease such as osteoarthritis and of dental problems. However, despite heavy wear and some evidence of decay (caries), abscesses and periodontal disease, the teeth of our Neolithic ancestors were surprisingly good, perhaps an indication of a diet devoid of sugar.

The time of birth was one of great danger for both mother and child and infant deaths were undoubtedly common, even though they are under-represented within the archaeological record. This could simply be due to survival: infant bones are very fragile and, as well as being the first to decay, may possibly not have been noticed by early excavators. It is also possible that newborn infants were not given the same burial as those who were considered to have become 'real' people, in the same way that babies in Roman times were not buried in formal cemeteries but in more domestic places such as under the floors of houses.

Life expectancy was also shorter, although precise figures are difficult to come by owing to the problems, still faced by those who study human remains today, of assessing age at death. The skeletons of children are easy to age (if not to assign to sex), as up to puberty they go through a series of well-defined changes, particularly in tooth development. Beyond this, age at death is often assessed on the basis of overall degeneration and tooth wear, but these are imprecise indicators and, while it is likely that the majority may well have died before the age of 40, there would have been individuals who lived for much longer, their age conferring great status and respect.

The evidence of early surgical intervention – apparently survivable.

The more settled nature of Neolithic life and the evidence of communally built monuments suggest the development of a society with some form of hierarchy. Whether or nor this was a society that cared for its weaker members is uncertain, but at this time there is the first evidence for direct surgical intervention in the form of trepanation. This involved the removal of a piece of bone from the skull, perhaps in an attempt to cure headaches or migraines, or to free trapped evil spirits. There may also have been a ritual component to this practice, which would have been carried out using stone tools and presumably little or no anaesthetic. Surprisingly, among the five recorded cases there is evidence in the form of healed edges of cut bone that some survived the operation.

In the Bronze Age the change from communal to single burials means that, despite the variety of burial practices employed throughout the period and the number of sites that have been excavated, only 291 individuals are available on which to base general observations about stature and health.

There is evidence that both men and women were becoming taller, men by 7cm (2½in) and women by 4cm (1½in). But although the average Bronze Age man was still only 172cm (less than 5ft 8in) tall, there must have been exceptions. William Cunnington noted that the skeleton found with all the wonderful gold objects in Bush Barrow was of a 'tall and robust man', sufficiently different from all the other skeletons they had seen to warrant comment. This increase in average height may be due to a higher calorie intake resulting from increased agricultural production. However, the effects of this more intensive farming can be seen in a substantial increase in joint problems and more dental disease. So there was more and possibly better food, but at the cost of greater wear and tear on the body and the risk of toothache.

For many years, ever since skulls from the islands of Arran and Bute were studied in detail in the 19th century, there have been attempts to identify distinct Neolithic and Bronze Age 'types' on the basis of head shape. Two categories were defined: individuals with narrow skulls (dolichocephalic) were thought to be Neolithic (the native inhabitants) while those whose skulls were broader (brachiocephalic) were Bronze Age in date and therefore considered to be incomers. Unfortunately, neat though this idea is (and it even fits in with changing barrow shape from the Neolithic into the Bronze Age), it is now apparent that head shape varied considerably at this time.

So by studying surviving bones it is possible to construct a picture of the physical makeup of these people – people who were generally not as tall as we are today and whose lives to us also seem comparatively short. Childbirth and infancy were times of great risk and infections that we routinely treat today with antibiotics would have been potentially life-threatening. There were the aches and pains of agricultural toil, the health problems associated with proximity to farm animals and issues with dental hygiene that would have resulted in extremely unpleasant breath.

Meat and two veg. Modern Soay sheep are the closest breed to ancient sheep/goats. Pignuts (top) and couch grass (above) would have provided edible roots.

But what about their lives? It is difficult to understand prehistoric society – the ways in which people organised their lives, the part that power and influence played and the social taboos that must have operated. Did people live in family groups? Or were they separated by age, sex or status? What rituals marked the vital passage from adolescence to adulthood? Elites must clearly have existed, but whether based on inheritance, wealth, strength or spirituality, we cannot say. Power could be used to motivate and organise, necessary for the construction of great monuments like Stonehenge. But at an ordinary, human level, these people must have had many of the basic needs that still drive us today, for food and shelter, warmth and clothing, companionship, love and affection, and fun.

The evidence for food comes from animal bones and preserved seeds and grains, with new data emerging from the study of residues preserved in cooking pots. The Age of Stonehenge began in an agricultural era and all the evidence suggests that farming intensified as time went on, so it is hardly surprising that domesticated animals and crops must have made up a large proportion of the diet. There is a tendency to view early agriculture as perhaps a less intensive version of what we see today in a rural environment, a landscape of neat fields and hedges, lanes and well managed clumps of trees. In reality, clearance of the wildwood, the dense broadleaved forest that covered the entire lowland of Britain, was piecemeal, and at first cultivation would have taken place in small clearings, more horticulture than farming. Only gradually would the mosaic of land use change as fresh clearings merged with those that were abandoned and overgrown to create a truly open landscape. There is also a tendency to equate farming with settling down, investment in a specific piece of land, whereas crops could have been planted and left to grow, and herds moved from one area of pasture to another.

The first major crops appear to be varieties of wheat and barley, but linseed was also grown as well as pulses: beans, peas and lentils. Cattle, pigs, sheep and goat were all reared for their meat and for their secondary products, like milk and wool. Sheep, especially the small goat-like animals of the Neolithic and Bronze Age, are hardy creatures, able to tolerate rough grazing, while pigs are happy to forage in woodland, eating acorns and beech mast in season. What is becoming increasingly obvious from recent excavations, like those at Durrington Walls, is the importance of pigs as feasting animals, with evidence of large-scale winter slaughter. But the prehistoric diet was not solely domestic in nature. Aurochs, giant wild cattle, roamed the countryside until well into the Bronze Age, rivers were full of fish and the remaining woodland sheltered red and roe deer. There was also a huge variety of wild foods that could be gathered in season. Acorns, blackberries, sloes, hazel nuts and crab apples were available to pick and eat straight off the branch, prehistoric 'fast food' (but far better for you than any modern equivalent). In effect, everything that had fed Mesolithic hunter-gatherers was still there, and the Neolithic and Bronze Age farmers that followed would have been stupid to ignore such an abundant source of free food.

Evidence of the Neolithic 'revolution': cultivated grain, the querns to grind it with and simple round-bottomed pots – the first pottery to appear in Britain.

So the components of the Stonehenge diet are known but how they were combined or served is only hinted at. The cultivated grains were ground on dished 'saddle' querns and the resulting flour, which contained a fair amount of grit, was presumably responsible for the greater tooth wear recorded at this time. The increasingly open nature of the landscape during the earlier part of the Bronze Age suggests more grazing, which may in turn result in a greater reliance on dairy products. But although the relationship of people with the natural world was changing, from one of mutual interdependence to one of domination, even these farmers may not have entirely settled down during the Age of Stonehenge. And whether they were settled or more nomadic has a great bearing on the next fundamental need – for shelter.

There tends to be an assumption that the dwellings of hunter-gatherers will be light and portable while those of farmers will be solid, durable and immovable. So the Mesolithic house at Howick on the Northumberland coast, built around 7000BC, was quite a surprise. To all intents and purposes built exactly like a later prehistoric round house, with walls of sturdy posts, it was in use for as much as a century. But Neolithic houses are more of a puzzle.

In Orkney they are exactly what would be expected: stone-built and with highly organised interior space. Doorways consistently face in the same direction, hearths are precisely placed and some houses are even fitted with stone-built furniture. But timber equivalents do not turn up on a regular basis in southern Britain. There are very occasional 'halls' or long houses, substantially built of posts with plank walls, but these are the exception rather than the rule. On the whole, recognisable Neolithic and early Bronze Age houses are absent from the archaeological record. But perhaps this is because we have been looking for the wrong sort of evidence, assuming that our 'farmers', having settled down, were living in permanent houses. What we should have been looking for were the traces of more ephemeral structures, of the sort that turned up at Durrington Walls in the 2005 and 2006 excavations.

In stark contrast to the massively built timber circles found within the henge, these small, lightly built 'huts' may not have been permanent dwellings but were perhaps lived in on a seasonal basis. The Stonehenge landscape could have been occupied all year round, with people either living in 'villages' or moving around within a small area, or may have had a far more mobile population that moved in at special times of the year, planting crops and returning later to harvest them. Were the little Durrington houses like beach huts, refurbished, swept out and repaired on an annual or seasonal basis? The beach hut analogy may be appropriate, as there seems to be far more evidence at this time for people living down on the south coast around what is now Bournemouth. Perhaps this was where the builders of Stonehenge and Durrington lived when not engaged in their great works.

So our builders had food and shelter and warmth from their hearths. Their clothing remains a mystery: perhaps garments made of hide during the Neolithic giving way to woven clothing as wild animals decreased and flocks of sheep grazed the downland grass. There is an unfortunate tendency to portray our prehistoric ancestors clothed in garments of rustic simplicity and to suggest that they were incapable of making proper shoes. But these were the people who built Stonehenge! Surely decent footwear would not have been beyond their capabilities?

What have been described so far are basic human needs; but prehistoric life should not be thought of as simply a struggle for survival. There must have been art, music and humour. There are rare examples of art in the form of decoratively carved chalk plaques, and the wonderfully exuberant treatment of Grooved Ware pots (if not the measured precision of Beaker decoration) suggests a love of ornament. Representations in chalk of what appear to be drums, together with occasional finds of bone flutes or whistles, can only hint at the music that may have accompanied both rituals and everyday life.

This then is as much of a general picture as we can build up of the lives of those who built Stonehenge, even though those whom we are able to study are likely to be far from ordinary people. But even among the ranks of the Bronze Age burials, where individuals come to the fore for the first time, there are three burials, excavated at and close to Stonehenge over the last 30 years, that stand out – not simply for the degree of analysis to which they have been subjected but by virtue of the stories they can tell. They are described here in the order in which they were discovered.

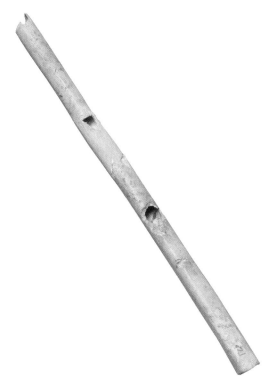

Music must have played a part in the lives of the builders of Stonehenge. This bone flute was discovered in a nearby barrow.

A decorated stone from the Irish passage grave of Newgrange. Later Neolithic decoration on stone and pottery is exuberant and flowing and may also have been applied to clothing, wooden objects and even skin.

The Stonehenge Archer, crouched in his grave in the Stonehenge ditch.

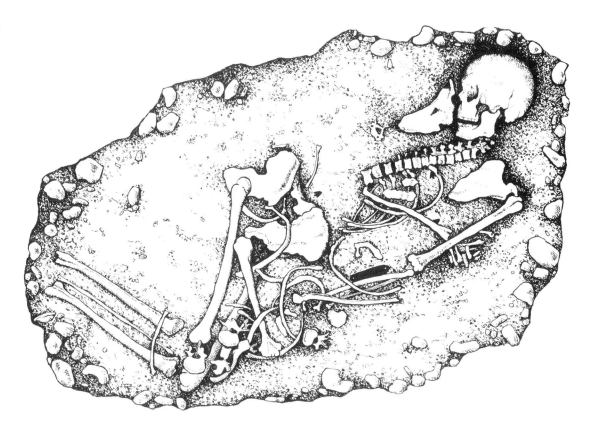

The lethal flint arrowheads, missing the tips that were found embedded in the archer's bones.

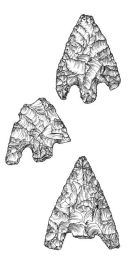

The Stonehenge Archer

In 1978 environmental specialist John Evans discovered a Beaker period burial in the ditch at Stonehenge, the crouched skeleton of a young man of about 30, buried with a stone wrist guard and three barbed-and-tanged flint arrowheads, some with their tips missing. Examination of the bones showed that the Stonehenge Archer had met a violent death, since the tips missing from some of the flint arrowheads were found embedded in his bones.

A more recent examination of the skeleton by human bone specialist Jackie McKinley showed that the archer was a strong, well-muscled man, and that his bones were starting to show the signs of hard work that we expect from this period. But the examination also threw more light on the way he had died. He may have been hit by as many as six separate arrows, three of which had hit bones and lost their tips in the process. The angle of the embedded tips, one of which was found in the back of the sternum (the breastbone) showed that at least some of the arrows had hit him from behind and that, though mortally wounded, he may have been finished off with an arrow at close range when he was lying helpless on the ground. His death was clearly not accidental.

Radiocarbon dating showed that the man was killed around 2300BC, and more recent analysis of isotopes from his teeth has shown that he was a local man, born and raised in southern England. But why had he met such a violent end, and why was he buried at Stonehenge? If he was the victim of murder it seems unlikely that he was buried by his killers as the ditch at Stonehenge would not have been an ideal place to secretly dispose of a corpse. He appears to have been buried with care, at what was at that time perhaps the most sacred place in the British Isles. So was he a sacrifice? Or did he crawl, mortally wounded, to a place which he felt could offer sanctuary?

Twenty-six years later the burial of another 'archer' was found, not at Stonehenge this time and, in terms of what he was buried with, clearly a very different sort of person.

The Amesbury Archer

In May 2002 a team from Wessex Archaeology was digging some Roman remains which lay on a housing scheme site at Amesbury, about 5km (3 miles) from Stonehenge, when they discovered an unexpected Bronze Age grave. The first hint that this was an extraordinary burial came when a gold hair ornament was discovered, and as the excavation progressed into the night the true richness of the person who was to become known as the Amesbury Archer became apparent.

The skeleton that lay within the large, probably timber-lined grave was of a man aged between 35 and 45, lying crouched, facing north and on his left side. A severe injury to his left knee meant that he would have been disabled for much of his life, walking with a limp and in constant pain. Radiocarbon dating of his bones showed that he was buried some time around 2300BC, the same time as the Stonehenge Archer, but the contrast between the contents of the two graves could not be greater. The Amesbury Archer turned out to have the richest grave ever found from the time of Stonehenge and, more importantly, from the time when metalworking was first introduced into Britain. Alongside the other grave goods – 16 finely worked barbed-and-tanged flint arrowheads, a pair of stone wrist guards that identified him as an archer, the bone pin and boar's tusks that would have held together and decorated his garments, and five Beaker pots – he had metal. There were three small knives made from copper that had come from France and Spain, and two gold ornaments thought to be for wrapping around a tress of hair – the earliest gold to be found in the British Isles. But there was also a peculiarly shaped 'cushion stone', thought to be a sort of anvil for working metal, its varying curves and edges providing a range of profiles over which to beat gold or copper. So the Amesbury Archer not only possessed some of the earliest metalwork to be found in the British Isles but there are hints that he may also have known the secrets of how to work it.

But perhaps the biggest surprise came when the results of the isotope analysis of his teeth came through, showing that he had probably come from Switzerland, or possibly Germany or Austria. Needless to say, this excited tabloid headlines on the

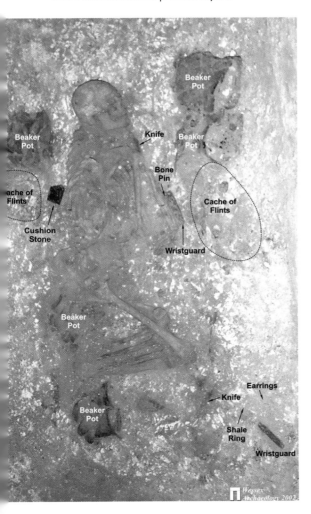

The grave of the Amesbury Archer, who was buried with a rich collection of precious objects.

The Amesbury Archer's symbols of power: a matching set of flint arrowheads, gold hair ornaments and a fine Beaker pot.

The Amesbury Archer's knives of French or Spanish copper.

lines of 'Steinhenge' (complete with stereotypical portly lederhosen-clad figure) suggesting that Stonehenge had been built by the Germans. On a more serious note, much has been made of the connection between this person, clearly someone of enormous wealth and prestige, and the construction of Stonehenge. The term 'King of Stonehenge' has been bandied around, but both the location and the dating of the burial do not support a close relationship with the building work that was going on at the time. The Amesbury Archer was buried at some distance from Stonehenge on the other side of the River Avon, which may at this time have been a symbolic boundary. And by the time he was buried, around 2300BC, the sarsen structures were either well under way or perhaps even completed. So it seems unlikely that an incomer, even one as wealthy as this, would have been able to move in on and have any major influence over such a well-established project as the building of Stonehenge. If human nature was the same in prehistory as it is today, then the establishment might well have snubbed such an ostentatious display of new wealth. Perhaps this is why he was not buried closer to Stonehenge.

The Boscombe Bowmen

A year after the discovery of the Amesbury Archer another extraordinary grave of approximately the same date was discovered during the digging of a water pipe trench at Boscombe, about 6km (4 miles) from Stonehenge. But this grave was unusual for very different reasons. It was the size that would be expected for a single person, but it contained the jumbled bones of seven individuals: three adult men, a teenage boy and three younger children. The most recognisable of the men was about 30–40 years old, buried in the crouched position that is so distinctive in burials from this period. At some time in his life he had broken his left thighbone very badly and, although it had healed, it may have been shorter and caused him to limp. The remains of three children were buried close to his head. One, perhaps no more than four years old, had been cremated, the remains of another, aged between five and six, had been disturbed while the third child, who was a little older, perhaps six or seven, was buried higher up in the grave and so had been added at a later date.

ISOTOPE ANALYSIS

The phrase 'you are what you eat' suggests that your body reflects the food that you consume, and that healthy food is necessary for a healthy body. Modern science is discovering that the phrase 'you are where you were born' can also be applied. In other words, ancient skeletons, or more specifically their teeth, can indicate the places where people lived as children.

The differing isotopes of two elements are particularly useful in these studies:

Oxygen – The isotope composition of oxygen varies with climatic zones and, as a result, water drunk by a child will provide information about the climatic environment in which that child grew up.

Strontium – This relates closely to the nature of the soil and underlying rock and can be taken up in both water and food.

These are the clues to location: by combining oxygen isotope data that indicate climatic zones with strontium isotope data that relate to geographical zones, it is possible to narrow down the place of a person's origin.

The clues can be found locked into teeth. Children's teeth go through a rapid process of growth during which they absorb information from isotopes until they mineralise, a process of hardening that happens at different ages for different teeth. Premolars mineralise between three and six years of age while the third molars, the last to erupt, mineralise much later, between the ages of nine and 13. As they mineralise, children's teeth lock in the evidence from isotopes that can show where they were living at that time. In this way each tooth is a snapshot of a particular time in that person's childhood development.

So, if a child was born in a particular area, defined by both oxygen and strontium data, and lived there until the age of seven, that information would be locked into their premolars. If they then moved at the age of 11 to an area with a very different isotopic signature, that information would be locked into their third molars when they mineralised a few years later. The evidence of that childhood movement would remain within that person's teeth for the rest of his or her life.

This is a powerful tool for answering questions about migration. Were people with pottery or metal from continental Europe the people who had brought it over with them or locals who had acquired new and fashionable goods? There are hints of the answers in the burials of the Amesbury Archer and the Boscombe Bowmen (chapter 9) but more testing is required before a definite answer can be given.

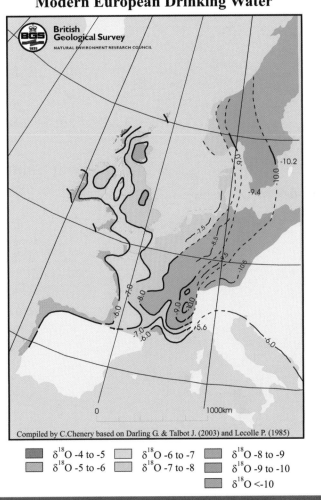

Oxygen Isotopes Values for Modern European Drinking Water

British Geological Survey
NATURAL ENVIRONMENT RESEARCH COUNCIL

-10.2
-9.4
-7.5
-8.5
-9.5
-10.5
-7.0
-8.0
-6.0
-9.0
-10.0
-7.0
-6.0
-5.6
-6.0

0   1000km

Compiled by C.Chenery based on Darling G. & Talbot J. (2003) and Lecolle P. (1985)

$\delta^{18}O$ -4 to -5 $\delta^{18}O$ -6 to -7 $\delta^{18}O$ -8 to -9
$\delta^{18}O$ -5 to -6 $\delta^{18}O$ -7 to -8 $\delta^{18}O$ -9 to -10
$\delta^{18}O$ <-10

Preparing tooth enamel samples for isotope analysis.

The strangely jumbled bones of the Boscombe Bowmen.

A Beaker pot, flint arrowheads and bone objects from the grave of the Boscombe Bowmen.

The strangest part of this whole burial was the way in which the bones of the other three individuals had been treated. These were the teenager and the other two men, who had both died aged between 25 and 30. What had been placed in the grave were not complete skeletons but selected parts, mainly substantial long bones and parts of skulls, together with a few smaller fragments. The surfaces of some of these bones appeared worn, so they must have been buried somewhere else or exposed to the elements and then stored before finally being laid to rest. The bones were arranged with some care on and around the corpse of the older man, with similar bones in clusters and the skulls laid together towards his feet.

This sort of burial, of jumbled (disarticulated) and worn bones, harks back to the deposits found in Neolithic long barrows but is strangely out of place here, in the Beaker period. Because this was a Beaker grave, containing eight Beaker pots – the highest number ever found in a single grave – together with a bone toggle, boars' tusks and the barbed-and-tanged flint arrowheads that are such a consistent feature of graves from this period.

There is the intriguing possibility that some of the people in the grave were related, as the skulls of the men and the teenager were of a similar shape and all had distinctive small bones between the separate skull plates. And, like the Amesbury Archer, oxygen and strontium isotopes suggested that they were not local and that between the ages of six and 13 they had all moved some distance from the place of their birth. Early results of the isotope work suggested that one place where they may have grown up was Wales (the source of the bluestones), which again generated predictable tabloid interest. Suddenly they were not only a 'band of brothers' but quite possibly the bluestone deliverymen. Statements appeared to the effect that 'the families of the Boscombe bowmen brought the bluestones with their own hands'. If this is the case, then the deliverymen would have had to be their grandparents several generations back, as the Welsh stones had arrived in the Stonehenge area at least 300 years before the bowmen.

More recent isotope analysis suggests that the picture is not quite so clear. The 'bowmen' definitely do not come from anywhere near Stonehenge but from an area of older rock which in Britain could mean Wales (the closest), but also Cornwall or north-west Scotland. Expand the search to the continent and their homes could have been in Brittany, Portugal or the Massif Central in France. They had certainly made a long journey, but along with their pots and weapons, did they also perhaps carry the bones of their ancestors to lie with them in their new land?

These newly discovered burials show that people from far and wide were drawn to Stonehenge, that it was a cultural and spiritual magnet, a place where new technology could be flaunted against a backdrop of ancient ideas and lasting traditions.

Stonehenge was truly an international monument, but which of these three contrasting graves contained the person who was the most closely involved with it? I would argue for the man who was found in the ditch. No outward signs of wealth and a violent death, but what a final resting place!

What is certain is that all of them, even if they were not the architects or the actual builders, would have either seen Stonehenge being built or heard tales of how it had been done. So they would have been able to answer the next big question: 'how was Stonehenge built?'

<table>
<tr><td>CHAPTER 10</td><td>How was Stonehenge built?</td></tr>
</table>

CHAPTER 10 How was Stonehenge built?

How they built Stonehenge...

No they didn't.

The sheer scale of Stonehenge, even leaving aside the distances over which the stones were transported, has led to a huge and growing fascination with the question of how it was built. The archaeology of the site provides some clues, but beyond these it has largely been experiments at varying scales that have enabled educated guesses to be made. But all experiments have their limitations. Even if one works and a stone is successfully moved or raised, this does not absolutely prove that this technique was used back in the Age of Stonehenge. All it means is that this particular method has been shown to work, and that it should therefore be allowed to join the ever-growing list of possibilities.

The previous chapter has given some idea, from the somewhat sparse evidence, of how people lived at the time of Stonehenge. But if the builders came from among these people what exactly were their self-imposed tasks? Just like any modern civil engineering project, the construction of Stonehenge can be broken down into a series of individual stages. It had to be designed, the raw materials had to be sourced and transported, the stones shaped, assembled and erected. This required architects, quantity surveyors, transport specialists, stonemasons and engineers. For a project of this scale, the labour requirements must have been huge and all those involved needed to be fed and sheltered.

Stage 1 – Design

This is perhaps the most difficult part of the whole process to grasp. Stonehenge developed in an apparently organic manner over more than 1,000 years, at the beginning of which some quite straightforward structures were built, like the ditch and bank and the circle of Aubrey Holes. But later there were elements requiring

OPPOSITE
The Sarsens of the outer circle throw long shadows in a low winter sun.

Propped up and ready to go – a potential monolith just below the summit of Carn Menyn.

considerable skills in both logistics and design. Who decided that this simple enclosure of wood and earth had to house a collection of stones brought from a distance that would have been beyond most people's imagination? Who, at a later date, came up with the idea of not only transporting even bigger stones but shaping and interlocking them into unique and complex structures? How were concepts like this explained? With drawings or models? And, perhaps a more significant question, why wasn't the 'architect' told to regain his (or her) grasp on reality?

We have no evidence for the planning that must have gone into Stonehenge yet it, and countless other structures of wood and stone throughout the British Isles, provide lasting evidence of the ability to count, survey and measure. In the 1960s Alexander Thom and his family carried out surveys of hundreds of stone circles from Brittany to Orkney, and decided on the basis of their plans that they were all built to a standard unit of measurement, the 'megalithic yard' of 82.9cm. The identification of such precision seems extraordinarily optimistic when the sites – ancient, eroded and fragmentary – are examined more closely. Attempts have been made to confirm the Thoms' observations, but they have all failed and the general consensus within the archaeological world is that the megalithic yard exists only in the modern mind.

Not having a megalithic yard does not mean that the builders of Stonehenge were unable to measure. No doubt those who went to collect the sarsens were equipped with the means to check the dimensions of their selected stones before dragging them back. But beyond a basic ability to measure, using lengths of rope or wood, how sophisticated were prehistoric surveying skills? The sarsen circle, for example, is an easy shape to lay out on the ground. All it requires is a central peg and a length of rope. But how were the positions of the 30 upright stones determined, the stones that divide the circle into precise segments each of 12 degrees? Is this evidence of sophisticated surveying skills or were the positions worked out by trial and error, by shuffling around templates that represented the footprints of the stones until the required symmetry and spacing had been achieved?

Within the sarsen circle, perhaps the most remarkable element of the whole complex stone structure, there is evidence of the ability to measure not just heights, but levels. The surviving uprights and lintels show that the builders had compensated for the north-facing slope on which Stonehenge lies to build a structure that across its diameter was level to within a few centimetres. This implies that they must have had not only an awareness of the horizontal but some form of levelling device, perhaps the long water-filled wooden trough that is still used in parts of the world today. Likewise, some form of plumb bob must have been used to ensure that stones were set vertically in their holes.

As the preceding chapter explained, we cannot find these architects, planners and surveyors among the rich burials of the Stonehenge area. The Amesbury Archer and the Boscombe Bowmen come onto the scene too late. Perhaps the bones of the original designers, the builders of the timber Stonehenge, are those that lie burnt in the ditch and the Aubrey Holes. But the builders in stone remain elusive; all we have left are their enduring achievements.

The bluestone circle and horseshoe are built of a variety of different Welsh stones.

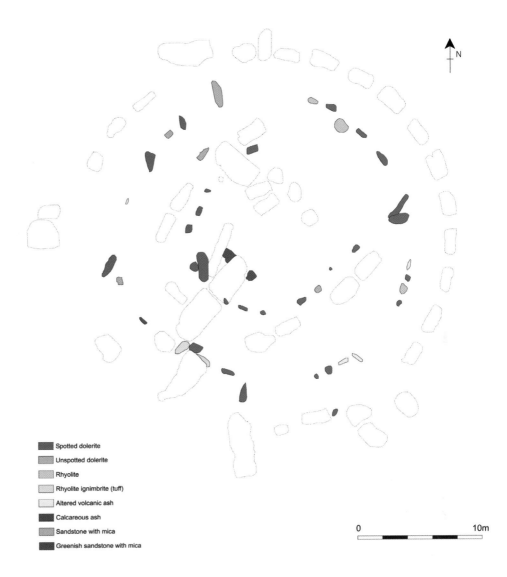

Spotted dolerite
Unspotted dolerite
Rhyolite
Rhyolite ignimbrite (tuff)
Altered volcanic ash
Calcareous ash
Sandstone with mica
Greenish sandstone with mica

0   10m

Stage 2 – Sourcing and transporting the raw materials

Of the two main types of stones used in the construction of Stonehenge, the earliest to arrive on site, and the most 'exotic', were the bluestones from Wales. There is no controversy about their geological source. In 1923 H H Thomas published an article entitled 'The source of the stones at Stonehenge' in which he demonstrated that spotted dolerite, the commonest of the bluestones (28 of the 33 that are visible at Stonehenge today), comes from the Carn Menyn area in the Preseli Mountains of west Wales. The remainder, a mixture of ryolite, volcanic ash and sandstone, also come from Wales but from sources that are more widely spaced.

Carn Menyn, the dolerite source, is a rugged hilltop of bare rock, a place of jagged pinnacles where the rock fractures naturally into convenient slabs and pillars. In this showroom for monoliths tempting stones lie everywhere; some even look as if they have been propped up and are ready for loading onto a sledge for the start of their long journey – perhaps more stones intended for Stonehenge that never made it?

The rocky outcrop of Carn Menyn in the Preseli Mountains of Wales – source of the bluestones.

So the source is certain, over 240km (150 miles) from Stonehenge. The debate is about how the stones got to Salisbury Plain: transported by people, or by ice? Each theory has its own highly articulate and convincing protagonists.

For many years Olwen Williams-Thorpe and her husband Richard, both geologists with the Open University, were the strongest supporters of the idea that the bluestones were transported to Salisbury Plain by glaciers during the last Ice Age. They argued that this could help to explain the variety of different rock types within the overall 'bluestone' category; they had all simply been scooped up by an unselective glacier and transported eastwards. Additional support for this theory was found in historic references to foreign stones littering the chalk of Salisbury Plain until cleared away in the 18th and 19th centuries. The final exhibit in their case for glacial transport was the famous Boles Barrow bluestone. This is a 300–400kg (660–880lb) block of spotted dolerite that has long been regarded as the boulder found in 1801 by William Cunnington inside a long barrow near Heytesbury on Salisbury Plain. As long barrows should comfortably predate even the earliest phase of Stonehenge, this has been taken to show that some bluestones must have been around on Salisbury Plain before the first such stones were raised at the henge.

However, there are problems with all aspects of this argument. If what was brought from Wales was not just building material but the components of an existing stone circle, then the mixed bag of bluestone types can be explained. The sole reference for the foreign stones, assumed to have included bluestones, comes from De Luc, a French geologist who visited Salisbury Plain between 1777 and 1809. However, a careful reading of his published work of 1811 reveals that the 'foreign stones' he was talking about were not on Salisbury Plain but in the Midlands. This leaves the Boles Barrow stone. Here the problem lies in the history of the stone from its recorded discovery in 1801 in the barrow to its identification as the block that now resides in Salisbury Museum and was in the grounds of Heytesbury House in 1920. That block had been there since before 1860 and was known as 'The Stonehenge Stone', which suggests that it may have come not from Boles Barrow but from Stonehenge itself. The story is complex and the documentary trail far from complete, but serious doubts as to whether these two stones are one and the same make this piece of evidence inadmissible.

Had Salisbury Plain really been littered with exotic stones it is highly unlikely that they would have gone unnoticed by keen observers like Stukeley or Colt Hoare. In the field today there seems little evidence of non-local stones of any size, and the villages that surround Stonehenge have none incorporated into any of their buildings and bridges. The final blow to the glacial transport theory was delivered by a study carried out in the 1970s that involved the examination of over 50,000 river gravel pebbles from 28 separate sites in the valleys that surround Stonehenge. The search was for 'erratics', pebbles that could have come from beyond the rivers' catchment areas. Not one was found.

Quite simply, the theory of glacial transport does not stand up to scrutiny and should be dismissed. So the stones must have been transported by people. Some archaeologists have argued against this, largely on the basis that no other stone circle in the British Isles includes stones that have been transported over a distance of more the a few miles. But this seems a rather strange argument as it is based on a denial of Stonehenge's unique character. On this basis, we should also refuse to accept the existence of the shaped and jointed stones, as they too are unique.

If the stones are accepted as having been moved by people, then the question of choice must be introduced: why bring stones all the way from Preseli when there was equally suitable building material much closer at hand? Part of the answer may lie in the contacts established between the two areas, Preseli and Wessex, at the time when there was a well-established long-distance trade in stone axes. The highly distinctive spotted dolerite appears to have been much prized at that time, and presumably grew in value and 'specialness' the further it travelled from its source. So a trade route, along which larger stones could potentially be passed, was already established and recent fieldwork in Preseli is discovering new monuments and starting to show that the source of the stones, as well as their final destination, was a place of ritual and ceremony.

Axe hammer of spotted dolerite from a Wiltshire barrow.

So rather than an expedition to bring back building materials from a deserted part of Wales, previously known only for its stone for axes, what may have happened was perhaps more akin to a cultural exchange. Hundreds of tons of bluestone pillars could not have been seized and removed without the blessing of those who occupied the area; so the stones must have been given willingly. But what exactly was the gift? Was it simply building stone or something with greater meaning – perhaps even the components of a stone circle? This would certainly help to explain the mixture of stone types as, if the stones had been selected purely on the grounds of being attractive and 'different', then they would almost certainly all have been of spotted dolerite.

Two possible routes from the Preseli Mountains to Stonehenge.

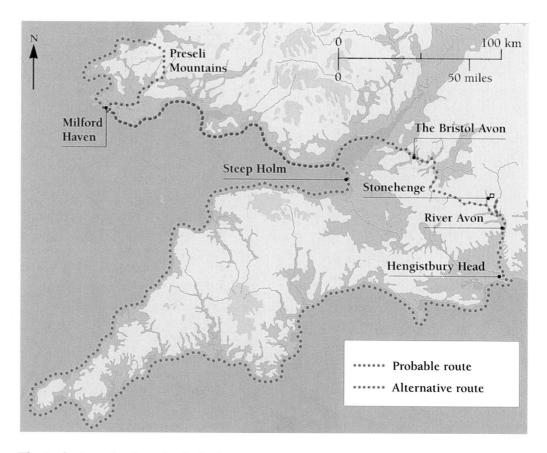

The inclusion of soft and relatively unattractive stones, such as the volcanic ash, suggests that these stones had already become special by virtue of their selection and incorporation within a sacred structure. There is also the possibility that the miniature trilithons of the 'decorated bluestone phase' stood not at Stonehenge but in Wales, perhaps supplying the inspiration for the huge sarsen examples that followed. This is pure guesswork, and could only be proved correct if a bluestone was discovered abandoned somewhere on the route from Preseli to Stonehenge and found to have been shaped rather than being just a simple unworked block.

The route taken by the bluestones has been the subject of much speculation, with alternatives that involve both land and sea. As the majority of the stones come from close to the Welsh coast, one suggestion is that they may have had only a short journey overland before being loaded onto rafts or boats and taken south round the Welsh coast to the Severn Estuary. From here on their route could have been a mixture of overland and river passage, with the neatest ending being a trip up the River Avon and a final short overland haul up the Avenue to Stonehenge. However, attractive though this idea is, the last part of the route does not fit with the known chronology as the bluestones, or at least some of them, arrived well before the Avenue was built. The alternative is for the bluestones to follow the same coastal route as far as the Bristol Channel but from there to be taken overland to Stonehenge. This is a much shorter distance and potentially far less hazardous, but would have involved far more effort.

Atkinson's experiments in the 1950s with schoolboys and punts demonstrated that bluestones were quite manageable on water, but the River Avon bears little resemblance to the wilder coastal waters that would have been encountered on the journey from Wales. However, even though we have no idea of the types of vessels available at that time, this means of transport must remain a possibility. Logistically it would seem sensible if, once loaded onto a boat or raft, the stone remained on that same vessel for the duration of the journey by water, even if the crew changed as the voyage progressed. The alternative was to go overland, although even the logical land routes would have involved some water crossing in order to avoid huge detours.

There is no immediately obvious land route. The terrain varies considerably from source to Stonehenge and this, together with local variations in vegetation, would have dictated the paths that were taken. For a land route the labour may have been organised along very different lines. Land would have been 'owned', so perhaps the stones were passed from group to group, each responsible for seeing the precious load through its own territory and safely handed on to the next in the chain. Local knowledge may have meant using different methods of transport, and changing 'vehicles' as the stone was handed over would have been a comparatively easy task. There would undoubtedly have been much less potential for disaster than moving a stone from one carrier to another on water.

Evidence of the loss of ancient skills was demonstrated by the ill-fated £100,000 Millennium Bluestone project that attempted to transport a bluestone (called 'Elvis Preseli') from its source to Stonehenge. The 17-mile trip to the estuary at Milford

Punting a replica bluestone on the River Avon – Atkinson's 1954 schoolboy experiment.

Sarsens in their natural setting on the Marlborough Downs (complete with BBC film crew).

Haven was accomplished slowly owing to a lack of the volunteers needed to drag the three-ton stone on its sledge. This ran on a plastic mat that was supposed to replicate ancient ground conditions as well as protecting the surface of the roads that it ran along. At Milford Haven the stone was slung between two replica ancient boats for the journey across the sea, but unfortunately slipped off its ropes and sank in over 16m (50ft) of water. Although the stone was eventually retrieved, additional problems with marine insurance meant that the project was abandoned and Elvis remained in Wales.

Unsurprisingly, the same arguments that are applied to the bluestones are also applied to the sarsens: that they were not transported to Stonehenge but were in the area already. And the same counter-arguments can be applied: why are there no natural sarsens of any size to be found in the villages that surround Stonehenge? There are, it has to be admitted, some sarsens in the area: in the village of Berwick St James, the 'Cuckoo Stone' close to Woodhenge and possibly some up by Robin Hood's Ball. But none of these is of any great size, and once again there is little evidence of the consistent use of sarsen as a local building material, unlike in and around Avebury (close to the source of the sarsens) where every house wall and cobbled surface is made from blocks of this hard stone.

Like the bluestones, the sarsens did not need to be quarried, but in their case merely prised out of the soil in which they lay, half buried like great beached whales. Some can still be seen in their natural setting on the Marlborough Downs, the survivors of centuries of destruction for building materials and to clear the land for farming. For the sarsens, where the requirements were for large matched stones that could be shaped to a precise specification, the selection process must have been very laborious. Stones that seemed from their upper sides to be acceptable would have had to be eased out and turned over so that every side could be inspected for

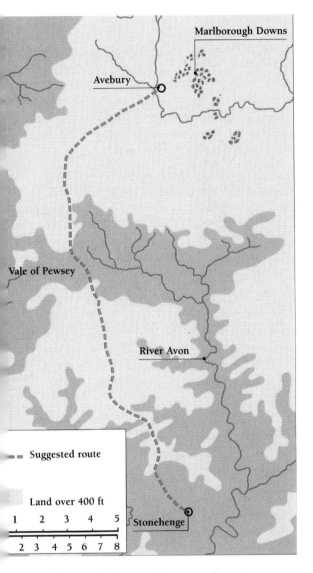

Marlborough Downs

Avebury

Vale of Pewsey

River Avon

■■ Suggested route

Land over 400 ft

1   2   3   4   5
2   3   4   5   6   7   8

Stonehenge

The most likely route of the sarsens from the Marlborough Downs to Stonehenge.

flaws or irregularities. This in itself is a huge task, as stones that ended up at a finished weight of over 40 tons must have been considerably heavier, possibly as much as 60 tons, in their raw, unshaped state.

There is an alterative. Like the bluestones in Wales, the Stonehenge sarsens could already have been extracted from their natural resting places and incorporated, in their raw unshaped state, into a stone circle (like those at Avebury). All that we need to find is the remains of a henge with at least 75 large empty stone-holes.

Defining the route taken by the sarsens is less problematic. With no water transport option it has to be close to the straightest possible line from the Avebury area to Stonehenge. This direct route drops down from the chalk that lies to the south of Avebury, before heading out across the low-lying and marshy Vale of Pewsey. It then climbs back up onto the chalk for the long home straight. It is this climb onto the gently rolling surface of the Plain that must have presented the greatest challenge to the transport teams and there has been much speculation about which is the easiest way up. The current favourite is Redhorn Hill, a steep but manageable climb, and still a considerable challenge whatever form of transport was being used.

This is where the debate becomes lively, on the subject of how you transport 40 tons or more of sarsen across undulating countryside and how many people it takes to provide the motive power. There have been decades of speculation, models have been made, theories developed and in recent years large-scale experiments have been carried out, offering some practical insights into this truly monumental task.

With almost all the suggested methods of transport that are outlined below, rope of some sort is a necessity. Hide can be used, thin strips plaited into thicker and stronger cords, but hide is a valuable commodity and also tends to have too much inbuilt elasticity. More readily available, and potentially more efficient, are vegetable fibres, including nettle, honeysuckle or the bark of trees such as lime.

But if you have some means of propelling the stone the question still remains – what do you pull it on? To suggest that the builders would simply have hauled such huge dead weights across open country without any means of reducing friction is an insult to their intelligence. So how do you reduce the friction and make the task easier?

There are ways of making the ground surface more slippery, perhaps by using chalk or clay; even ice has been suggested. Ice would undoubtedly provide a surface with the lowest friction but would be difficult to create (chalk absorbs water very quickly) and would limit the time when the work could be done to when temperatures were below freezing (difficult to guarantee). There would also be the problem of gravity. To move a stone uphill on ice would be impossible. Downhill it would become a 40-ton toboggan.

The 'traditional' method, one that is a firm favourite and shown in many reconstructions, is the use of round wooden rollers, basically tree trunks of a uniform diameter, stripped of their side branches. The stone either sits directly on the rollers or on a simple wooden sledge on top of them. Experiments with weights of up to about ten tons have shown that rollers do work but require very firm ground in order not to dig in and have a tendency to bunch up. Removing the rollers from the back and bringing them to the front is also a potentially hazardous job, especially when the stone has gained some momentum.

The largest experiment on the building of Stonehenge was carried out in 1994 as part of a BBC2 television series entitled *Secrets of Lost Empires,* in which great construction challenges from the past were re-examined by modern engineers. The author was involved in this experiment, his job to make sure that only appropriately prehistoric technology was employed. Engineer Mark Whitby was given the task of reconstructing the Great Trilithon, the largest structure at Stonehenge, using only materials that were available to the original builders. The 'stones' were not authentic; the two 40-ton uprights and the ten-ton lintel were replicated in concrete which is fortunately almost precisely the same density and weight as sarsen. Mark's chosen delivery method was to build a simple sledge, basically a large thick slab of oak which would slide on a pair of parallel squared oak rails that were set slightly into the ground a short distance apart. The sledge had a keel fixed to its underside; a long squared beam that sat between the two rails and kept the sledge running straight and true.

The idea was simple, and the carpentry well within the capabilities of Neolithic builders who would have split the oak with wooden wedges and used stone tools for the detailed work. It worked very well, but there was one unforeseen problem: getting

The 'traditional' method of moving a large stone – on wooden rollers.

Mark Whitby's method of moving a 40-ton replica sarsen used a wooden sledge running on greased rails.

it started. The sledge and rails were greased but the pressure exerted by 40 tons of concrete caused the two flat surfaces to stick together and breaking this 'stiction' took huge effort. Once freed, the keel worked well in its guide slot and the stone could be towed down, and more significantly up, a one-in-ten slope by a team of 170 volunteers hauling on four (admittedly modern) ropes. Given that the haulers included a number of tug-of-war teams, plus firemen and rugby players, the true prehistoric figure, given the smaller stature of the original builders, is likely to have been slightly over 200. This is the first real indication of the number of people it would have taken to move the largest stones – large, but nowhere near the figure of 1,100 (rising to 1,500 for the steepest parts of the route) estimated by Atkinson in 1956.

There are, however, a number of alternative methods of moving large stones. One way of avoiding the use of ropes is to 'row' the stone, a method devised by Gordon Pipes, the leading light behind a group known as the 'Stonehengineers'. Gordon's method involves the stone sitting on a simple wooden structure designed to keep it raised slightly above the ground. Wooden beams are placed close to the long sides of the stone, fulcrums on which an array of levers will pivot (this is the reason for the stone being raised, to allow the levers to be placed underneath it). With the levers all in place, downwards pressure will raise the stone and its support off the ground, and if the lifting team, keeping the pressure on the levers, all walk in the same direction, the raised stone will move a short distance in the opposite direction. The levers are removed and replaced and the process repeated, and in this way the stone slowly 'crabs' its way forwards. This method has been demonstrated to work well with a ten-ton weight but it has yet to be determined whether it would be as easy to control the levers, which would have to be both longer and more numerous, with a 40-ton stone.

The 'Stonehengineers' using long levers to 'row' a 10-ton replica stone.

An even more ingenious method, which as yet remains untested at any reasonable scale, has been promoted by at least two independent experimental engineers. The 'Bedlam roller' (a large working model made by Bruce Bedlam) and 'Michael's Roller' (a model created by Mike Slade) both involve encasing the entire stone in a circular timber casing, effectively creating a 40-ton garden roller. There seem to be several fundamental drawbacks to this method. Keeping the timber casing intact would be difficult given the stresses imposed upon it by the enormous weight of the enclosed stone. Both versions are shown lashed around with rope, but over rough terrain the ropes would soon fray and fail. But a greater problem would seem to be one of control. Across level ground a roller would not be difficult to guide or to stop. Uphill, the problem would be to prevent it running backwards and crushing the team involved in moving it. But the most terrifying prospect is what would happen on a downhill slope.

One problem with many of the experiments that have been carried out is the assumption that moving the stones involved only one method of transport. What is far more likely is that a combination of methods was used along the stones' route, differing according to the varying conditions encountered along the way. Stones may have been rowed up slopes, where steady progress rather then speed is the essence, but there is no advantage in using this method on level ground or on downslopes where rollers or sledges are far more energy efficient. There is also no way of knowing over what length of time the deliveries took place: was a dedicated team of stone movers employed full time, supported by the labours of their communities, or were stones moved on an annual basis, each one accompanied by appropriate celebrations? The requirement for at least roughly matched stones would suggest that, once earmarked, stones would have been transported as soon as

The author at 'Foamhenge' in the summer of 2005. Why isn't the Altar Stone in the right place?

possible. It would have been disastrous to reach the halfway stage in the construction of what was a coherent plan and realise that the materials needed to complete it were no longer available.

Whatever methods were used, around 80 massive sarsens were delivered – well over 1,000 tons of stone – selected for size and perhaps even roughly trimmed. They were ready for the next stage in the construction process.

Stage 3 – Shaping the stones

In 2005, as part of a television programme entitled *Stonehenge, the ultimate experiment – live,* the first full-sized replica of Stonehenge was created, nicknamed 'Foamhenge'! Its creators claimed that their involvement had given them some insight into the task faced by the prehistoric builders. But in 2005 the stones were not only transported by train and lorry, they were crafted from polystyrene foam and shaped with hot wires and industrial sanders, in the indoor comfort of an aircraft hanger in Northamptonshire. The builders of the real Stonehenge were faced with an altogether different task: how to smooth and shape their raw blocks of stone, stone that is as hard as granite, with a toolkit that consisted entirely of other stones.

Sarsen can be 'knapped' in the same way as flint, a process in which pieces are removed from the edge of the parent block by a sharp blow with another stone. But the forces involved in removing stone in this way are large and knapping is not good at creating rectangular shapes, so this could have been only the first and crudest stage in the shaping process. Beyond this, the smooth flat surfaces exhibited by many of the sarsens can only be created by pounding away with stone tools, removing the waste stone as tiny chips or powder. The tools used were smaller blocks of sarsen which, whatever shape they started out, eventually became circular through constant pounding. Many of these 'mauls', the smallest the size of an orange, the largest bigger than a football (presumably the oranges started off as footballs), have been found packing stone holes. They provide the only tangible evidence of how the stones were shaped, as the first metals that were introduced during the course of Stonehenge's construction, copper and bronze, would have been useless against sarsen. The only other aid would have been the use of fire which, when applied directly to stone such as sarsen, will cause the surface to crumble and therefore become easier to remove by hammering.

Visible on the surface of the sarsens is a range of finishes – although 4,000 years or more of weathering may have eroded whatever final finish the stones were given. Some, including the back of a fallen trilithon upright, have beautifully rippled surfaces suggesting that the first stage of the tooling was carried out by working in parallel shallow grooves, with the intention of eventually battering down the intervening ridges. Other faces have a finely 'pecked' finish, one stage short of a completely polished look. The practicality of the Stonehenge builders can be seen in these varying surface finishes. The fine finish never extends below ground, showing that they were not prepared to waste effort on something that would not be visible. Likewise, there is a

The finely rippled surface finish on an upright sarsen.

The bulge at the base of Stone 55 shows how much stone was removed to create its regular shape.

large protruding bulge at the base of Stone 55, the fallen upright of the Great Trilithon. This would also have been below ground so, as well as saving the effort of removing it, the builders left a heavy mass at the stone's base which must have initially helped to stabilise it. The bulge also provides a graphic demonstration of just how much stone had to be removed to achieve the slab-like profile of the upper part of the stone.

It has been suggested that, because the fine tooling of the stones ceases at ground level, the final finish must have been applied when the stones had been set upright. But this would have been very difficult to achieve and, whatever method or combination of methods were used, it seems almost certain that the stones were worked while they were lying flat on the ground, being turned over when one face was finished and a new one was to be started.

The effort required to shape the stones is incalculable given that there is no way of understanding their original dimensions. But even the creation of the elaborate joints that lock the stones together must have taken months, if not years, of solid labour. The mortice holes are substantial, but what is even more remarkable is the effort required in order to leave the corresponding tenons standing proud. Where stones were worked into subtle tapers and curves, like the components of the sarsen circle, wooden formers may have been used to confirm dimensions and shape. Whether or not joints fitted as they were intended may have been checked while stones still lay on the ground. Better to discover errors at this stage than when they are high in the air. There is a tantalising hint that something may have gone wrong on the fallen lintel of the Great Trilithon. On one side are finished mortice holes, great basins that would each hold gallons of water, but on the other side are two embryonic mortices, shallow hollows that hint at a mistake on the part of the stone shapers. Presumably prehistoric builders swore.

The wreckage of the Great Trilithon: Stone 56 towers over its fallen lintel.

Chipping and pounding, using a continuous supply of mauls that grew smaller, split and were discarded, the stone shapers created the 75 precise building blocks that went into the sarsen circle and trilithons. The debris from this shaping process undoubtedly contributed to the 'Stonehenge layer', a mixed bag that covers the whole of the enclosure inside the bank and contains everything from stone chips and flint tools to more modern debris, broken bottles and bullets.

So the stones, which had been dragged to site and laboriously shaped, were ready for the next stage.

Friction stakes helped the replica upright to slide into place in its stone-hole.

Stage 4 – Raising the uprights

Antler picks were again used, this time to dig the holes that would take the upright stones. The holes vary considerably in depth, for the simple reason that the stones are not of uniform length and it is much easier to dig out comparatively soft chalk than to remove excess hard stone from the base of a huge sarsen (or even a small bluestone). The holes also provide clues about how the stones were raised. Those that have been examined are consistently ramped, with one vertical side and one sloping one, down which the base of the stone was slid. Traces of small upright wooden posts on the opposite, vertical side are most likely friction stakes to assist the stone to slide against the edge of the hole and prevent too much crumbling.

Placing the stones in their holes and raising them to the vertical has always been assumed to be a fairly straightforward task that could be accomplished by means of human effort, leverage and ropes. But for the *Secrets of Lost Empires* experiment engineer Mark Whitby devised an ingenious method that, while at first seeming complex, relied on the simple principles of forces and leverage and would have been well within the capabilities of the original builders.

A sloping ramp of earth was built against the hole into which the stone was to be raised, its higher end (the end closest to the hole) terminating in a solid block. This ramp end, which was of concrete but could easily have been built of heavy timbers, was the pivot point. The stone, on its wooden sledge, was then dragged up the ramp until its end overhung the hole. A bundle of smaller 'tilting stones' was then dragged slowly up its length. When these reached the end of the stone, they tipped the balance and the stone rotated over the pivot point and dropped neatly into the hole. On the day this worked spectacularly well, and had all the elements of a great drama: the preparation, the anticipation and the expectation that something could go horribly wrong. Had this method been used by the original builders, it would surely have given a huge boost to the prestige of whoever set it up, whether engineer or priest (or both).

Mark Whitby's 'tilting stones' in action as the replica stone rose up and dropped into its prepared hole.

Surprisingly, after the unqualified success of this stage of the process which left the upright sitting at an angle of less than 20 degrees to the vertical, moving it through those last few degrees proved far more difficult. Direct leverage could not be applied so ropes attached to the top of the stone were used. Even using an A-frame (essentially a vertical lever) to multiply the force of the pullers by a factor of four, it still took over 100 men on the ropes to pull the stone to the vertical.

Other means of dropping the uprights into their holes have been suggested, but all share one common factor: the need to raise the end of the stone high above its hole and let either gravity take over or assist the tilting process by the use of small weights.

With the uprights in place, safely shored up but with their holes not finally packed with chalk and stone debris, the final stage of construction is Stonehenge's crowning glory.

Stage 5 – Placing the lintels

There are several alternative suggestions as to how this task was accomplished. Once again there is a method that, by virtue of having been illustrated in many guidebooks, has become the firm favourite. This involves the construction of a wooden platform, a simple latticework structure of overlapping timbers that gains its stability from its own mass and the weight of the stone that it carries. To start with, the lintel is placed on the ground adjacent to its uprights and levers are used to lift it, one end at a time. As each end is raised, timbers are placed beneath it before the process is repeated. So the lintel rises on a growing platform that, by incorporating longer timbers, can be tied in with the uprights to provide additional stability. As the main platform grows in height, smaller platforms are needed on either side for the teams on the levers. Once at the required height the lintel can be 'crabbed' across, again using levers, before being lowered onto its uprights. One of the advantages of this method is that it provides a comparatively stable working

The replica lintel rising steadily on its timber crib, in this case made of railway sleepers.

The scaffolding ramp (representing one made of earth) that Mark Whitby used to raise the lintel.

platform on which final adjustments to the joints could be made in comparative safety. The material requirements are simple: the timber would have been readily available and would work whether squared or left round (although this would require the ends to be notched, like the walls of a log cabin). There is also the added advantage that the timbers could be reused, with the next platform going up at the same time as the previous one was being dismantled.

The alternative suggested methods mostly involve the use of some sort of ramp up which the lintel is hauled sideways. In 1990 an experiment by the Czech Pavel Pavel demonstrated that this method works, when a five-ton lintel was dragged up sloping timbers onto a pair of 3.9m (13ft)-high uprights. Surprisingly this could be accomplished using only 10 labourers.

For *Secrets of Lost Empires* Mark Whitby chose a variation of this method, building a huge 30-degree ramp of scaffolding (not strictly available to the Neolithic builders but apparently representing an earthen ramp). Once again wooden rails were used as a guide up which the lintel, lashed to a modified wooden sledge, was hauled. At some point the lintel and sledge had to change direction from the slope of the ramp to a horizontal plane that would take them the last few feet to the top of the uprights. Mark's solution was to leave the rails sticking up in the air but to partly saw through them at the appropriate point, the idea being that the weight of the stone would cause them to break and drop to the horizontal. This worked, but provided the only truly dangerous moment of the whole experiment when the lintel, still propelled by a team who could not stop pulling in time, hurtled across the short distance to the uprights and was only stopped from crashing over the edge by the two protruding concrete tenons. This method is a possibility, but the materials and effort required to erect, consolidate and then dismantle such huge ramps of earth and chalk suggest that a simpler method would have been chosen.

There is one other intriguing method of raising a horizontal stone that has been demonstrated by an American team working with concrete blocks weighing up to 10 tons. This involves rocking the stone over a central pivot point which, if the stone is careful balanced, can be achieved with very little force. With one end of the stone raised, a thin piece of packing timber can be inserted on the raised end side of the central pivot point. That end is then lowered and a similar packing piece is inserted on the other side of the pivot point. Each time the ends of the stone are raised and lowered once, the stone will rise by the height of the inserted packing pieces. It is a slow process but requires very little force (and consequently very few people) to raise a large weight. The only real problem would be maintaining stability with a 10-ton lintel poised at a height of over 6m (20ft) above the ground. There is also the problem of then moving it sideways onto its uprights.

But even with the stones standing and the lintels in place, there was still work to be done.

Stage 6 – Decoration

As has been described, representations of many axes and at least one dagger were pecked into the sarsen uprights, presumably using smaller versions of the 'mauls' used to carry out the shaping and fashion the joints. What survive are the outlines but these may originally have been picked out in natural colours, chalk white, browns and reds from earth pigments. The decoration was almost certainly carried out after the stones were in place, not simply because the shapes suggest a date well after the stones were raised, but because they are all low down on the stones, at a height that could have been reached by someone standing on the ground.

The effort required

Exactly how much effort was required to build Stonehenge? There are some elements of the overall project for which this cannot be calculated. Without a clear idea of routes, the labour requirements for moving the bluestones is a mystery. Without knowing how much stone was removed, the same problem arises for the shaping of the sarsens. And how much time was invested in the infrastructure required for each stage of the construction, the long-vanished timbers and trackways?

However, recent experiments suggest that the sarsens would have taken around 100,000 days of labour to move, or 500 days with the optimum sized team of 200. In other words, with full-time working they could have been brought to Stonehenge within two years or, if transportation was part-time, possibly seasonal, comfortably within a decade. The uprights are estimated to have taken around 18,000 days of labour (150 people working for 120 days) and the lintels a further 2,900 days (145 days for a team of 20). So, given a tremendous concentration of effort, the sarsen structures at Stonehenge could have been built within a period of three years. The chronology, however, suggests otherwise.

The replica uprights in position ready to receive their lintel.

Fascination with the question of how Stonehenge was built will undoubtedly continue. New methods of moving, shaping and erecting the stones will be devised and, with luck, tested, perhaps even on the original concrete 'stones' made for the BBC experiment which are still, at the time of writing, available for use by anyone with the capability of moving them from their resting place on the Salisbury Plain Military Training Area.

Those involved with the *Secrets of Lost Empires* experiment were concerned that showing how Stonehenge might have been built would somehow demystify the process and make Stonehenge seem less special, less of an achievement. We should not have worried. The experiment made us more aware than ever of the problems and the dangers faced by the original builders and we were left with an increased sense of wonder that so much had been achieved by our ancient ancestors.

So, while we may have gone some way to answering the question of how Stonehenge was built, the remaining question – and perhaps the one that is the most difficult to answer – is why?

CHAPTER 11   **Why was Stonehenge built?**

When the late Richard Atkinson was asked questions about Stonehenge that began with the word 'why' his response was blunt:

> ... there is one short, simple and perfectly correct answer: We do not know.

On that basis this chapter should stop right now. But despite Atkinson's pessimistic outlook it still seems worth trying to find some answers to this, the most challenging of the big questions about Stonehenge. Tackling it involves going beyond the hard evidence of archaeological fact and scientific analysis and attempting to understand the minds of the people who built Stonehenge – their hopes, fears and motivations. But this is difficult, if not impossible. Did they share our concepts of past, present and future, or right and left, sacred and profane? Did they associate light and dark with good and evil? What place did they think they occupied in the material world? What meanings did they give to the elements that made up their daily lives: earth and sky, water, wood and stone?

Stonehenge – early morning, December 2003.

It is always difficult to interpret remains from the ancient past, before written history. Some places appear to have had an obvious function, a hill-top fortification, for example, or a mound that contains a burial. But even such obvious structures may have hidden meanings: perhaps the 'fort' was more about enhancing the social status and prestige of the people who had it built than about defence. Perhaps the 'burial mound' was not simply somewhere to place a dead body but a way of marking out territory, a pre-literate title deed laying claim to a piece of land. Archaeology can provide us with artefacts, dates and structures, it can hint at how things were made, traded and used; but it can only give us glimpses, through these places and objects, into the prehistoric mind. So trying to work out the purpose (or purposes) behind the building of a structure as long-lived and complex as Stonehenge is a real problem.

This has not deterred generations of antiquarians, archaeologists, scientists from other disciplines, interested amateurs and, to be frank, lots of crackpots from coming up with theories about the purpose of Stonehenge that are more or less plausible. Even amongst the ranks of archaeologists ideas vary hugely, with the same piece of physical evidence being used at times in support of two (or more) widely differing theories. Much of the more serious archaeological discussion is bound up in terminology so deliberately arcane as to be unintelligible to those outside this select circle (and quite possibly some who are within it). So this chapter will attempt to take some of these ideas, strip them of their jargon and subject them to some hard questioning.

Let us begin with Stonehenge itself and then move on to its place within the landscape. It is easy to start with things that Stonehenge is clearly not, such as defensive. Its small ditch and bank, even if they are the right way round to offer protection, would never have kept anyone out, except in a symbolic way, just as today's rope barriers do. We could cross them but we don't because we know that we shouldn't. Nor does it look as if anyone lived there although, at the time when our ancient ancestors were thought to live in 'pit dwellings' (a convenient explanation for all the rubbish pits that litter prehistoric settlement sites), there were suggestions that the small amounts of debris found in the Stonehenge ditch were evidence that it was occupied. But this was a short-lived theory and even those who in more recent times have suggested that the stones were there simply to hold up the roof timbers of an enormous circular building acknowledge that this would have been no ordinary house.

Excavation has clearly shown that Stonehenge went through a brief stage as a place of burial, when cremated human bones were placed in the upper levels of the Aubrey Holes and in the ditch and bank. But this seems to have been a comparatively short-lived phase and was clearly not its prime function.

So where does this leave us? Perhaps not with any one defined function, as Stonehenge was built and used over a period of 1,400 years, during which time its meaning and use may well have changed just as the landscape, the economy and people's lives may also have changed. But throughout this long period, Stonehenge

Two works of art – one ephemeral, one enduring. Crop circle south of Stonehenge, 7th July 1996.

is consistently devoid of any obvious practical function and, in requiring enormous effort and resources to build if not to maintain, falls neatly into the category, beloved by archaeologists, of 'ritual' or 'ceremonial'. A visitor from another planet might interpret the golf courses that now litter the British countryside in very much the same way. Cynics suggest that these terms simply cover up archaeologists' total inability to make any sensible suggestions about the purpose of many prehistoric sites. They may be right. So, 'ritual' or ceremonial' are to us the very antithesis of functional, but perhaps sites that fall into these categories were entirely functional to the people who built them, as essential a part of everyday life as buildings that provided shelter.

The idea that Stonehenge was some sort of temple was not new even when championed by William Stukeley in the early 18th century. Unfortunately, by relying on classical writers he managed to get the builders and the priests entirely wrong. But in 18th-century academic society, where the past was measured on a

First light. Stonehenge, midsummer 2004.

biblical timescale and where ancient sites like Stonehenge tended to be interpreted from a position of faith, the idea stuck. Stonehenge was a temple but to which gods? By the early years of the 19th century enough ancient sites had been excavated to show that, unlike in the Roman era, the age of Stonehenge was not one of idols and recognisable gods. So who, or what, was being worshipped?

It became apparent that the answer must lie in the heavens. From the beginning of Phase 3 Stonehenge has an axis, an imaginary line that, once the central stone structure is complete, runs from between the two uprights of the Great Trilithon, through the open end of the two horseshoe structures and out through the slightly wider gap between uprights 1 and 30 of the sarsen circle. Project this line further and it skirts the Slaughter Stone, passes close to one side of the Heel Stone and heads off down the line of the Avenue. Stukeley realised the importance of this axis and saw that, facing north-east from the centre of the stones, it corresponded with the point on the horizon where the sun rose at midsummer day, the longest day of the year. He also observed that, looking out from the centre of Stonehenge with your back against the Great Trilithon, the sun did not first rise precisely over the Heel Stone but slightly to the left of it. This, though, was a minor detail and was explained when the pair to the Heel Stone was discovered in 1979. Stonehenge became widely accepted as an ancient temple to the sun, and took the first steps on the road to becoming, in the minds of some, a prehistoric observatory.

It is difficult to grasp how different from ours the world of the Stonehenge builders must have been. On the whole we are insulated from the natural world. It produces our food but we are largely unaware of (or perhaps do not want to know about) the processes of production. We register the changing seasons but our houses, work places and cars, heated or air conditioned at whim, mean that their variations have

The annual cycles of the sun and moon (after Ruggles).

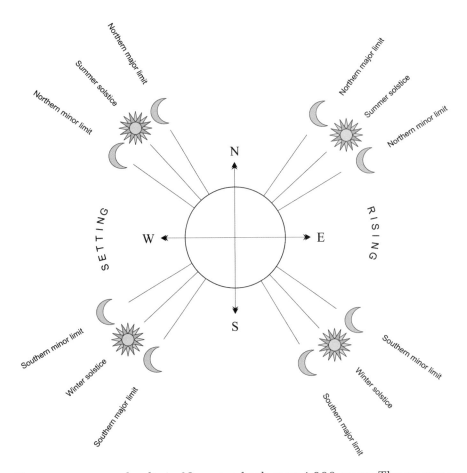

little effect on our everyday lives. Now step back over 4,000 years. The seasons would have meant extremes of heat and cold. Throughout the year food would have gone from being abundant at times to extremely scarce at others; feast or famine in their truest sense. In a world devoid of artificial light, except for firelight and the lamps and candles that we assume must have been used, there would have been a much greater awareness of natural illumination, from the sun and from the moon. Today, when most of us live in areas swamped by light pollution it is difficult to appreciate just how bright moonlight can be. But when this was all that you had there must have been a great awareness of cycles of change, of the way in which these two vital sources of light moved around the sky. A careful and patient observer would have been able to chart these regular cycles.

The sun follows an annual cycle of around 365 days with sunrise/sunset being at their most northerly points at the time of the longest day of the year, the summer solstice, around 21st June in our modern calendar. Conversely, these events are at their most southerly points on the shortest day, half a year away at the winter solstice on 21st December. In between these extremes come the vernal (spring) equinox around 21st March and the autumnal equinox around 21st September. Using the modern concepts of north, south, east and west, what can be observed throughout the annual solar cycle is as follows. At the time of the autumn equinox the sun rises almost due east and crosses directly overhead before setting in the west.

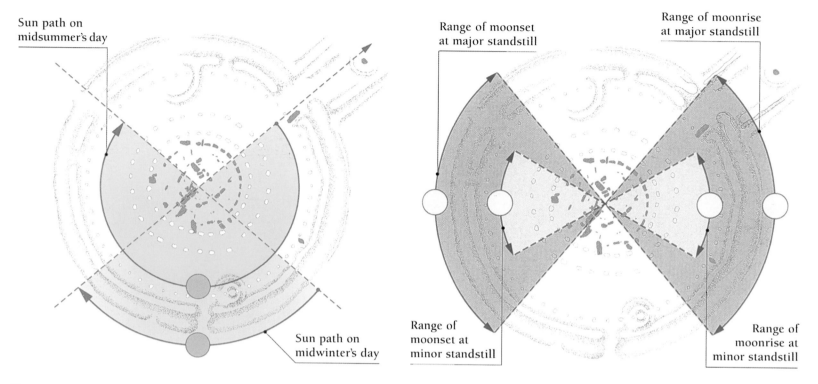

Sun path on midsummer's day

Range of moonset at major standstill

Range of moonrise at major standstill

Sun path on midwinter's day

Range of moonset at minor standstill

Range of moonrise at minor standstill

The movements of the sun and moon in relation to the layout of Stonehenge.

At this time day and night are of almost equal length. Throughout October and November, with each shortening day, the sun rises and sets further south until the most southerly limits are reached at about the time of the winter solstice. Around this time, for a few days, the positions on the horizon of both sunrise and sunset hardly seem to move. Then they set off north again, passing the point of the spring equinox where they are once again almost precisely east–west before arriving at their most northerly points around 21st June. Here, around the time of the longest day, the sun again stands still for a few days, rising and setting at almost the same points, before heading south again towards the autumnal equinox and the completion of yet another annual cycle.

The movement around the horizon of the points at which the sun rises and sets is fairly rapid and plotting these points and their northern and southern extremities would have been comparatively simple. The observation of a very few of these annual cycles would have revealed the consistent position of the sun at the times of greatest darkness and greatest light. What would have been too small to be observed and recorded at this time is the minute change each year in the position of these extreme points. This movement, of one-seventieth of a degree over the course of a century (or less than two-thirds of a degree since construction started at Stonehenge) is caused by slight variations in the tilt of the earth's axis. In the late 19th century both Flinders Petrie (the man responsible for numbering the stones) and the astronomer Sir Norman Lockyer attempted to use this slight change to define a construction date for Stonehenge by astronomical means. Petrie arrived at a date of AD730, which pleased him as it confirmed his theory that Stonehenge was a royal burial ground dating to the time after the end of the Roman occupation.

Lockyer, prepared to accept any alignment that fitted his theories and to change them if something better turned up, decided that Stonehenge had been built around 1680BC. This was not a bad guess for its time but this is effectively what it was – a guess 'supported' by a totally uncritical use of astronomical data.

The other great heavenly body, the moon, follows a much more rapid cycle of movement in which moonrise and moonset move from their northernmost to southernmost limits and back again in the course of only a month. But unlike the sun, the movements of the moon have a further cycle. Take, for example, the point on the horizon where the moon rises. The most northerly point at which this can be observed is called the northern moonrise major standstill. The point of rising will then move southwards until it reaches another limit, known as the minor standstill. The same thing happens with the opposite points at which the moon sets and here too are a major and a minor standstill. The complete cycle performed by these movements, going from major standstill to minor and back again to major, takes 18.6 years to complete. Once identified, this cycle would have had to be observed and recorded several times before it could be fully understood. This would probably not have been feasible within the much shorter lifetime of an individual at the time of Stonehenge.

The march of the Druids, 1958.

Stone 56, the tallest of the sarsens, silhouetted against a dramatic midwinter sunset.

If the builders of Stonehenge had observed and recorded these phenomena, then they would have realised that on each side of a north–south line there were six important directions, two for the sun and four for the moon. The vernal and autumnal equinoxes add a possible seventh. But the question is, did they really observe these directions and, if so, are they actually embodied within the geometry of Stonehenge and the layout of its surrounding landscape?

A fundamental problem is defining a precise geometry for Stonehenge as it now is. There are, within the structure itself, an almost infinite number of potential alignment points. There are the stones themselves, both inner and outer, each of which can furnish a number of points from their various sides and corners. In seeking proof for the use of his 'megalithic yard' Alexander Thom invested the layout of the stones with an overstated precision that reappears in the search for alignments. Many of the stones have been replaced or reset; and there is the question of ground level at the time that they were raised, which was higher than it is today owing to the surface of the chalk dissolving over the millennia, a difference that affects the overall ground plan. Quite simply, it is difficult to find credible precision in the eroded and restored stones of Stonehenge.

Then there are the elements of the earthworks, the ditches and banks and finally, as a result of all the 20th-century excavations, the now invisible holes that held timbers, vanished stones or, in some cases, nothing at all. But how, in seeking alignments, are these elements to be used? The published plans show the eroded edges of holes that would have been smaller and better defined when first dug, of which some would have held posts; but should a central point be used, or one side or another? Looking out from Stonehenge, the immediate landscape offers a tempting array of potential alignment points, mainly in the barrows that lie on every surrounding ridge top. But beyond these are long-distance sight lines too, to far horizons, each with their own distinctive natural character and many again capped with barrows and other earthworks.

So given the range of potential alignments and the vast array of possible points from which to construct them, is there any correlation? And if so, can this be proved to be deliberate or is it simply a matter of chance?

Sir Norman Lockyer found lots of alignments, proving in the process that you could indeed find any alignment you wanted if you were sufficiently uncritical with your selection of alignment points. But his work also had the effect of convincing many archaeologists that all Stonehenge astronomy was bunkum. Even in the face of such professional opposition, however, the association of Stonehenge with the solstice survived, cemented throughout the 20th century by the regular rituals conducted by various bands of Druids at both the summer and winter solstices. To many people Stonehenge, with its convincing solar associations, became an ancient observatory with astronomical alignments built into its solid structure. And in the decades that immediately followed the Second World War, radical changes in society meant radical changes in the way that Stonehenge was viewed. Society was becoming increasingly secular, with economics and science replacing religion. The 1960s were a time of great technological advance with the advent of computers which were both novel and exciting, a force for future good capable of solving baffling mathematical problems – perhaps even the question of why Stonehenge had been built. To American astronomer Gerald S Hawkins Stonehenge was the Neolithic equivalent of the futuristic machine he used to plot the movement of the stars. In the layout of its earthworks and stones and their alignments with features in the surrounding landscape he saw evidence that it had been designed as a sophisticated computer, the heart of an observatory to monitor the movements of the sun, the moon and the stars. These theories appeared in print in 1965, in the ambitiously titled and controversial *Stonehenge Decoded*. Here was the proof: the old computer of Stonehenge checked out by his new machine.

Hawkins checked the position of 165 points within and around Stonehenge and created a series of alignments. These he checked against the rising and setting points of a wide range of celestial bodies – planets and bright stars, the sun and the moon – calculating where they had been in 1500BC. The planets and stars did not work, but the sun's movements fitted perfectly with alignments he had identified and there was an almost total correlation with those of the moon. All of this, and a theory that the 56 Aubrey Holes were an eclipse predictor, convinced Hawkins that these alignments could not have occurred by chance – proof not only of the skills of the Stonehenge surveyors and builders but of an overall purpose for the great construction.

So Stonehenge was a giant observatory. There was something appealing about an answer to the great question of why Stonehenge was built, and it seemed fitting that the answer should have been provided by a computer, the modern electronic descendant of the ancient ancestral machine that stood on Salisbury Plain. Like Stukeley's Druids, Hawkins' ideas expressed in *Stonehenge Decoded* became both popular and widely accepted. The archaeological establishment, however, continued to have its doubts; Atkinson made his scepticism public fairly rapidly in an article published in *Antiquity* entitled 'Moonshine on Stonehenge'. And there is the question of definition: just what do we mean by astronomy? In the modern sense it is the process of observing the sky, just one facet of Western analytical science. But why should astronomy have interested the builders of Stonehenge? Perhaps because what they were interested in was not the observations themselves but the meanings that they embodied. What they may have been looking for was a way of making sense of events on earth by linking them with observable astronomical events. More astrology than astronomy.

So what is the truth – if such a thing can be said to exist when we try to look back through the mists of prehistory?

The voice of reason in what can become at times a debate not about evidence but about belief – if you want to believe that Stonehenge is a complex observatory then that is what you will believe – is Professor Clive Ruggles of Leicester University. His opinion is that the ideas of Gerald Hawkins and others of a similar inclination simply do not stand up to detailed reassessment. There appears to be no convincing

Celebrating the summer solstice in 2001.

evidence that, at any time during its long period of construction, Stonehenge deliberately incorporated a great many precise astronomical alignments, or that its layout served as any sort of eclipse predictor. In his own words: '...there is no reason whatever to suppose that at any stage the site functioned as an astronomical observatory – at least in any sense that would be meaningful to a modern astronomer'.

So does Stonehenge really incorporate any of the alignments representing the movement of the sun and moon that have already been described? Clive Ruggles thinks that some of them can be dismissed as irrelevant, including the whole concept of equinox. He is firmly of the opinion that this is a modern idea, not significant or of any interest to the ancient observers and identifiable only by dividing either the physical distance (between the sun's two extreme points) or time (in days) between the two solstice events.

Likewise, as far as the movements of the moon are concerned, he feels that the lunar standstills are also ideas that exist within the framework of modern scientific thinking and are unlikely to have had any meaning at the time of Stonehenge. Moreover, the southern limit of the moon is, in his opinion, of little importance as it occurs close to midsummer when the light of the moon makes virtually no difference to the overall brightness of a short summer night. Interestingly, the northern limit is a very different matter as this happens in midwinter when the presence or absence of a full or near full moon can mean the difference between a very long dark night and one that has at least some comforting illumination.

However, despite all this scepticism some links between the layout of Stonehenge and those alignments that have survived Clive Ruggles' critical eye can still be seen.

This is not, however, the case with Stonehenge 1, whose position within the landscape does not seem to be influenced by any astronomical considerations and where little can be read into the orientations of its two entrances. In contrast to what happens later, the view from the centre of this first simple earthwork enclosure actually shuts out the midsummer sun.

Moving on to Stonehenge 2, the timber phase, a persistent idea first suggested in 1966 by Peter Newnham, an amateur astronomer, is that the entrance postholes were used to mark moonrises over a number of the 18.6 year cycles (at least 112 years) in order to establish a precise direction for the northern lunar limit. There are some problems with this idea. It is unlikely that posts of this size would have stood for that length of time and, in addition, some of the arguments put forward in its support depend on the postholes being earlier than the enclosure (which is now considered highly unlikely). So while there is still the possibility that these uprights did mark lunar observations, their precision cannot have been as great as has been previously suggested.

The idea has also been put forward, by both Rodney Castledden and Aubrey Burl, that the distribution of artefacts of bone, stone, pottery and antler within the ditch, bank and Aubrey Holes reflects astronomical symbolism. To Burl, offerings of cremated bone mark the transition from lunar to solar worship. Despite the restrictions placed upon this interpretation by the absence of any information from the unexcavated half of the site, this is an interesting idea especially in the light of what happens next at Stonehenge.

In contrast to Stonehenge 1 and 2, where there seems to be little firm evidence for intentional lunar orientation, the evidence for a solar solstice alignment within Stonehenge 3 is strong. The slight realignment of the enclosure entrance and the raising of the first bluestone structure possibly with the Altar Stone in a focal position create an axis that, with a declination of +24 degrees to the north-east and −24 degrees to the south-west, appears to deliberately mark the line of the midsummer sunrise and midwinter sunset. The rectangle marked out by the four Station Stones also appears to have some significance, aligned in one direction with the new Phase 3i axis but in the other direction (declination +/- 29 degrees) fitting with major moon rising and setting events in summer and winter. Is this simply a coincidence or did Stonehenge now embrace both solar and lunar symbolism?

From this point onwards all subsequent additions and modifications follow this new axis. Through the open ends of the two horseshoes of sarsen and bluestone and the wider gap between Stones 1 and 30 of the sarsen circle, the line heads off to the Slaughter Stone and its companions, passes between the Heel Stone and its recently discovered pair and continues down the Avenue. This 'solar corridor', as it has been described, works in two diametrically opposing directions. On a flaming midsummer dawn the golden orb of the rising sun, once it has broken free of the horizon, sends shafts of light down this corridor into the very heart of the stones. Its rays penetrate the horseshoes of bluestone and sarsen and creep on until they light up the Altar Stone that lies at the foot of the Great Trilithon.

The dying sun at the turn of the year: sunset at the winter solstice.

Six months later, at midwinter, the setting sun plunges to earth over the Altar Stone and down the narrow gap between the uprights of the Great Trilithon. Sunset at this time of the year can be rapid, and at times today a blood-red winter sun appears to pulse like a giant beating heart as it slides down the side of the one remaining upright of the Great Trilithon. Both of these events are spectacular and very special – the summer sun at its most powerful bringing life and warmth and the winter sun at its most vulnerable, enfeebled, barely able to melt the frosts – perhaps even dying?

This alignment is not unique to Stonehenge. Within the surrounding landscape the entrances of both Woodhenge and Coneybury Henge also face north-east, the latter slightly adjusted to take account of a different horizon. There are also solar alignments at Durrington Walls, but here reversed, the southern circle looking precisely towards the midwinter sunrise and the newly discovered avenue leading into the henge roughly in the direction of the midsummer sunset.

Further afield, at the great passage grave of Newgrange in Ireland, the huge mound covers a long passageway leading into a central burial chamber. Above the passageway is a 'light box', a carefully constructed peep-hole that allows the first rays of the sun at midwinter dawn to illuminate the central chamber. It is an extraordinary sight to witness the finger of light moving along the floor of the passage, creeping towards its final goal. This is quite deliberate: there is no ambiguity at New Grange and it only functions in this way at midwinter.

The same is true at Maeshowe, a Neolithic chambered cairn on Orkney, where the setting midwinter sun briefly illuminates the passageway that leads into the mound and the back wall of the central chamber.

View from Newgrange of a midwinter dawn in the Boyne Valley.

At dawn on the winter solstice the rays of the rising sun send a shaft of light into the central chamber at Newgrange.

On the basis of the evidence outlined above it does not seem unreasonable to suggest that Stonehenge, in incorporating solar solstice alignments, may be regarded as at least a giant calendar marking the changing seasons, even if not an observatory. But a further question remains: Stonehenge functions in this way at both midwinter and midsummer, so was it built for both these events or just one? Today it is far more tempting to gather and celebrate towards the end of June when the nights are long and comparatively warm; but would midsummer have meant anything to the original builders? It is not a particularly significant time in the agricultural calendar – far too early in the year, before summer appears even to have started, to contemplate shortening days and an impending winter. Surely midwinter would have been a time of far greater significance to people who were investing more and more of their efforts in a sedentary agricultural way of life? The autumn saw shortening days, dwindling stocks of stored food, the onset of cold, dark and perhaps anxiety. Would the dying sun be reborn to provide the light and warmth that would mean that crops would grow and animals thrive? Or would it fade away and leave a world of perpetual darkness and death? Perhaps this was why Stonehenge was built: to mark this time of change, the turning of the year when the sun stood still for a few heart-stopping days and then, if all was well, moved on and guaranteed another year of life.

Professor Timothy Darvill of Bournemouth University who, along with Geoff Wainwright, has been conducting fieldwork around the source of the bluestones in the Preseli Mountains, has another suggestion as to why Stonehenge should be seen as a life giver. In Preseli there is said to be an association between sacred springs, the waters of which are reputed to possess healing qualities, and the rocks that surround them. Professor Darvill suggests that the bluestones themselves may have been thought to have healing powers and that this may explain why they were brought to Stonehenge. Maybe this is the origin of the medieval myths and legends concerning the magical power of the stones and why for so long people collected fragments of them as talismans. Perhaps Stonehenge became a place of pilgrimage, the Lourdes of ancient Wessex, although there are far too few skeletons available for study to support the suggestion that the surrounding barrows are full of the bones of the infirm or disabled.

So perhaps Stonehenge really was a temple and this term, with all its overtones of specific gods or votive objects, is still the most appropriate way to explain why so much effort was expended to build something so truly monumental. If Stukeley was right, then should we regard Stonehenge as the prehistoric equivalent of the huge cathedral that still dominates the town of Salisbury a few miles to the south? Here our understanding of the Christian faith and of the social and economic structure of medieval society means that we can accept a building that provides such a contrast to the domestic structures of wood and thatch that clustered at a respectful distance from its walls. Here, in a town created for economy and function, are elements of 'sacred geography', the same forces that were at work in the landscape surrounding Stonehenge thousands of years earlier. Within this landscape barrows and other ritual sites may have been laid out according to principles of cosmology,

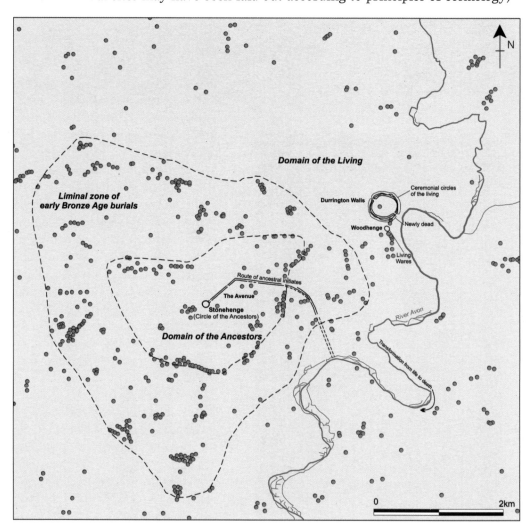

Mike Parker Pearson suggests that the Stonehenge landscape can be divided onto zones: for the living, for the dead and for those on the journey between these two states.

228

Frosty cobwebs festoon the Heel Stone – January 2007.

a broader view that included not just the immediate world of earth and stone but the less tangible one of sun, moon and stars.

Suggesting that a landscape may have been laid out according to such principles does not necessarily mean that it should be regarded as a purely 'ritual landscape'. This implies a landscape that is devoid of everyday activity, of the places where people lived and went about their daily business. This is certainly not the case in the vicinity of Stonehenge where, despite the huge number of monuments concerned with ceremony and burial, there are also traces of industry and settlement, albeit in a very fragmentary state. And why should these two facets of prehistoric life be mutually exclusive? Ritual would almost certainly have been woven into the fabric of everyday life, into the way people interacted, the use of different types of pottery and tools, the foods that were permissible to eat. So living within a landscape populated by the ancestors would have seemed quite normal. This is not to say there may not have been some exclusions within this landscape; zones close to Stonehenge itself where taboos operated, perhaps the zone between the stones and the barrows that ring them on the immediate horizon.

There have been many recent attempts to explain the Stonehenge landscape, some based on spreads of surface finds, some on the analysis of barrow contents, yet more on recreations of the ancient topography of the area devoid of modern clutter. 'Viewsheds' (the envelopes of visibility from certain monuments or locations) have been examined and the landscape viewed as something to be experienced. But what all these many and varied studies have in common is that they are all in some way trying to guess what the people who built Stonehenge and laid out this landscape were thinking when they did it. And this is not easy.

A new and thought-provoking view of the Stonehenge landscape has recently been proposed by archaeologist Mike Parker Pearson of Sheffield University and his Madagascan colleague, Ramilisonina. Under the title 'Stonehenge for the Ancestors: the stones pass on the message' they use a formal analogy between contemporary Madagascan society and that of Neolithic Britain, both of which erect standing stones. In the former, standing stones, 'vatolahy' ('man stones'), are associated with the dead, their very hardness symbolising the process of human ageing that culminates in death – the ultimate hardening. So when this scheme is extended to the monuments around Stonehenge, those of wood, such as Woodhenge and the circles within Durrington Walls, become the ceremonial circles of the living while Stonehenge, of cold stone, must therefore be the circle of the ancestors. By extension the area that immediately surrounds Stonehenge itself, bounded by the barrow groups that lie on the immediate horizon, becomes the domain of the ancestors. This is separated from the domain of the living (the Durrington area) by a spiritual no-go area that acts as a buffer between the living and the dead. But even given this division of the landscape, links between the dead and the living are suggested. The newly dead (in the domain of the living) make the first part of their journey from life to death down the River Avon. At the point downstream where the river meets the Avenue they move to dry land along what is described as the route of ancestral initiates until they reach the heart of the domain of the dead.

Dawn on the River Avon – January 2007.

An interesting view, and one that sees Stonehenge not as a living temple, celebrating renewal through the cycles of the sun's movements, but as a place of death visited by few after its construction and certainly not a place of celebration. That was reserved for the circles of the living, where the evidence of pig bones in great quantities suggests midwinter feasting.

But there are dangers in making such direct comparisons, as the two authors admit: modern Madagascar is not Neolithic Wessex and their descriptions of the moment at which the meaning of Stonehenge was suddenly apparent are as worrying as Hawkins' 'discovery' that Stonehenge was a computer. Where, for example, are all the dead that made that journey from the land of the living? The only Neolithic or Bronze Age dead at Stonehenge (if you discount the arrow-riddled body in the ditch) are those whose cremated remains lie in the ditch and Aubrey Holes, before the Avenue was constructed. Why is there evidence of settlement within the Domain of the Ancestors (on the King Barrow Ridge) and why, just because Stonehenge does not have the quantities of feasting debris that Durrington has, could it still not have been a living temple, a place of celebration not death?

The analogy with Salisbury Cathedral has already been made. Perhaps this can be extended. In the same way that Christmas was and still is celebrated at the cathedral followed traditionally by feasting at home with family and friends, so perhaps a feast of roast pork in the houses of the living was the traditional way to follow a midwinter visit to Stonehenge. It may well even have involved a cleansing in the river at the point where the Avenue meets it, a very spiritual experience in the dead of winter.

Perhaps at some time in the future science will create a time machine. At that moment all archaeologists would be instantly redundant. But if I am still around at that time I would like to make one trip, to Stonehenge at midwinter in 2000BC. I hope that I would find lots of people there: I would be very disappointed if I did not. But until that hypothetical time, the real answer to the question of 'why' is the one that was given by Richard Atkinson at the start of this chapter – 'we do not know'. But this will not stop us carrying on guessing.

CHAPTER 12 Stonehenge – the story so far

The previous chapters have described the physical structure of Stonehenge, placed it in its landscape and in its wider context, outlined the history of its discovery and investigation over the centuries and have finally attempted to answer the questions of how it was built, who built it and why.

What follows is a narrative, a story that combines facts and theory to offer a personal view of the Age of Stonehenge. It is an attempt to bring to life this remote past and its people, using the hard evidence that we have uncovered about Stonehenge and the landscape around it but without straying into unreasonable speculation or whimsy. I have allowed myself a personal view – poetic licence perhaps – in one or two places; but nothing suggested here is based on anything other than fact or allowable possibility.

In describing the landscape historic names associated with monuments will be used, together with modern concepts of direction and time.

Prelude c 7000BC

The story of Stonehenge begins long before the ditch was dug and the stones arrived, three and a half thousand years earlier during the Mesolithic or Middle Stone Age period. This was the time when Britain had only just become an island, separated from the mainland of Europe by the rising seas that were a result of the final melting of the glacial ice. The land that we now call Salisbury Plain was covered in open hazel and pine woodland, dotted with clearings of rough savannah grassland, and the valleys were filled with willow and reeds. Within this landscape scattered bands of people lived as part of nature, hunting and gathering wild foods, always moving, their shelters and their stone tools as light as they could make them.

For some reason which we cannot pretend to understand, a band of these people did something that was quite out of character. Within what may already have been a large clearing in the woodland they used their sharp-edged flint axes to cut down full-grown pine trees, at least four of them, which they set upright in holes dug into the chalk. The posts were probably not very tall, given that the holes in which they were placed were quite shallow and the sides were straight, so the trunks had to be dropped in upright. Whether they were carved or decorated in some other way, whether they stood in a clearing or whether they celebrated something special in the natural world, we cannot tell. But they were a way of marking that place. They provide us with our first point of reference in the landscape.

4000BC

Three thousand years later the pine forests had gone, the warming climate having forced them further north allowing in a mixed woodland of oak and ash, lime and birch, hazel and willow. At first this was a wildwood, as untamed as the earlier pine forests had been. But new ideas had crossed the Channel from the European mainland: the use of pottery instead of vessels of skin and bark, new ways of grinding smooth axes of flint and stone and new ways to find food. So now when trees were felled it was for a purpose: to clear land to plant crops of wheat and barley and to create clearings where cattle, pigs and sheep could graze. These were the people of the Neolithic – the New Stone Age – living partly as their ancestors had done, partly as farmers and herders.

One summer, on Coneybury Hill perched above the valley of the River Avon, a group of these people gathered to feast in a woodland clearing. We don't know whether they gathered there for regular feasts or simply for this one big party, but they certainly ate well. They had slaughtered some of their cattle and had been hunting and fishing. They ate venison from red and roe deer, they had killed a wild pig and from the river came beaver and trout. The food was cooked and served in round-bottomed pots, hand-formed and fired in bonfires, simple vessels that were undecorated except where they had been burnished to a dull shine. Thirty-seven pots, from large cooking vessels to small cups, were used and smashed, perhaps accidentally or maybe as part of some ritual concerned with the feasting. But the reason we know so much about this feast is because of what happened afterwards. They dug a huge pit into the chalk, perhaps using the antlers of the deer they had killed and eaten, and into this pit they swept all the debris from the feast: the bones, the broken pots, ash from the cooking fires and the flint tools used to hunt, to cut up the meat and to scrape the hides clean. Today we take photographs of a special occasion and the rubbish goes into the bin. To these people this may have been a way of remembering this event, of marking a spot where something special happened. It seems to have worked; this place stayed special for over a thousand years.

Marking the land was becoming important to these farmers and herders of the earlier part of the Neolithic period. Even though as hunters and gatherers they must have identified parts of the landscape that they felt were theirs, in which only they had the right to search for food, beginning to settle down meant a new relationship with the land. There was, for the first time, a sense of ownership and they were looking for ways to express it. So on the crests of hills, some gentle and sweeping, some dramatic, they built houses for the bones of their ancestors, bones that had either been buried for a while or had been picked clean by the wind and rain and the birds. And on both sides of these houses they dug long quarry ditches and over the houses they piled up the chalk. These white mounds, eight of them within this landscape ranging in size from a tiny one on Normanton Down to a monster near the Winterbourne Stoke Crossroads, were a visible statement: 'these are our ancient dead – this is our land'.

It was not surprising that people wanted to claim this land. It was a good place to live. The soil was fertile and easily worked with digging sticks and simple wooden ploughs. The woods provided timber for buildings and fuel for fires and with careful management would continue to do so long into the future. The woodland gave somewhere for pigs to roam and forage for food, and sheltered wild animals that could be hunted for meat and skins. There was clean water in the rivers and streams, fish to be caught and beavers trapped, and good flint for tools could easily be dug from the chalk. But although this land, now claimed by the ancestors asleep in their tombs, gave everything that was needed for everyday life, more was needed – places to gather and celebrate. So they collected antlers and began digging more ditches.

To the north-west of Stonehenge, on the crest of a low ridge, two rough, meandering circles of ditches were dug; not neatly but more like a string of oval pits, each perhaps the contribution made by a small family group to this communal site. By each short ditch the chalk was piled up to make a low bank. As the work continued the builders camped outside the enclosure, leaving their flint tools scattered on the grass but clearing away the more obvious signs of their presence, burying broken pots and the remains of their food in small but carefully dug pits, miniature versions of the great feasting pit on Coneybury Hill. What they had built with their combined labour was a place to meet and feast, a place to conduct the ceremonies that started their dead on the journey to the next world. A place to exchange gossip and strange possessions, shiny pottery from far in the south-west of the country, axes of stone that were not as sharp as flint but were warm in colour and looked and felt special. A place to settle old arguments, to laugh and flirt, to find a partner. The first ceremonial circles; circles within circles.

But there were other ways of marking the land. Just to the north of Stonehenge, between two low ridges, long shallow ditches were dug, not quite straight but shifting direction at times as if to readjust to some greater scheme. At one end lay a long low burial mound, already old and grass-covered. The ditches that marked the sides of this construction, and the banks that were piled up next to them, were parallel, and when they reached each of the two low ridges they turned inwards and joined up to make a huge elongated ditched enclosure. At both ends the ditches were dug deeper and wider and the banks were broader and taller. Was this a way of dividing the land, of separating the land of the ceremonial circle to the north from the land to the south where something similar was soon to be built? Or was it a way of forging links? Was the large mound at the western end perhaps meant to imitate the existing long barrow at the east? Were the long side ditches of the enclosure a way of bringing together two separate groups of people? And was the most significant part of this great enclosure maybe the place in the middle where it dips down into a shallow dry valley, out of sight of either end? This would have been a suitably neutral place to meet. The soft turf within this great enclosure may have seen processions, ceremonies, perhaps even races. But ancient feet leave no trace on soft downland grass.

Just beyond the western end of this great enclosure, along the perfectly flat crest of a low chalk ridge, more long ditches were dug to create a miniature version of it. At first the ditches were tiny, little more than furrows in the chalk, but they served, along with their banks, to mark out another long narrow space that also had a larger ditch at its end. But this was clearly not grand enough, so the ditches were dug deeper and the enclosure was doubled in length – but was then instantly abandoned. On the gleaming white floor of the newly dug ditch the workers laid down their antler picks and rakes and shovelled back the chalk that they had only just dug out. What was the reason for this seemingly illogical behaviour? Perhaps the digging, the effort that was expended, was the important thing, not the end product. Or perhaps it was symbolic, marking the end of the time of long mounds and long enclosures, a time to move on to something new.

The landscape had changed enormously since the sound of flint axe on timber had marked the tentative beginnings of an age in which people started to tame nature rather than live as part of it. Large areas of woodland still remained but now the land was a mosaic, a patchwork of cleared areas, some open and grassy where animals grazed, some cultivated in small plots, at first little more than gardens, then growing to larger fields. Patches of scrub, bushes of hazel, hawthorn and juniper marked places that had been cleared but then abandoned to nature. In one of the cleared areas work now started on something that was be a focus for more than 1,000 years – a simple circular ditch.

The people who dug that first circular ditch of what was to become Stonehenge can have had no idea that very close by, but 3,500 years earlier, timbers had been raised in pits to celebrate something special about that particular place in the landscape. Those pine posts had long gone, along with the pine trees around them, and even the oak woodland that replaced them had been cleared away making it easy to lay out the plan of what was to be dug. Using a wooden peg and a rope of hide or twisted fibre they marked out a circle in the springy grazed turf. They carefully noted the places where entrances were to be left, and the digging began. In some ways this was just like the old enclosure to the north, a ditch that was dug in short sections, irregular oval pits with bases at different levels and sides that sloped at different angles. Once again each small pit may have been the work of a family, perhaps from close by or perhaps drawn from further away by the lure of one last enclosure built in the old way. So they turned up to camp nearby, to dig as children played, casting an eye on the work that was going on to either side to become, by their small labour, a part of something much greater. Antler picks were swung and the loosened blocky chalk was levered out and carted away in skins and baskets, piled up mainly into a bank on the inside of the ditch but with small amounts laid in a low bank on the outside. And then the chalk walls that separated the individual pits were roughly knocked through and the ditch was finished.

There were bonuses to helping with this task. In the soft chalk lay lumps of hard flint, useful for so many tools and not to be passed over. So in the lulls between digging another sound could be heard, of stone and antler striking flint as lumps were tested to see whether they were sound – good for tools – or flawed rubbish, leaving the ditch floor in places trampled and littered with rejected flakes. The builders must have been aware that this was not quite like the enclosures of old, but something new. Yet when ancient bones and antlers, preserved for generations, were placed with ceremony on the floor of the ditch close to the two entrances, suddenly it was as if this new work had been there for all time.

As the seasons passed frost and rain ate at the sides of the ditch and, as the chalk crumbled and loose turf slipped in, its profile softened. Grass grew on what had once been bare white chalk. But after only a few generations the new enclosure started to bristle with upright timber posts: oak from the remaining woodlands, which were shrinking even more as pasture and arable fields took a greater hold on the landscape. Posts were set up in the centre of the enclosure and in the main entrance neat rows formed screens that restricted entry. From the smaller southern entrance lines of posts, perhaps linked with panels of woven branches, guided the visitor along a sinuous path to the centre of the enclosure. And then there were the 56 pits, set in a regular circle close to the inner edge of the bank. Each was dug larger than the timber that it was intended to take and after the post was put in place the space around it was firmly packed with flint and chalk.

Years passed, and on the chalk hills and valleys that surrounded the enclosure everyday life went on with crops being sown and animals tended. Flint was dug for tools to hunt and chop, to cut and skin. Clay from the river valleys was mixed with crushed stone and flint, then formed into pots that emerged red-brown or black and sooty from their firing in bonfires. Life was still fragile: the young and the old were especially at the mercy of famine or disease. But the important dead were no longer buried in houses under long chalk mounds. For a select few there was a new way of travelling the route from the land of the living to the land of the dead. Close to the enclosure with its gently decaying timbers a new smell wafted in the breeze, a sweet smell like roasting pork. On tall pyres the dead were consumed by flame, reduced in hours to twisted fragments of whitened bone. When nothing was left but scorched earth and fine white ash that blew in the wind, those that had tended the pyre came to collect the bones and take some of them for burial in the enclosure. They were placed with care in shallow holes scooped into the soils that filled the ditch, in the slumped bank and in the tops of some of the pits that had formed a circle just inside the bank, their posts now rotted or withdrawn. Slender bone pins were left with some of them and one very special person was laid to rest with a beautiful macehead of polished stone, striped and gleaming, a symbol of power from one world to take to the next. The enclosure had become a place of the dead.

Despite the centuries of felling – for the timber needed for buildings and as fuel for warming fires – some parts of the landscape retained many of their trees. So when digging started again on Coneybury Hill, over a thousand years since the great feast had taken place, the hill was still wooded. The pit in which the debris had been buried would still have been visible as a wide shallow depression, perhaps prompting the idea that this was somehow a special place, worthy of commemoration. Whatever the reason, a small oval enclosure was dug here, its single entrance pointing north-east imitating the first Stonehenge. This new ditch was not shallow and irregular like those of the earlier enclosures; the builders dug deep with their antler picks, to nearly twice the height of a man. The chalk from the steep-sided ditch was piled up to form a bank, outside the ditch – so not as a barrier but a place from which to view the events that took place within. As if to further create the effect of an amphitheatre great care was taken to level the interior, with the chalk on the gently sloping hilltop dug away before pits were excavated, a circle of small posts set up and sharpened wooden stakes driven into the ground, encircling the pits and creating fences. This back-to-front arrangement of the deep ditch and its tall bank was a new idea; but this was still a place of feasting – not once but many times. Cattle were slaughtered and the meat roasted, the scorched bones tossed into the ditch along with new and exuberantly decorated pottery, its surface moulded and incised with lines and spirals. And elsewhere in the ditch were bones that told a different story: an arthritic dog, not a pet but a tool for hunting and herding and, most curious of all, a white-tailed sea eagle. Great oaks from little acorns grow and perhaps the small enclosure on Coneybury Hill was the seed for what was about to start growing just to the north. As the woodland closed in around this first henge, work started on something far greater on the west bank of the River Avon.

All over Britain great constructions were being planned: huge ditches and banks, great circles of oak posts, vast mounds of earth and stone, all of which would require planning and organisation. Someone, or some group of people, had the authority to bring together those who were living scattered around the countryside, to collect the hundreds of antlers that would be needed as digging tools, to arrange for the workers to be housed and fed – and all this while remaining anonymous, not buried with great finery and wealth so that we can point them out as architects, engineers or priests.

In a sheltered hollow on the bank of the river Avon a village had grown up, a cluster of small square houses huddled together in fenced enclosures, with walls of woven wood and mud and roofs thatched with reeds. Smoke drifted out from the comforting fires that burnt in the centre of each of their neat, well-swept chalk floors and at midwinter the air was full of the sweet smell of roasting pig. At this time, when the days were cold and dark, they walked up the slope, along the track that was surfaced with gravel and flint from the bed of the river, to where the great circle of timber stood. Such a contrast to their small neat houses; here each post was the trunk of a great oak, some hundreds of years old, sought out in the woods that still lined the valley sides, felled with flint axes and then dragged by sheer determination to its place in this strange new structure. Some posts were so big, so heavy, that they could not simply be dropped into a hole. Special pits were dug with one sloping side and down this slope the timber was slid before being hauled upright against the opposite vertical side of the pit. While the post was held in place with ropes the pit was filled with chalk, broken picks, stone, anything that was to hand, all packed in to keep the post firm and upright.

As time went by the track grew and was resurfaced, pointing the way of the sun as it rose on midsummer day. More circles of timber, chalk-dug ditches, houses that were not for the living but the dead, spread across the shallow valley until the time came to encircle them, protect them, show to the world just how special this place had become. So hundreds laboured, digging ditches that were nearly four times the height of a man and eight times as wide. After months of back-breaking work it must have seemed as if they had just scratched the surface. Antler picks constantly broke or simply wore out and as the ditches gradually deepened the only way to get out was to cut steps in the steep chalk sides. Each change of weather made the task different. In the sunshine chalk dust stiffened the hair, clogged and irritated noses and eyes. In the wet the chalk became as slippery as ice and work was slow. And all the time as the work slowly progressed there was time for ceremony, time for feasting, at midsummer when there were new children to celebrate, and at midwinter when there were fears that the sun would never return to bring light and warmth and life. The work carried on for year after year, the ditch getting deeper, the bank growing and spreading until it was finished – a vast chalk circle, ten times the size of the one on Coneybury Hill. This was magnificent and the people of the river margin could be rightly proud. But it was not only here that people toiled to build great works. Those who farmed just to the west and lived in their own small square houses on the King Barrow Ridge could look west into the natural amphitheatre ringed with low ridges, and see an amazing transformation taking place at the enclosure that was to become Stonehenge.

The people who lived in this landscape knew about stone. They made their tools from the black flint that lay in the chalk – arrowheads for hunting, knives and scrapers for cutting meat and preparing hides, chipped and polished axes for tree felling and woodworking. A wealthy few had smooth polished axes of stone, green and grey, banded and spotted, axes that had been passed from hand to hand until they were far from their quarries in Wales or the Lake District. The further they travelled, the more 'foreign' they became – and the more special. But no-one here had the skills of building in stone; they built in 'soft' materials, raising mounds of chalk and uprights of timber, posts that no matter how big they were would eventually rot and disappear. The closest place where the houses of the dead were made of enduring stone lay to the north, a good day's walk across the rolling chalk where huge brown boulders lay half buried in the earth. All this changed as stones started to arrive at Stonehenge. Some were sarsens, the brown stones from the north; four small, unshaped boulders that were set up close to the inner edge of the bank and two massive stones, nearly twice the height of a man, raised as a pair just outside the north-east entrance. Moving these was a huge task, the day's hard walk to the place where they were found becoming weeks of toil, of strain and frustration that taxed strength and ingenuity. Six stones – surely that was enough?

It was not. More stones started to arrive and these were very different. Some were like the axes that the people had seen before, white-spotted and greeny-blue, but others were unfamiliar. They were not huge – in fact they were much smaller than the timber posts that had been raised at Durrington Walls – but stone is heavy and each one weighed more than 60 men. It was said that they had come from a rocky land, ten days' walk away, a land that lay beyond water that could only be crossed in boats or on wooden rafts. In this land, on bare and windswept hilltops, the elements broke stone into natural pillars that the people who lived there took and shaped, just as they shaped the axes, and set up in circles and ovals. This is what came as a gift from this far-off land – specially picked stones, stones which already had a sacred meaning and which now had a new home.

A few chosen people had made the long journey to the place where the stones came from; they had gone there to talk, to explain their vision for Stonehenge, to ask for help from all those who lived along the way. For however these stones were to be moved, whether by passing them from one tribe to another or by sending teams to the place where they were to be found, it was going to require help, food and shelter, ropes and wood, boats and rafts. It was a great task, driven by ambition, and one that would unite people as they had never been united before.

As more of the strange stones arrived, dragged across the downs on wooden sledges, their progress eased by rollers, preparations were made to change the face of the old enclosure where the only trace of the old timbers was the circle of shallow depressions running round the inside of the bank. More holes were dug, closer to the centre, strange elongated pits, almost bone-shaped, with deeper ends where the new stones were set up in pairs. It looked like the start of two circles, two arcs, running in parallel but then, just as they started to take shape, work stopped. Perhaps for some reason the supply of stones dried up, the huge effort of transporting them over such a great distance proving too much for the communities along the route. Or perhaps there was simply a change of plan. Whatever the reason, the bluestones were removed from their pits leaving the enclosure once again bare except for the four small rough sarsens and the two larger ones standing sentinel outside the entrance. To those who moved stones, who dug and backfilled pits, this may have seemed like the end. But in fact this was just the beginning: plans were already being drawn up for something truly remarkable.

All this time there was, in the minds of those who planned and built, a growing awareness of the heavens. The moon moved swiftly, darting across the sky, its full light a blessing on dark winter nights. But the sun marked out the year, from the long warm days of summer to the short cold days of winter when its rays seemed feeble, unable to warm and coax growth from the earth. It sometimes hid, and a terrifying blackness spread across the earth when there should have been light. The sun was the giver of life but there were fears that it could just as easily take life away. So when the plans were made for what was to happen next, they recognised those two most important times in the sun's year – the longest day at midsummer and the shortest at midwinter. The entrance to the enclosure had already been shifted slightly and the ditches reworked, so that it pointed to that part of the horizon where the sun rose on the longest day, its golden orb shimmering between the two large upright stones that stood just outside the entrance. And now it was time to mark this special alignment inside the old enclosure with a magnificent stone building.

The place where the brown sarsens could be found lay one day's walk to the north, over the dry plain and across a fertile valley to the chalk beyond. On this far chalk, many years before, the rough stones had been used to build the houses that held the bones of ancestors, stone caves that could be reopened time and time again, hidden under long earth mounds. Now, in an echo of the massive timber circles that were still being built at Durrington Walls, the henge at Avebury was growing too, its ditch and bank on an equally massive scale, its circles of stone unformed by anything but nature though carefully selected for their shape.

To this area came people from Stonehenge with a shopping list of stones. They needed something quite specific: more than 75 stones, not all the same and not just roughly matched in terms of size and shape. They needed permission to prospect in the shallow valleys where the stones lay half-buried and when this was granted they set out, searching, digging beside and under likely stones, checking for flaws, levering them over to look at every side. In each rough boulder they had to be able to see the finished stone and sometimes, after much effort, they were disappointed.

Once a stone had passed inspection – when it was agreed that it was the right size and free from obvious flaws – the masons started work trimming off the excess stone, roughly shaping and smoothing. There was no point in transporting any unnecessary weight and it was far better to discover hidden flaws at this stage. But this was just part of the whole great scheme. As the masons pounded away with their stone mauls, others felled trees to make levers and rollers, carpenters split and hewed timber creating sturdy sledges that would bear the stones, and the young and the old wove ropes from stripped bark, nettle fibre and honeysuckle. Meanwhile the route from Avebury to Stonehenge was being prepared. Every inch of it was walked over, examined in minute detail and discussed at length. Steep climbs that would defeat even the greatest efforts were noted and avoided. Trees and scrubby bushes were cleared away, piled up nearby to provide replacement levers and rollers as well as fuel for camp fires along the way. Boggy patches in the one wide valley that had to be crossed were identified and reinforced with mats of criss-crossed branches until they were firm under foot. To see a precious stone sink irretrievably into a morass would be a terrible disaster.

Finally the route was prepared, the first trimmed stone was lashed to its sledge and everything was ready. But no-one had ever done anything like this before, no-one had moved stones of this size over such a distance, so it was with great trepidation that 200 people took the strain on the ropes and on the order 'pull', they pulled. At first nothing happened; the ropes creaked and stretched but the stone remained obstinate. Finally, kick-started by the judicious application of some large levers, and to the sound of great jubilation, it started to move. The epic journey of the sarsens had begun. This was the beginning of months, stretching into years, of toil, sweat and blood, frustration and joy. Frustration as ropes parted and timber splintered, as rain made the exposed chalk as slippery as ice, as frost froze fingers and feet. Frustration as those who dragged the stones became ill or simply exhausted. There were times when the fields and family called and there were not enough people to pull on the ropes. Times when a stone was temporarily abandoned to sit sullen and defiant, resisting all attempts to move it.

Much of the land over which the stones inched towards Stonehenge was gently rolling and there was delight when a stone rolled effortlessly downhill, with those who moved the rollers running to catch up and place them in front of the stone. It was at times like these, however, that the accidents happened, when the young and inexperienced, or sometimes the old and slow, failed to realise the speed and the unstoppable power of the stone as it slid downhill. There were screams of pain as fingers, hands, even whole arms were trapped and crushed; but worse was the silence that came when a life was lost.

After the easier downslopes came the inevitable uphill struggle that was to follow. At these times every able-bodied man, woman and child would come to help, congregating to add their weight and efforts to ropes and levers, to offer encouragement and refreshment to the exhausted workers.

And there was joy too, joy in shared effort, in recalling the day's triumphs as meat was shared around the fire, joy in each familiar landmark that showed how far along the route they had come, joy in cresting the last ridge and seeing the final destination and the excitement of those who waited. Each stone was greeted with jubilation and exhilaration, examined and marvelled over. Each weary band of stone movers were greeted as heroes and their tales of triumph and disaster were retold again and again to a new audience.

So was that it? Were these stones, roughly shaped but still far more elegant than any other stone set up in Britain, simply to be raised upright? And if so then why were they of so many different sizes? There was a clue to the answer. It lay in the few bluestones – dwarfed by these newcomers – that stood inside the enclosure, stones that stood in pairs with each vertical couple supporting a horizontal lintel stone, like small neat doorways. The lintels sat firm on their slender supports, fixed in place with simple invisible joints. Each lintel had two hollows on its underside and these sat over protruding 'pegs', lumps that stuck up from the tops of the uprights. Such methods of fixing were familiar to every woodworker of that age. This was the plan: more stone doorways, but this time made from much bigger stones.

So now Stonehenge rang with the sound of stone on stone as, with the ground carpeted in chippings and the air filled with dust, the great boulders from Avebury gradually took on their final shape. It was the most massive stones, four times as long as a man was tall, the most difficult ones to find in the first place, that were the first to be shaped. Under careful supervision, with shapes and dimensions checked regularly with wooden forms and rules, edges were smoothed, sides were tapered and joints were created. The positions of the hollows were marked out with chalk on the pale surface of the stone and then, with stone and sand and water, deep basins were cut. There were mistakes: when work started on the greatest lintel of them all and the hollows were just beginning to take shape, the order came to turn the stone over and start again. All that work for nothing.

The hollows were easy enough, just a matter of patience. What was harder was making the lump that was to fit into the hollow. This was a soul-destroying task which meant removing all of the surrounding stone, pounding away, careful not to damage the stone that you needed to leave, seeing this little lump grow, constantly inspected until someone in authority decided that it stuck up enough to fulfil its function. Then on to the next.

Finally the first of the stones were ready to be raised, the two tallest that would form the greatest of the doorways, facing the rising midsummer sun. One had been shaped to perfection, the pride of Stonehenge; elegantly tapered, its surface gently

STONEHENGE – THE STORY SO FAR

rippled by the marks of the stone hammers that had done the first rough pounding, followed by the smaller, fist-sized balls of sarsen that had provided the final finish. It was a work of art. Its pair was not quite so elegant; there had been problems in finding a suitable matching stone and it was only just tall enough. Its bulbous base had been left unworked, a great protruding heel that had saved labour and also provided weight low down in the hope of making it more stable. While all the stones were still lying on the ground the fit of the lintel had been checked as it was eased into place. All seemed well, but would it fit when the stones were upright?

Holes were dug, picks of antler once again pressed into service to hew deep pits, each with one sloping side like the holes that held the wooden posts at Durrington Walls. The pits were not the same depth but were carefully measured, again and again; the tops of the stones had to be exactly level – any adjustment to them once they were upright was too awful to contemplate. It would mean yet more stone-working but this time on a platform perched high above the ground.

Raising the stones called for ingenuity. There had been much discussion, sometimes even heated argument. Models had been made, small pits dug and wooden 'stones' tilted into place. Much time had been spent on preparing for this event, building a sloping ramp of timber and earth behind the stone-hole next to its sloping side, a ramp which ended at a solid wall of stout timbers. Up this ramp the great stone was dragged, until its base hung far over the hole in which wooden stakes had been placed upright to protect its vertical side. Here it lay, so close to its final resting place but not quite ready yet. Then, along its sloping length a smaller stone was dragged, inching along until, with creaks and groans, the big stone rose up to lie horizontal, balanced on the reinforced end of its ramp. This was the moment that would bring triumph or disaster, that would leave the engineers who had designed and prepared this spectacle either more powerful than before, or in disgrace. One last pull on the ropes sent the small stone sliding, accelerating down the remaining length of the balanced stone until its weight finally tipped the balance and the great sarsen rose up and settled into its hole, crushing the wooden stakes which had served their purpose. Dust settled, ropes slackened and cheers rang out as everyone rushed forward to see where the stone had landed. Perfect. But more effort was needed with ropes and levers to ease it through the final arc until it sat vertical. There it stood, propped with timbers, guyed with stout ropes. But now was not the time to fix it in firmly; that would come only when the lintel was in place.

The second stone, with its heavy bulbous base, was lowered into its shallower hole. It was time for the lintel to be placed on top but the uprights were more than three times the height of the tallest man and weighed as much as 150 men. How was it to be raised so high?

The answer lay in the small, straight, round logs, each with notches cut close to both ends, that were stacked inside the old enclosure. The lintel was dragged across until it lay at the foot of the uprights and then, with wooden levers, one end was raised up and logs were slid underneath it before it was gently lowered on top of the logs. The process was repeated at the other end and as logs were inserted with each lift the stone rose steadily on its bed of interlaced timbers, their ends locked together with those simple notched joints. These were easy to make to those who had just created far more complicated joints in hard stone.

The lintel rose swiftly on the growing stack of logs passed up from hand to hand, with smaller stacks built at either end to support the men whose weight on the levers raised the stone. Soon it was just above the tops of the uprights and then, with great care, it was crabbed across to sit poised, the hollows under the lintel directly above the stone knobs that stuck up from the tops of the uprights. This was the moment of truth: would they fit together? Logs were removed and with a grinding of stone on stone the huge lintel settled in place, the uprights in their cocoons of timber shifting slightly, easing down a little under this additional weight. But it had worked. They fitted and it was time to pack the upright stones in place, filling their holes with stone chips, broken antlers, chalk, flint, all rammed down hard until they stood firm and immovable.

What a spectacular achievement, to complete the first and the largest of the stone doorways. There was a new confidence now; the remaining four were all smaller, so compared to this first monster there would be no problems in raising them in the same way. But these five doorways only accounted for 15 stones; what about the remaining 60 or so?

As the remaining trilthons took their place in the growing horseshoe work started on shaping the remaining sarsens. Three were set aside to be placed in a line across the entrance to the enclosure and it seemed obvious, even to those who knew nothing of the secrets of the place, that those that were left could easily be divided into two groups. There were 30 that had to be uprights, great flat slabs, not as big as the sarsens that had already been set up but still big, and 30 smaller stones that must be their lintels. But how were these to stand? As 15 more 'doorways' or as something more complicated? The answer came when instructions were given to shape the stones. Each upright was to have two protruding lumps, one close to each end of the flat top of the stone. Two lumps left standing, although a little more complicated than just one, in fact required the removal of less stone. The lintels were a different matter though and their complicated shape required careful explanation. For a start they were not straight-sided; their long parallel sides had to be gently and precisely curved to the contours of a long curved piece of timber which served as a pattern. The top and bottom had to be precisely flat and there were the customary hollows on the underside. But joints were also required on the ends of each lintel: on one end a vertical hollow groove and on the other a corresponding ridge or tongue. As these extraordinary joints were explained, the stoneworkers realised that what they would be creating was a smooth ring of stone, suspended high above the ground.

There was no room for error here. Dimensions and joints were checked regularly and, as each lintel was declared perfect, it went to join the growing arc laid out on the soft turf, tongue in groove, creeping closer together until the circle was complete and the work of raising the stones could begin.

This was more complicated than even the elaborate stone joints could suggest. The great plan called for the circle to be level but the ground on which it was to be built sloped gently down in the direction of the midsummer sun. The difference in height from one side of the circle to the other could be measured easily with long wooden troughs filled with water, which always showed what was level and what sloped. So the uprights had to be carefully sorted, the taller ones placed on the downslope side and the shorter ones upslope, and the holes all had to be dug to exactly the right depth. There was much calculating and arguing, checking and rechecking, making sure that the wider gap was left opposite the entrance to the enclosure before work started on digging out the stone holes.

Soon the henge was a hive of activity as teams of workers dug holes, built ramps, hauled stones, propped uprights and built and dismantled the platforms that lifted the elegant lintels. The air was full of the sounds of hammering stones, of flint axe on timber, of oaths and laughter. There were arguments over who was to use the levers next, about who had frayed the best piece of rope, but gradually in dust and heat and hubbub, the circle grew. Each lintel that settled in place, each end joint that slotted together, brought relief and excitement. Yes, they had fitted together on the ground but there was still anxiety about what would happen when they were balanced high in the air. It all worked perfectly, stone fitting stone; but then disaster struck. As the final upright toppled into place a crack deep inside, a flaw that had hidden itself from the stoneworkers, split the stone in half, leaving only a short stub in the hole where a tall upright should have stood.

The symmetry was ruined and a desperate search of the downs where the stones had been found revealed the awful truth; there were none left that were big enough to replace the one that had shattered. But what had been built was still an awe-inspiring structure, a triumph of design and engineering. And at times during the building work, when the workers laid down their tools and left the stones where they lay, when the henge fell silent, everyone remembered why all this effort was necessary. At midsummer, as the strong sun rose over the old rough stones, they gave thanks for the light and warmth that it offered so freely. And at midwinter, when the feeble sun set between the tallest of the uprights, those that braved the cold prayed the sun would once again grow in strength and warm their aching bones.

But the ceremonies were not just confined to Stonehenge. There were times when those who lived in the scattered farms around came together to celebrate and feast at the old neglected henge on Coneybury Hill, as their ancestors had done over a thousand years before, and at the timber circles of Durrington Walls great winter feasts of pig meat followed the more sombre celebrations at the new stones.

Among those who came to gaze at the power of human hands and inventive minds were strangers, men from over the seas who spoke a strange language and whose daggers were not of stone but shone like the sun itself. These men were different; they drank from fine red pottery vessels and their arrows were tipped with flint points that swept back into cruel barbs. They came to look, but they were not welcome – they had no part in what was being built. This was the old way, old ideas translated from short-lived timber to everlasting stone and the builders had all the old skills that they needed to build what they believed in.

But the newcomers, men who talked of a land of towering snowy mountains, did have some new and extraordinary skills. Their leader, a lame man who was there with a younger companion, could take green rock, crush it to a powder and melt it like butter over a fire until it glowed like the sun and flowed like the thickest cream. He could pour this melted rock into moulds of stone and out came dull blades that made water hiss and bubble. But rub them with sand and the bright lights reappeared. This was metal; and there was an even brighter kind that flashed in the light. The stranger could beat tiny lumps of it over a curiously shaped stone until it stretched and grew but still kept its brilliance. This was what he and his friends folded into small neat tubes and wore wrapped around braids in their hair.

Everyone wanted to possess a dagger that shone, to wear brilliance in their hair, but these new metals were rare and only for the very wealthy. The new arrowheads, though, were made of flint and flint was for everyone, so there was nothing to stop copies being made. It was the same with the flat plates of fine stone that the newcomers wore strapped to their forearms to provide some protection from the lash of the bowstring. Stone was the old way and the people of Stonehenge knew how to fashion it.

These newcomers may not have been accepted but when both their leader and his companion died one winter curiosity drove the locals to the funeral, on a ridge on the opposite side of the river. Even their burial ways were strange, laying the man's body crouched on its side, as if asleep, in a deep chalk grave. He still wore his fine clothes and the brilliant gold in his hair and to the astonishment of those who watched and were unfamiliar with the ways of these people, into that grave went all his worldly possessions: his three copper knives, his five fine pots, his arrows and wrist guards and even the curiously shaped stone that signified his trade. Burying such wealth, and all for use in the next world. The low mound of chalk that was piled up over the grave was just the first to rise in the landscape around Stonehenge. Some covered the graves of strangers, the men and women who brought the shining metal, but others were for those who had laboured at Stonehenge, buried alone in the new way, their just reward a resting place within sight of their great creation.

But there was one man who was given an even more special burial place. They had found his body early one morning, lying in the shallow depression that was all that now marked the ditch of Stonehenge. The arrow shafts that stuck from his body at awkward angles were evidence of a violent death and the bloodstains on the grass showed how he had crawled, mortally wounded, until dispatched by one final arrow in the back. This was shocking; everyone knew him, he lived closed by and had laboured hard at the raising of the stones. But worse still blood had been spilt on sacred turf, not spilt accidentally in the building work – that was just part of the sacrifice that went into the labour – but spilt in anger, and a life had been taken. There was only one solution: to bury him where he lay, to let him lie in death where he had toiled in life and hope that the gods would look after him. So a grave was dug, down through the layers of soil that had filled the ditch over the centuries, through bloodstained turf and white chalk, through chips of sarsen and bluestone until it was deep enough. And there he was laid, still wearing the stone wrist guard that he had been so proud of, curled up, at peace.

But soon this dark episode in the history of Stonehenge was forgotten as once again work started to make Stonehenge even more elaborate, even more special. The great sarsen circle and horseshoe had been completed generations before and after the debris of construction had been cleared away the henge had become a place of tranquillity. For most of the year the only sounds to be heard were the bleating of the sheep that cropped the short grass and the sounds of birds – the harsh grating of the rooks that roosted in the nearby trees and the melody of the skylarks that soared high overhead. Then once again the peace was shattered and the voices that were heard were not the hushed voices of prayer but the raised voices of engineers and workers as they argued over what was to happen next.

To the surprise of the assembled workers, drafted in from the farms and villages that had become such a prominent feature of the surrounding landscape, their first task was to recover the bluestones which had languished, neglected and moss-covered, for centuries. Scrubbed and cleaned, the protruding tenons battered off from the tops of those that had at one stage held up lintels, they were set up in arrangements that echoed those already built in sarsen. The tallest and most slender, including some with elaborate vertical tongues and grooves the purpose of which had long been forgotten, were set in an oval that lay inside the sarsen horseshoe. The remainder, including the hollowed lintels, formed a circle just inside the sarsen ring. But then even these plans changed. Stones were taken from the inner oval to make a horseshoe that echoed the layout of the huge doorways and the left-over stones were set up in the crowded bluestone circle. The final act was to place a large slab of a peculiar red-brown stone, unlike any other in the henge, flat at the back of the horseshoe in the shadow of the tallest of the sarsens. If Stonehenge was a place of worship then this must be the altar. Surely there could be no more rearrangement? There were certainly no more stones available but that did not mean that there would be no more work.

Stonehenge had started over 30 generations earlier with the digging of a ditch and now there was more digging to be done. Once again antler picks swung in the sunlight and white gashes reached out from the enclosure entrance – ditches and banks down across the grassy slopes in the direction of the summer sunrise. Surveyors paced out the lines, at intervals hammering in stakes to mark the points where the ditches changed course. The diggers followed blindly, straight down across the bottom of the shallow valley, turn left, up the slope, across the ridge, then a gentle curve and down to the river where cool water eased dry throats and washed off the sweat and chalk. This was now the way into Stonehenge, a way of contemplation, the stones appearing and disappearing as those walking got nearer and a route to be taken only after the waters of the river had cleansed and purified the body.

The sight that now greeted anyone cresting the low ridges surrounding Stonehenge was unlike anything they could have seen before, anywhere. At first sight it looked like the framework for a circular building, solid, complex, set in the middle of a bowl of hills on a rolling plain. Come closer and the realisation struck that this was not a building of wood but of stone, stone upon stone, stones of different colours, stones that were smooth and fitted seamlessly together as if carved from one solid block. Closer still, as close as was allowed, and their true beauty was apparent; works of art that shone in the sun and glittered in the moonlight.

Most of those who came to visit and marvel could approach no closer than the old encircling ditch – not so much a physical barrier as a divide between the world of ordinary men and those with special knowledge. From here all that could be seen was a forest of stones, small gaps allowing the merest glimpses of the interior and, at special times, of the mysteries that were taking place. At midwinter, as the sun set, those gathered in the cold needed the reassurance that those inside the stones were communicating with the gods on their behalf. Reassurance came with the toing and froing of priests, with the flickering light of flaming torches, with sparks and sweet-smelling smoke and with sound of voices in prayer. All would be well again, the sun would return.

All this effort had gone into this one, wonderful place, but the landscape in which it lay remained far from unchanged. Over time the needs of growing flocks for more grazing land and of farmers for fields to grow their crops shrank the surviving woodlands. But there were still some great oaks, their acorns autumn food for the rooting pigs that would provide the meat for winter feasts, trees that were sacred and could only be sacrificed for a very special purpose. They had been cut to make the great timber circles at Durrington Walls, circles that had seen generations of feasts but were now decayed and rotting. And now they were to be cut for one last timber circle, perched high above the river close to the huge riverside henge. They did it the old way: they dug a circular ditch, piled the chalk up to make an outside bank and left an entrance facing the midsummer sunrise. Inside rose a forest of posts, ring upon ring, varying in size from slender poles to great trunks so big that they needed to be set in holes with sloping sides. In the centre, under a cairn of flint, they laid the body of a child, a child whose life had been short as was the case for so many but who had played among the rising timbers. Death was always a sadness but they offered the child's life to the gods to bring good fortune to their new henge.

In some ways the building of the new henge of wood was a futile gesture. The time of the henges was over; those who farmed the chalk and traded with people far away no longer wanted to toil together to build great places of worship. They wanted fine pots and beads, shiny metal, daggers and glittering gold, possessions that would show everyone how wealthy they were in life. They wanted to be buried under white chalk mounds so that everyone could see how powerful they were in death. So the white mounds rose on every hilltop, big and small, and the funeral pyres burned once again as some chose that their ashes rather than their bones should lie in the earth.

But even in this materialistic age Stonehenge, now truly ancient, continued to exert its influence and magic. It was not abandoned. Hordes still gathered at those special times of the year and some of the greatest stones were even decorated with carvings of the new symbols of power: axes and daggers of bronze. Around Stonehenge clustered the most elaborate of the cemeteries of burial mounds. On the ridge tops closest to the stones lay some of the largest, the fanciest in form and the richest: massive mounds to the east close to where the entrance avenue led to the stones; mounds shaped like giant bells to the north, close to the line of the ancient cursus; to the south mounds shaped like beautiful circular targets and the burial of a tall strong man with so much gold that he shone like the sun. The people who lay under the mounds were rich and mighty, the elite of a powerful region. But they still wanted to be buried as close as possible to the greatest symbol of old power, within sight of Stonehenge.

Even as Stonehenge moved towards the twilight of its life there were those who tried to resurrect its old powers by one last gesture. Two rings of shallow pits were dug outside the now ancient sarsen circle but whatever the plan may have been it was all too late: the pits never did hold stones or timbers and they were soon forgotten.

The white mounds were now green with grass, the stones that had once glistened were softened by lichen and moss, their differences masked by time. Now land was wealth and when ditches were dug it was not to celebrate the gods but to create boundaries. Villages grew up, huddles of round houses of wattle, daub and thatch, and gradually their small, neat fields reached out into the sacred landscape. Old beliefs were forgotten, old monuments ignored. The banks of the Cursus were now no more than field boundaries, its interior a ploughed field.

For over fifteen hundred years the simple enclosure and the structures of timber and then stone that were built within it had dominated the landscape of that part of Salisbury Plain and the lives of the people who lived close by. They had toiled to build it, not questioning the need for such enormous efforts and enjoying the companionship of shared labour. They had gathered there to help ensure the return of the sun to bring warmth and life and had feasted well. But now the world had changed. Those who could melt rocks had started the change, men who could capture the sun in shining metal and who showed the way to wealth and power. So the potency of Stonehenge dwindled as each year the numbers that gathered grew smaller and those that did come were the old and the frail. And then there came a time when, imperceptibly, Stonehenge became a place of the past – no longer a living temple but an ancient curiosity, a marvel from the time of the ancestors. For generations tales were told of how it had been built, of the land far away that had provided the small stones and of the great gatherings that had once been held there. Visitors from afar still came, drawn by its reputation, no longer excluded from its sacred interior, to stand surrounded by stones that stood on stones.

The Age of Stonehenge was over.

Postcript: Stonehenge today… and tomorrow

As I hope the preceding chapters have demonstrated, Stonehenge and its surrounding landscape have changed over the millennia, over the centuries and, in quite radical ways, over the last few decades. The numbers of visitors have grown as first railways and carriages, then buses and cars provided greater access to the countryside. As the numbers of visitors grew so too did concerns for the long-term preservation of Stonehenge. Gravel replaced grass within the stones and then finally in 1978 the heart of the site was closed off to the everyday visitor, accessible only on special occasions. Subtle changes have also taken place in the landscape: fences removed or tucked out of sight and visitors encouraged, with not much success, to venture out and explore more of the surrounding ancient sites.

But despite these changes there has been a growing awareness, almost since the car park and underpass were built in 1968, that the presentation of Stonehenge and its landscape is far from ideal. As visitor numbers have grown the facilities have struggled to cope with ticket sales and the desire of visitors for toilets, souvenirs and refreshments. Far worse, there has been nowhere to provide information so, beyond guidebooks and more recently audio tours, the wider picture went largely unexplained.

The situation got so bad that in 1993 the visitor facilities were labeled as a 'national disgrace' by a House of Commons Public Accounts Committee. But by this time there were moves to improve the situation, to grasp the twin challenges of where and how to provide appropriate facilities for visitors and what to do about the

roads. These two elements are inextricably linked. There is no point in moving the intrusive facilities away from the stones to recreate a more tranquil backdrop if the landscape is still bisected by the A303 with its constant stream of traffic; no point in enhancing the immediate surroundings of Stonehenge if the A344 still passes by within touching distance of the Heel Stone.

There have been attempts to find a solution to these challenges for over 27 years now, with a succession of suggested sites for a new visitor centre ranging from the infinitely sensible to the downright ridiculous. Solutions for the A303 have ranged from on-line improvements, either on the surface or in a covered cutting, to a wide selection of routes that swept either north or south, but all still within the World Heritage Site. Both local and archaeological opinion has been polarised, but what is on offer towards the end of 2006 (government decisions and finance allowing) seems to me to offer an acceptable solution. The proposal for the A303 is to place it in a 2.1km (1.6 mile) bored tunnel past Stonehenge, from just east of the King Barrow Ridge to just west of the low ridge that lies along the A303 to the south-west of Stonehenge. This would mean that, from Stonehenge, the A303 would disappear from sight. Combine this with the removal of the A344 and there is the potential to create a road- and traffic-free landscape.

The current, and in my mind the best, suggestion for the visitor centre is to place it close to the Countess roundabout on the A303 (the Amesbury turning). This is outside the World Heritage Site and would necessitate visitors travelling into the Stonehenge landscape on low impact 'land trains' before walking the final part of their journey. I have often argued that this is the only way that Stonehenge can properly be appreciated – approached from a visitor centre where the site and its landscape can be introduced and then with an increasing sense of wonder as the stones first come into view, grow larger and are finally reached.

So where are we now? In September 2006 the new visitor centre, with its striking yet unobtrusive buildings, was given planning permission from Salisbury District Council but was then called in for a Public Enquiry. That planning permission was conditional on a solution being found for the A303 which, although the inspector at the public enquiry effectively said that the bored tunnel was the only acceptable option, at time of writing still awaits a government decision. So both of the key elements in the joint scheme that could finally bring about the beneficial changes that Stonehenge needs are in limbo.

By the time this book reaches the bookshops decisions will have been made, decisions that will affect the way we view Stonehenge well into the future. Just as certain is that archaeological excavations will continue to change our understanding of both Stonehenge and its landscape.

This is why this book really is 'Stonehenge – the story so far'.

Picture credits

Except where listed, images are (c) English Heritage, (c) National Monuments Record or (c) Crown copyright.NMR. Reference numbers for NMR images are given where known.

Every effort has been made to identify copyright holders. We apologise in advance for any unintentional omissions, which we would be pleased to correct in any subsequent edition of the book.

Aerial-cam: 40b; David Algar: 114b; Dave Batchelor: 206; Martin Bell/Alex Brown: 154; Bodleian Library: 62t (Gough Maps 41k f24), 64; Bridgeman Art Library/V&A Museum: 84; BBC Hulton Picture library: 89; British Geological Survey: 109, 191; British Library 56 (Egerton MS30 28 f140 r), 58, 62b (Gen c 24, f64v); Kath Buxton: 152; The Master and Fellows of Corpus Christi College, Cambridge: 59 (MS 194, f57r); English Heritage/NMR: title page, 8–9, 10 (NMRAA007999),11,13,15 (NMR15041/25), 17, 18t, 18b (NMR ALO922/021), 19, 20, 21, 23, 24, 26, 27t, 28, 29t, 29b (NMR5783), 31, 32, 33, 34–5, 36(NMR), 37(NMR), 38r , 39 (NMR15075-19), 45, 46t (NMR), 47 (NMR24078-16), 48 (NMR24078-06), 49 (NMR), 53, 55, 65, 87 (NMR BB95/50010), 90 NMR no ref), 95b (NMR BB67/429), 100 (NMR AL)913/039/01), 101t (ALO914/113/01), 103, 104, 107 (NMR MPBW colln), 113 (NMR MPBW colln), 114t (NMR MPBW colln), 114m (NMR MPBW colln), 115t, 115b (NMR 2.42/5 P52379), 116(NMR 888 P50792), 118 (NMR 17626 P51729/30), 122 (NMR ALO914/044/01A 4152/26), 123t (NMR MPBW colln), 125 (NMR MPBW colln), 126 (NMR MPBW colln), 127, 128r (NMR P50216), 128l (NMR 50/419 P50384) 129 (NMR 1270 P51162), 130 (NMR A6498/28 ALO918/054/01), 132 (NMR MPBW colln/T Fuller), 133 (NMR ALO915/038/01) 134, 137 (NMR24078-13), 138, 139, 144t (NMR), 144b (NMR), 145t (NMR), 145b (NMR 15380-33), 147, 150, 151, 155, 156, 160, 165, 167, 169, 172, 175, 176, 177, 178, 188bl, 195, 200, 201 (NMR 1.70/26 P51701), 203, 209, 215, 217 (NMR 15453-02), 220, 221 (NMR 36/255 P50241), 224, 226, 249; English Heritage/ Sarah Cottam: 16, 22, 40t, 43, 121, 149, 197, 219, 228; English Heritage/Peter Dunn: 41, 141t, 166, 168, 171, 173, 174; Guinness Archive, Diageo Ireland: 131; Archive/Getty Images: 90; Imperial War Museum: 97; Jan Pohribny: 51, 52; National Trust Photo Library: 71t, 76; Norman Parkinson Archive, London: 143; Punch Cartoon Library: 91 (30 Aug 1899); Julian Richards: 25, 27b, 38l, 46b, 136t, 148, 157, 158, 159, 162, 181, 187b, 193, 196, 198, 202, 204, 205, 207, 208, 210, 211, 212, 213, 218, 222, 227, 229, 230; author's collection: 6, 61b, 72–3, 74, 77, 78t, 81, 88, 91b, 98, 108, 111, 117, 119, 123b, 178, 180 (photo Bill Locke), 194; Charlotte Roberts: 184t; Salisbury and South Wiltshire Museum: 63b, 66, 67, 68, 69, 85; 99, 101b, 105, 135, 136b, 139b, 141b, 142, 163, 164, 199; Society of Antiquaries of London: 96; Geoff Wainwright: 140; Wessex Archaeology: 183, 184b, 189, 190, 192: Wessex Archaeology/Jane Brayne: 182, 186, 188t/br; Clifford Williams: 161; Wiltshire Heritage Museum, Devizes: 59, 70, 71b, 78b, 79, 80, 82, 83, 92, 93, 187t; Wiltshire Record Office: 95t

Places to visit

No serious visit to Stonehenge and its landscape can be considered complete without visiting two Wiltshire museums.

Salisbury and South Wiltshire Museum, 65 the Close, Salisbury SP1 2EN (tel 01722 332151) includes amongst its galleries one dedicated to Stonehenge where finds from the site, including those that relate to the Stonehenge Archer, are displayed. Alongside the finds from Durrington Walls, their prehistoric gallery also displays the Amesbury Archer and his spectacular array of grave goods.

The jewel in the crown of the Wiltshire Heritage Museum, 41 Long Street, Devizes SN10 1NS (tel 01380 727369) is the Stourhead Collection, the finds amassed by Sir Richard Colt Hoare and William Cunnington during their campaigns of barrow excavation in the early 19th century. These include finds from all the major barrow cemeteries that surround Stonehenge, including the wonderful Bush Barrow gold.

Further reading

There are lots of books about Stonehenge, some good, some bad, some eccentric in their approach and many simply outdated because ideas and understanding change alongside advances in archaeological science. Under no circumstances should anyone read my earlier Stonehenge (Batsford and English Heritage, 1991) which falls very firmly into this latter category.

What follows is a short list of recommended reading with an explanation in each case of what the particular book has to offer. Each book itself has a bibliography that can be used to lead the reader down further avenues of exploration.

Stonehenge in its landscape: 20th-century excavations
R M J Cleal, K E Walker and R Montague, English Heritage Archaeological Report 10 1995

This is the definitive report on all the excavations carried out at Stonehenge and on associated features such as the Avenue during the 20th century. It is a heavy book, in more ways than one, but does contain all the detail that you will ever need about Stonehenge.

The Stonehenge Environs Project
Julian Richards, English Heritage Archaeological Report 16 1990

This gives the details of all the landscape studies carried out during the 1980s, the fieldwalking and the sample excavations of both monuments and flint scatters. It is detailed and, like most archaeological reports, dull to read.

Stonehenge World Heritage Site, an archaeological research framework
edited by Timothy Darvill, English Heritage and Bournemouth University 2005

Distinctive because of its acid yellow cover, this is an incredibly useful book as it draws together contributions from a wide range of scholars with different interests in Stonehenge and its landscape, to debate what we know and what we would like to know. Some of the content is couched in the language of modern theoretical archaeology and may therefore be incomprehensible to non-specialists, but it is worth persevering with.

Science and Stonehenge
edited by Barry Cunliffe and Colin Renfrew, Proceedings of the British Academy 92, British Academy and Oxford University Press 1997

This volume draws together the results of a conference held in 1996 and includes contributions on dating, the environment, astronomy and engineering. Some of these contributions have been superseded by more recent publications by the same author but this is still a useful volume.

Stonehenge Complete
Christopher Chippindale, new edition, Thames and Hudson 2004

When this book first appeared in 1983 it was billed as 'everything important, interesting or odd that has been written or painted, discovered or imagined about the most extraordinary ancient building in the world.' Still, after more than 20 years, a lively look at the fascinating social history of Stonehenge.

Stonehenge – a history in photographs
Julian Richards, English Heritage, 2004

This is exactly what it says it is: a history of Stonehenge and the changes that have taken place over the past 150 years, through the eye of the camera. It is not just a series of interesting photographs with captions, but a genuine narrative.

Hengeworld
Mike Pitts, Arrow, 2001

A lively and entertaining approach to the story of the Neolithic and the extraordinary monuments that it spawned. A good read.

Stonehenge
Richard Atkinson, Hamish Hamilton, 1956

Although obviously very dated, it is interesting to look at the original work on Stonehenge, written after the first few seasons of post-war excavation.

Stonehenge, making space
Barbara Bender, Berg 1998
and
Who owns Stonehenge
Christopher Chippindale, Paul Devereux, Peter Fowler, Rhys Jones and Tim Sebastian, Batsford 1990

Together these take an interesting look at Stonehenge and its recent contested history.

Astronomy in prehistoric Britain and Ireland
Clive Ruggles, Yale University Press 1999

Should be read by anyone interested in ancient astronomy whether connected with Stonehenge or beyond.

And finally, if attempts are to be made to interest the next generation in Stonehenge and convince them that history can be fun, then why not try

The amazing pop-up Stonehenge
Julian Richards, English Heritage 2005